THE
MEGHA DUTA
OR
CLOUD MESSENGER:

A POEM,
IN THE SANSKRIT LANGUAGE,

BY

KALIDASA.

TRANSLATED INTO ENGLISH VERSE,
WITH
NOTES AND ILLUSTRATIONS.

BY

H. H. WILSON, M.A.F.R.S. &c. &c.
Boden Professor of Sanskrit in the University of Oxford.

SECOND EDITION

GYAN

Published by

Gyan Publishing House
5, Ansari Road
Daryaganj, New Delhi-110002
Phone: 011-47034999, 9811692060
E-mail: books@gyanbooks.com

Distribution Network
gyanbooks.com
India, USA, Canada, UK, Australia, France

ISBN : 978-81-212-2574-8 (HB)
First Published, 1843

2nd Impression 2021

Printed at: Gyan Press, Delhi.

The
Megha Duta or Cloud Messenger
Author : H. H. Wilson

THE

MEGHA DÚTA

OR

CLOUD MESSENGER:

A Poem

IN THE SANSKRIT LANGUAGE,

BY

KÁLIDÁSA.

TRANSLATED INTO ENGLISH VERSE,

WITH

NOTES AND ILLUSTRATIONS,

BY H. H. WILSON, M.A. F.R.S. &c. &c.

BODEN PROFESSOR OF SANSKRIT IN THE UNIVERSITY OF OXFORD.

SECOND EDITION.

LONDON:

PRINTED BY RICHARD WATTS,

PRINTER TO THE EAST-INDIA COLLEGE.

MDCCCXLIII.

PREFACE.

THE advantages that have been found to result from the publication of the First Book of the Hitopadesa, and the Selections from the Mahábhárata, as Class-books for the East-India College, have induced Professor Johnson to prepare an edition of the Megha Dúta, or Cloud Messenger, for the same purpose, on a similar plan.

The Text of the Megha Dúta was printed in the year 1813, at Calcutta. It has the faults of most of the early-printed Sanskrit books;—the words are altogether unseparated, and the Text is not always accurate. In the present edition, these defects have been remedied; the faulty passages have been corrected; and the words have been detached wherever their separation was consistent with an observance of the laws that regulate euphonic combination. A Glossary, intended to serve at once as a Lexicon and a Grammar to the Text, compiled by Professor Johnson, is added to the publication.

As the style of the poem is more difficult than that of the preceding Class-books, Professor Johnson has considered it desirable to reprint the Translation in English Verse, which was the principal object of the original publication in Calcutta; for, as considerable freedom, or, it may sometimes be thought, license, was taken in that Translation, its use will not, it is to be expected, preclude the necessity of mental effort on the part of the Student, in order to develope the sense of the Sanskrit Text, whilst it may not unallowably lighten his labour, by furnishing him with a general notion of its purport. I have acquiesced in the republication, in the hope that it will afford no greater help than it is designed to render; for experience has satisfied me that the aid of Translations, in the study of any language, except for a short time, perhaps, in the earliest stage of it, is exceedingly mischievous and deceptive. It induces carelessness, encourages indolence, exercises no faculty but the memory, and employs that faculty with so little energy of application, that the impressions received are faint and superficial, and fade and are effaced almost as soon as they are made. The progress effected with such assistance is a mere waste of even the scant expenditure of time and trouble with which it has been attained; for it is unreal—a mere mockery—as the learner will soon discover, to his surprise, and, if he feel rightly, to his mortification, when he tries his strength upon passages unprovided with such illusory aid, and finds that he is as little able to understand them as if his studies were yet to be begun. It has been with some reluctance, therefore, that I have assented to the proposition; and have done so only in the trust that the verse translation will by no means obviate the necessity of independent exertion.

The Translation of the Megha Dúta was the first attempt made by me to interest European readers in the results of my Sanskrit studies. It has the imperfections of a juvenile work; and the Translator has no doubt sometimes not only departed from his original further than was necessary, but further than was justifiable; and has occasionally mistaken its meaning. Some of the mistakes I have corrected; and in some instances have altered the arrangement of the lines, so as to adhere more nearly to the order of the original. I have not cared, however, to render the version much closer or more faithful; as even had I been inclined to take the trouble, the circumstance of the book becoming a class-book would have deterred me from the attempt: but it is very possible, that whatever poetical fidelity the version may possess, might have been injured by verbal approximation, and that the attempt to give a more literal likeness of the poem of Kálidása would only have impaired the similitude of its expression.

I have gone over the Notes with more attention, and have continued the information they convey to the present time. I have added some, and omitted some, especially those which were designed to place the parallel passages of European poets in contiguity with the language and sentiments of the Indian bard. Such analogies will readily suggest themselves to well-educated minds; and it cannot be necessary to endeavour to prove to them, that Imagination, Feeling, and Taste, are not exclusively the products of the Western Hemisphere.

The Megha Dúta, or Cloud Messenger, is recommended to a Student of Sanskrit by its style and by its subject. The style is somewhat difficult, but the difficulty arises from no faults of conception or construction. There must, of course, be some unfamiliar imagery, some figures of purely local associations, in every foreign—in every Oriental composition; but, with a few possible exceptions, the Megha Dúta contains no ideas that may not be readily apprehended by European intellect. It has no miserable conceits, no enigmatical puzzles, which bewilder a poetic reader, and overwhelm a prosaïc one with despair; and which, when the riddle is solved, offer no compensation for the labour of solution. The language, although remarkable for the richness of its compounds, is not disfigured by their extravagance: the order of the sentences is in general the natural one, with no more violent inversion than is indispensable for the convenience of the rhythm. The metre combines melody and dignity in a very extraordinary manner; and will bear an advantageous comparison, in both respects, with the best specimens of uniform verse in the poetry of any language, living or dead.

The subject of the poem is simple and ingenious: a Yaksha, a divinity of an inferior order, an attendant upon the god of riches, Kuvera, and one of a class which, as it appears from the poem, is characterized by a benevolent spirit, a gentle temper, and an affectionate disposition, has incurred the displeasure of his sovereign, and has been condemned by him to a twelvemonths' exile from his home. In the solitary but sacred forest in which he spends the period of his banishment, the Yaksha's most urgent care is to find an opportunity of conveying intelligence and consolation to his wife; and, in the wildness of his grief, he fancies that he discovers a friendly messsenger in a cloud—one of those noble masses which seem almost instinct with life, as they traverse a tropical sky in the commencement of the Monsoon, and move with slow and solemn progression from the equatorial ocean to the snows of the Himálaya. In the spirit of this bold but not unnatural personification, the Yaksha addresses the Cloud, and entrusts to it the message he yearns to despatch to the absent object of his attachment. He describes the direction in which the Cloud is to travel—one marked out for it, indeed, by the eternal laws of nature; and takes this opportunity of alluding to the most important scenes of Hindu mythology and tradition;—not with the dulness of prosaïc detail, but with that true poetic pencil which, by a few happy touches, brings the subject of the description vividly before the mind's eye. Arrived at the end of the journey, the condition of his beloved wife is the theme of the exile's anticipations, and is dwelt upon with equal delicacy and truth; and the poem terminates with the message that is intended to assuage her grief and animate her hopes. The whole of this part of the composition is distinguished by the graceful expression of natural and amiable feelings, and cannot fail to leave a favourable impression of the national character; whilst the merely descriptive portion introduces the student to a knowledge of a variety of objects of local, traditional, and mythological value, with which it is his duty to become familiar; and which he will, when in India, contemplate with additional interest and pleasure, from his previous acquaintance with the verses of Kálidása.

Little is known of the literary history of the Megha Dúta. It is, by common assent, attributed to Kálidása, a celebrated poet, who is reputed to have been one of the ornaments of the Court of Vikramáditya, king of Ujayin, whose reign, used as a chronological epoch by the Hindus, is placed 56 years before the Christian æra. There is no reason to dispute the truth of these traditions. The poem undoubtedly belongs to a classical period of Hindu Literature; and that period, there is reason to believe, did not long survive the first centuries of Christianity. At a later date, the Poets were men of more scholarship than imagination, and substituted an overwrought display of the powers of the language for the unforced utterance of the dictates of the feeling or the fancy. This is not the case with the Megha Dúta; and although it is rather of a more sustained elevation of language than other works attributed to the same author, particularly his dramatic compositions, Sakuntalá, and Vikramá and Urvasí, yet there is a community of character in them, a similar fidelity to nature, a like delicacy and tenderness of feeling, and the same felicity of description, gracefulness of imagery, and elegance of expression, which leave it sufficiently probable that they are the works of the same master-hand. There are, indeed, in the Vikramá and Urvasí especially, passages which call the Megha Dúta to recollection; and in one place, where the deserted monarch inquires of the passing Cloud whither Urvasí has fled, we have the germ of the perhaps later poem, the Cloud Messenger. Of the other works attributed to Kálidása, the Ritu-sanhára, Raghuvansa, Málavikágnimitra, Kumára-sambhava, Sringára-tilaka, Prasnottara-málá, Hásyárnava, and Sruta-bodha, some of them are certainly not of his composition.

The Text of the Megha Dúta has been the subject of very industrious illustration, and, as noticed in the Preface to the first edition, the copy then consulted comprehended no fewer than six commentaries. This Manuscript, the property of Mr. Colebrooke, is now in the Library at the India House, and has been made use of by Professor Johnson in the present edition. The text of the poem has been also printed at Bonn, from Manuscripts in the Royal Libraries of Paris and Copenhagen, by Mr. Gildemeister, with Notes of various readings, and a useful Glossary.

MEGHA DÚTA,

OR

CLOUD MESSENGER.

कश्चित् कान्ताविरहगुरुणा स्वाधिकारप्रमत्तः
शापेनास्तं गमितमहिमा वर्षभोग्येन भर्तुः ॥

WHERE Rámagiri's cool, dark woods extend,
And those pure streams, where Síta bathed, descend;

ANNOTATIONS.

Verse 1. Rámagiri] Is a compound term signifying The mountain of Ráma, and may be applied to any of those hills in which the hero resided during his exile or peregrinations. His first and most celebrated residence was the mountain Chitrakúta in Bundelcund, now known by the name of Comptah, and still a place of sanctity and pilgrimage. We find that tradition has assigned to another mountain, a part of the Kimoor range, the honour of affording him, and his companions, Sítá and Lakshmana, a temporary asylum, upon his progress to the south; and it is consequently held in veneration by the neighbouring villagers: see Capt. Blunt's journey from Chunarghur to Yertnagoodum, Asiatic Researches, vii. 60. An account of a journey from Mirzapore to Nagpore, however, in the Asiatic Annual Register for 1806, has determined the situation of the scene of the present poem to be in the vicinity of the latter city. The modern name of the mountain is there stated to be Ramtéc: it is marked in the maps, Ramtege; but I understand the proper word is Rámtinki, which, in the Marhatta language, has probably the same import as Rámagiri, The hill of Ráma. It is situated but a short distance to the north of Nagpore; and is covered with buildings consecrated to Ráma and his associates, which receive the periodical visits of numerous and devout pilgrims.

Verse 2. Where Síta bathed.] In his exile, Ráma was accompanied by his younger brother, Lakshmana, and his faithful consort Sítá, or, as she is called in the original, the daughter of

Janaka,

यक्षश्चक्रे जनकतनयास्नानपुण्योदकेषु
स्निग्धच्छायातरुषु वसतिं रामगिर्य्याश्रमेषु ॥ १ ॥

Spoiled of his glories, severed from his wife,
A banished Yaksha passed his lonely life: 4
Doomed, by his lord's stern sentence, to sustain
Twelve tedious months of solitude and pain.

ANNOTATIONS.

Janaka, until the latter was carried off by the demon or giant Rávańa: see the Rámáyańa. The performance of her ablutions in the springs of the mountain is here stated to have rendered their water the object of religious veneration.

Verse 4. A Yaksha] Is a demigod, of which there exists a Gańa or class. They have few peculiar attributes, and are regarded only as the companions or attendants of Kuvera, the god of wealth. The word is derived from यक्ष 'to worship'; either, because they minister to Kuvera, are reverenced themselves by men, or are beloved by the Apsaras, the courtezans of Indra's heaven. They have, however, their own female companions, or wives; as appears by the poem. One writer, cited and censured by a Commentator on the Amara Kosha, derives the name from जक्ष 'to eat,' because he says they devour children. Occasionally, indeed, the Yakshas appear as imps of evil; but, in general, their character is perfectly inoffensive.

Verse 5.] The lord of the Yakshas is Kuvera, who, in Hindu mythology, performs the functions of the Grecian Plutus. He is the god of wealth, and master of nine inestimable treasures. His capital is situated on mount Kailása, and inhabited by Yakshas, Kinnaras, and other inferior deities. He has a variety of appellations alluding to these circumstances, but is most commonly designated by the one here employed. The term is expressive of his deformity, being derived from कु 'vile,' and वेर 'body'; and he is described as having three legs, and but eight teeth. No images of him occur, nor is any particular worship paid to him; and in these respects there is a considerable analogy between him and his Grecian parallel. Plutus is described as blind, malignant, and cowardly; and seems to have received but very slender homage from Greek or Roman devotion. The term "sentence," here used, is, more literally, 'curse.' The text also states that it was incurred by a neglect of duty, the Yaksha having been heedless in his office, स्वाधिकारप्रमत्तः. According to the Commentators, he was the warder of the gate of Kuvera's garden; and, quitting his post for a season, allowed Indra's elephant to commit a trespass, and trample down the flower-beds.

तस्मिन्नद्रौ कतिचिदबलाविप्रयुक्तः स कामी
नीत्वा मासान् कनकवलयभ्रंशरिक्तप्रकोष्ठः ॥
आषाढस्य प्रथमदिवसे मेघमाश्लिष्टसानुं
वप्रक्रीडापरिणतगजप्रेक्षणीयं ददर्श ॥ २ ॥

To these drear hills through circling days confined,
In dull unvaried grief, the god repined;
And sorrow, withering every youthful charm,
Had slipped the golden bracelet from his arm;
When with Ásárha's glooms the air was hung,
And one dark Cloud around the mountain clung;
In form, some elephant, whose sportive rage,
Ramparts, scarce equal to his might, engage.

ANNOTATIONS.

Verse 10. Had slipped the golden bracelet from his arm.] This is a favourite idea with Hindu poets, and repeatedly occurs: thus, in the elegant drama of Sakuntalá, Dushmanta says:

इदमशिशिरैरन्तस्तापाद्विवर्णमणीकृतं
निशि निशि भुजन्यस्तापाङ्गप्रसारिभिरश्रुभिः ।
अनभिलुलितज्याघाताङ्कान्मुहुर्मणिबन्धनात्
कनकवलयं स्रस्तं स्रस्तं मया प्रतिसार्य्यते ॥

or, in Sir William Jones's version, "This golden bracelet, sullied by the flame which preys on me, and which no dew mitigates, but the tears gushing nightly from my eyes, has fallen again and again on my wrist, and has been replaced on my emaciated arm."

Verse 11. When with Ásárha's glooms.] The month Áshád'ha or Ashár'ha comprehends the latter part of June and the commencement of July, and is the period about which the south-west monsoon, or rainy season, usually sets in.

Verse 13. In form, some elephant.] Thus, in the Purána Sarvaswa, clouds are described as महिषाश्च वराहाश्च मत्तमातङ्गरूपिणः 'Shaped like buffaloes, boars, and wild elephants.' In Chapman's Bussy D'Ambois, they are said to assume,

In our faulty apprehensions,
The forms of dragons, lions, elephants.

And

तस्य स्थित्वा कथमपि पुरः केतकाधानहेतो-
रन्तर्बाष्पश्चिरमनुचरो राजराजस्य दध्यौ ॥
मेघालोके भवति सुखिनो ऽप्यन्यथावृत्ति चेतः
कण्ठाश्लेषप्रणयिनि जने किम्पुनर्दूरसंस्थे ॥ ३ ॥

Long on the mass of mead-reviving dew
The heavenly exile fixed his eager view;
And still the melancholy tear suppressed,
Though bitterest sorrow wrung his heaving breast.
For e'en the happy husband, as he folds
His cherished partner in his arms, beholds
This gathering darkness with a troubled heart:
What must they feel, whom fate and distance part!
Such were the Yaksha's thoughts; but fancy found
Some solace in the glooms that deepened round;

ANNOTATIONS.

And Shakspeare, although he omits the elephant, gives them, with his usual overflow of imagery, a great variety of shapes:—

Sometimes we see a cloud that's dragonish,
A vapour sometimes like a bear or lion,
A towered citadel, a pendant rock,
A forked mountain, or blue promontory,
With trees upon 't, that nod unto the world,
And mock our eyes with air.

ANTHONY & CLEOPATRA.

Verse 20. For e'en the happy husband.] The commencement of the rainy season being peculiarly delightful in Hindustan, from the contrast it affords to the sultry weather immediately preceding it, and the refreshing sensations it excites, becomes, to the lover and the poet, the same source of love and tenderness, as the season of Spring is to the young and poetical, in Europe.

प्रत्यासन्ने नभसि दयिताजीवितालम्बनार्थी
जीमूतेन स्वकुशलमयीं हारयिष्यन् प्रवृत्तिम् ॥
स प्रत्यग्रैः कुटजकुसुमैः कल्पितार्घाय तस्मै
प्रीतः प्रीतिप्रमुखवचनं स्वागतं व्याजहार ॥ ४ ॥

धूमज्योतिःसलिलमरुतां सन्निपातः क्व मेघः
सन्देशार्थाः क्व पटुकरणैः प्राणिभिः प्रापणीयाः ॥
इत्यौत्सुक्यादपरिगणयन् गुह्यकस्तं ययाचे
कामार्त्ता हि प्रकृतिकृपणाश्चेतनाचेतनेषु ॥ ५ ॥

And bade him hail amidst the labouring air,
A friendly envoy to his distant fair;
Who, charged with grateful tidings, might impart
New life and pleasure to her drooping heart.

Cheered with the thought, he culled each budding flower,
And wildly wooed the fertilizing power;
(For who, a prey to agonizing grief,
Explores not idlest sources for relief;
And, as to creatures sensible of pain,
To lifeless nature loves not to complain?)
Due homage offered, and oblations made,
The Yaksha thus the Cloud majestic prayed:—

ANNOTATIONS.

Verse 35. **And oblations made.]** The oblation of the blossoms of the Kuťaja, 'a small tree,' (Wrightea antidysenterica) is called Argha (अर्घ) in the original, a religious rite, which seems to be analogous to the libation of the earlier periods of the Grecian ritual. अर्घ, in the Amara Kosha, is described as a species of worship, and is perhaps more properly the act of offering

जातं वंशे भुवनविदिते पुष्करावर्त्तकानां
जानामि त्वां प्रकृतिपुरुषं कामरूपं मघोनः ॥

Hail, friend of Indra, counsellor divine,
Illustrious offspring of a glorious line! 38

ANNOTATIONS.

offering a libation to a venerable person, or to a deity; although it also implies the oblation itself, otherwise denominated अर्घ्य. This oblation, of which water forms the basis, is presented in a cup, a shell, or any metallic oblong and boat-shaped vessel. The vessel in the spoken dialects is called by a similar name ارگها 'Argha.' Indeed, Mr. Wilford states, Asiatic Researches, iii. 364, and viii. 274, that Argha, in Sanskrit, means 'a boat;' whence he deduces the ship Argo, &c.; and whence, with Mr. Bryant's assistance, we may deduce the Ark of Scripture. The Sanskrit word, however, has not been found in any of the vocabularies of the language, with the import Mr. Wilford has assigned to it.

The oblation called Argha or Arghya, generally considered, comprises eight articles, thus enumerated:

आपः क्षीरं कुशाग्राणि दधि सर्पिश्च तण्डुलाः ।
यवाः सिद्धार्थकं चैव अष्टाङ्गार्घ्यं प्रकीर्त्तितम् ॥

"The eight-fold Arghya is formed of water, milk, the points of Kuśa-grass, curds, clarified "butter, rice, barley, and white mustard." In the Áchára Darśa of Śrídatta, in a passage quoted from the Déví Puráńa, they are stated somewhat differently; thus,

रक्तबिल्वाक्षतैः पुष्पैर्दधिदूर्व्वाकुशैस्तिलैः ।
सामान्यः सर्व्वदेवानामर्घोऽयं परिकीर्त्तितः ॥

"The general Argha, proper for any of the gods, consists of saffron, the Bél, unbroken grain, "flowers, curds, Dúrba-grass, Kuśa-grass, and Sesamum." Water is not mentioned here, being considered as the vehicle of the whole: the same author adds, that should any of these not be procurable, they may be supplied by the imagination:

अभावे दधिदूर्व्वादेर्मानसं वा प्रकल्पयेत् ॥

Besides the Argha common to all the gods, there are peculiar ones for separate deities: thus we find a few new-blown buds are sufficient for a cloud; and in the Sarvaswa Puráńa, the Argha for the Sun is thus enumerated,

चन्दनोदकसम्मिश्रं दत्त्वार्घ्यं कुसुमं रवेः ॥

"Having presented an Arghya to the Sun, of water mixed with sandal, and flowers:" and an oblation to the same planet, as given by Mr. Colebrooke, Asiatic Researches, ch. v. 357, is said to consist

तेनार्थित्वं त्वयि विधिवशाद्दूरबन्धुर्गतो ऽहं

Wearer of shapes at will; thy worth I know,
And bold entrust thee with my fated woe:

ANNOTATIONS.

consist of Tila, flowers, barley, water and red sanders. Water alóne is also sufficient to constitute the A.gha. In the articles which form the Argha of the Hindus, as well as in the mode of presentation, that of pouring it out, or libating, we trace its analogy with the ancient libation. Of course, wine could never enter into Hindu offerings of this kind; but we find that the Greeks had their *νηφάλια ἱερὰ* or 'sober sacrifices,' from which wine was excluded. These were of four kinds: *τὰ ὑδρόσπονδα*, 'libations of water,' *τὰ μελίσπονδα* 'of honey,' *τὰ γαλακτόσπονδα* 'of milk,' and *τὰ ἐλαιόσπονδα* 'of oil;' which liquors were sometimes mixed with one another. According to Porphyry, most of the libations in the primitive times were *νηφάλιοι*. See Potter's Antiquities of Greece. We have here, then, three of the four fluid substances of an Argha, as first enumerated above, if we may compare the clarified butter with the oil: honey would, of course, be omitted on the same account as wine, being a prohibited article in Hindu law. With respect to the solid parts of the offering, a reference to the same authority will shew that they consisted of green herbs, grains, fruits, flowers, and frankincense; analogous to the grasses, rice, barley, flowers, sandal, &c. of the Sanskrit formulæ.

Verse 37. Hail, friend of Indra!] Indra is the sovereign deity of Swarga, or the Hindu Olympus. The cloud is here considered as his friend or counsellor, in allusion to his functions as regent of the atmosphere, where he appears in the character of the Jupiter Tonans, or Νεφεληγερέτα Ζεύς. The appellative मघवत्, used in the original, is considered, by Etymologists, as irregularly derived from the passive form of मह, 'to adore,' 'to worship.'

Verse 38. Illustrious offspring of a glorious line.] According to the original, "Descended from the celebrated line of the Pushkarávarttakas," translated, in a prose version of this passage, "Diluvian Clouds:" see Colebrooke on Sanskrit and Prakrit Prosody, Asiatic Researches, Vol. X. Clouds, agreeably to the Brahmáńda Puráńa, are divided into three classes, according to their origin from fire, the breath of Brahmá, or the wings of the mountains, which were cut off by Indra (पक्ष). These latter are also called पुष्करावर्त्तक, being especially the receptacles of water. Thus, in the Puráńa Sarvaswa,

पुष्करा नाम ते मेघा बृहन्तस्तोयमत्सराः
पुष्करावर्त्तकास्तेन कारणेनेह शब्दिताः ॥

"The clouds called Pushkara are those large clouds which are insatiable of water; and, on

याच्ञा मोघा वरमधिगुणे नाधमे लब्धकामा ॥ ६ ॥
सन्तप्तानां त्वमसि शरणं तत् पयोद प्रियाया-
स्सन्देशं मे हर धनपतिक्रोधविश्लेषितस्य ॥

For, better far, solicitation fail
With high desert, than with the base prevail.

Thou art the wretch's aid, affliction's friend;
To me, unfortunate, thy succour lend: 44
My lonely state compassionate behold,
Who mourn the vengeance of the god of gold;

ANNOTATIONS.

" on that account, they are called in this world, Pushkarávarttakas." So also it is said, upon the authority of the Váyu, Linga, and Matsya Puránas, "The third class of clouds is that of " the Pakshaja, or those which were originally the wings of the mountains that were cut off " by Indra. These are also termed Pushkarávarttakas, from their including water in their " vortices. They are the largest and most formidable of all; and those which, at the end of the " Yugas and Kalpas, pour down the waters of the Deluge." Vishńu Puráńa, p. 231, note.

Verse 39. Wearer of shapes at will;] Or Kámarúpa; from काम 'desire,' and रूप 'form,' 'shape': thus Socrates, in the "Clouds:"

Σω. Γίνονται πανθ' ὅτι ἂν βώλωνται.

Soc. Why, then,
Clouds can assume what shapes they will, believe me!

CUMBERLAND's Translation.

Verse 40. For, better far, solicitation fail &c.] This is a sentiment of rather an original strain, and indicates considerable elevation of mind. Something of the same kind occurs in Massinger's play of the "Bondman;" where Pisander says,

I'd rather fall under so just a judge,
Than be acquitted by a judge corrupt
And partial in his censure.

Verse 46. The god of gold,] Kuvera. See above.

गन्तव्या ते वसतिरलका नाम यक्षेश्वराणां
वाह्योद्यानस्थितहरशिरश्चन्द्रिकाधौतहर्म्या ॥ ७ ॥

त्वामारूढं पवनपदवीमुद्गृहीतालकान्ताः
प्रेक्षिष्यन्ते पथिकवनिताः प्रत्ययादाश्वसन्त्यः ॥
कस्सन्नद्धे विरहविधुरां त्वय्युपेक्षेत जायां
न स्यादन्योऽप्यहमिव जनो यः पराधीनवृत्तिः ॥ ८ ॥

Condemned amidst these dreary rocks to pine,
And all I wish, and all I love, resign.

Where dwell the Yakshas in their sparkling fields,
And Śiva's crescent groves surrounding gilds,
Direct thy licensed journey, and relate
To her who mourns in Alaká, my fate.
There shalt thou find the partner of my woes,
True to her faith, and stranger to repose;

ANNOTATIONS.

Verse 50. Where Śiva's crescent realms surrounding gilds.] The crest of Śiva is the new moon, which is sometimes described as forming a third eye in his forehead. The Himálaya mountains, amongst which we shall hereafter find Kailása to be situated, are Śiva's favourite haunts. He also resides occasionally on that mountain, and is represented as the particular friend and frequent guest of Kuvera.

Verse 52. I have here taken a liberty with the order of the original, and brought the description of the Yaksha's wife a little in advance, in order to preserve the description which follows, of the Cloud's progress, more connected. The Hindu poets are not very solicitous in general about arrangement; but it is possible that in this case I may not have improved upon that of Kálidás. The 10th stanza of the Sanskrit corresponds with these lines.

Verse 53. Alaká is the capital of Kuvera, and the residence of his dependent deities.

मन्दं मन्दं नुदति पवनश्चानुकूलो यथा त्वां
वामश्चायं नदति मधुरं चातकस्ते सगर्वः ॥
गर्भाधानक्षमपरिचयं नूनमाबद्धमाला-
सेविष्यन्ते नयनसुभगं खे भवन्तं बलाकाः ॥ ९ ॥

तां चावश्यं दिवसगणनातत्परामेकपत्नी-
मव्यापन्नामविहतगतिर्द्रक्ष्यसि भ्रातृजायाम् ॥
आशाबन्धः कुसुमसदृशं प्रायशो ह्यङ्गनानां
सद्यःपाति प्रणयि हृदयं विप्रयोगे रुणद्धि ॥ १० ॥

Her task to weep our destiny severe,
And count the moments of the lingering year:
A painful life she leads, but still she lives,
While hope its aid invigorating gives;
For female hearts, though fragile as the flower,
Are firm, when closed by hope's investing power.

Still, as thou mountest on thine airy flight,
Shall widowed wives behold thee with delight,
With eager gaze, their long locks drawn apart,
Whilst hope re-animates each drooping heart:
Nor less shall husbands, as thy course they trace,
Expect at hand a faithful wife's embrace;
Unless, like me, in servitude they bend,
And on another's lordly will depend.

कर्तुं यच्च प्रभवति महीमुच्छिलीन्ध्रातपत्रां
तच्छ्रुत्वा ते श्रवणसुभगं गर्ज्जितं मानसोत्काः ॥

The gentle breeze shall fan thy stately way,
In sportive wreathes the Cranes around thee play;
Pleased on thy left the Chátaka, along
Pursue thy path, and cheer it with his song; 72

ANNOTATIONS.

Verse 70. Valáká (बलाका) is said, in Mr. Colebrooke's Amara Kosha, to mean a 'small crane.' The word is always feminine, and perhaps therefore means the female bird only. Indeed, some of the Commentators on this poem call it the female of the Vaka (बक), Ardea Torra and Putea. The rainy season is that of their gestation; which explains their attachment to the Cloud, and the allusion to its impregnating faculty mentioned in the text of the original, गर्भाधानक्षणपरिचयम्.—The periodical journeys and orderly flight of this kind of bird have long furnished classical poetry with embellishments: they are frequently alluded to by Homer, as are the wild geese, of which mention is also made below:—thus, in the Iliad, Book ii. 459:

Τῶν δ', ὥστ' ὀρνίθων πετεηνῶν ἔθνεα πολλὰ,
Χηνῶν, ἢ γεράνων, ἢ κύκνων δουλιχοδείρων,
'Ασίῳ ἐν λειμῶνι, Καϋστρίου ἀμφὶ ῥέεθρα.

Not less their number than th' embodied cranes,
Or milk-white swans in Asia's watery plains,
That o'er the windings of Caÿster's springs
Stretch their long necks and clap their rustling wings. Pope.

The translator has omitted the geese. Milton also describes the flight of these birds:

So steers the prudent Crane
Her annual voyage, borne on winds. Paradise Lost, vii. 436.

And again, line 442:

Others on silver lakes and rivers bathed
Their downy breast.——
——Yet oft they quit
The dank, and, rising on stiff penons, tower
The mid aërial sky.

Verse 71. The Chátaka is a bird supposed to drink no water but rain-water: of course he always

आकैलासाद्बिसकिशलयच्छेदपाथेयवन्त-
स्सम्पत्स्यन्ते नभसि भवतो राजहंसास्सहायाः ॥ ११ ॥

And when thy thunders soothe the parching earth,
And showers, expected, raise her mushroom birth;
The Swans for mount Kailása shall prepare,
And track thy course attendant through the air. 76

ANNOTATIONS.

always makes a prominent figure in the description of wet or cloudy weather. Thus in the rainy season of our author's (ऋतुसंहार) 'Rĭtu Sanhára,' or Assemblage of Seasons:

तृषाकुलैश्चातकपक्षिणां कुलैः
प्रयाचितास्तोयभरावलम्बिनः ।
प्रयान्ति मन्दं नववारिधारिणो
वलाहकाः श्रोत्रमनोहरस्वनाः ॥

The thirsty Chátaka impatient eyes
The promised waters of the labouring skies;
Where heavy Clouds, with low but pleasing song,
In slow procession murmuring move along.

The Chátaka is the Cuculus Melanoleucus. The term वाम is rendered by the Commentators in general 'left,' on the left side; but Rámanát'h Tarkalankára interprets it 'beautiful'; and maintains that the cry of birds, to be auspicious, should be upon the right side, not upon the left. Bharuta Malliku, however, cites astrological writers to prove that the Chátaka is one of the exceptions to this rule:

वर्हिणश्चातकाश्चाषा ये च पुंसञ्ज्ञिताः खगाः ।
मृगा वा वामगा हृष्टाः सैन्यसम्पन्नलप्रदाः ॥

"Peacocks, Chátakas, Cháshas (blue jays), and other male birds, occasionally also antelopes, "going cheerfully along the left, give good fortune to the host." The Greek notions agreed with those of Rámanát'h, and considered the flight of birds upon the right side to be auspicious: the Romans made it the left; but this difference arose from the situation of the observer, as in both cases the auspicious quarter was the east; the *οἰωνοπόλος* facing the north, and Aruspex the south. In general, according to the Hindus, those omens which occur upon the left side are unpropitious.

Verse 75. "The Rájahansas, desirous of going to the lake Mánasa, shall accompany thee "as far as Kailása, having laid in their provisions from the new shoots of the filaments of the "stalk of the lotus." This is the closer reading of the text. Kailása is, properly speaking, a mytho-

आपृच्छस्व प्रियसखममुं तुङ्गमालिङ्ग्य शैलं
वन्द्यैः पुंसां रघुपतिपदैरङ्कितं मेखलासु ॥
काले काले भवति भवतो यस्य संयोगमेत्य
स्नेहव्यक्तिश्चिरविरहजं मुञ्चतो वाष्पमुष्णम् ॥ १२ ॥

मार्गं तावच्छृणु कथयतस्त्वत्प्रयाणानुरूपं
सन्देशं मे तदनु जलद श्रोष्यसि श्रोत्रपेयम् ॥
खिन्नः खिन्नः शिखरिषु पदं न्यस्य गन्तासि यत्र
क्षीणः क्षीणः परिलघुपयः स्रोतसां चोपयुज्य ॥ १३ ॥

Short be thy farewell to this hill addressed;
This hill with Ráma's holy feet imprest;
Thine ancient friend, whose scorching sorrows mourn
Thy frequent absence and delayed return.

Yet ere thine ear can drink what love inspires,
The lengthened way my guiding aid requires.
Oft on whose path full many a lofty hill
Shall ease thy toils, and many a cooling rill.

ANNOTATIONS.

a mythological mountain; but the name is also applied to the lofty range that runs parallel with the Himálaya, on the north of that chain. The lake Mánasa lies between the two ranges: and it is quite true, that it is the especial resort of the wild grey goose at the beginning of the rainy season; "Those birds finding in the rocks bordering on the lake an "agreeable and safe asylum, when the swell of the rivers in the rains and the inundation of "the plains conceal their usual food." Moorcroft's Journey to Mánasarovara: Asiatic Researches, xii. 466. The Rájahansa is described as a kind of goose with white body and red legs and bill; whence Mr. Ellis affirms that it is properly applicable to the Phœnicopteros or flamingo. Asiatic Researches, xiv. 28, note.

Verse 78. With Ráma's holy feet imprest.] In the original text we have, "marked with the steps of Raghupati, venerated of men." This appellation is given to Ráma, as the most distinguished,

अद्रेः शृङ्गं वहति पवनः किंस्विदित्युन्मुखीभि-
र्दृष्टोच्छ्रायश्चकितचकितं मुग्धसिद्धाङ्गनाभिः ॥
स्थानादस्मात् सरसनिचुलादुत्पतोदङ्मुखः खं

Rise from these streams, and seek the upper sky;
Then to the north with daring pinions fly.
The beauteous Sylphs shall mark thee with amaze,
As backward bent thou strik'st their upward gaze,
In doubt if by the gale abruptly torn,
Some mountain-peak along the air is borne.
The ponderous Elephants, who prop the skies,
Shall view thy form expansive with surprise;

ANNOTATIONS.

guished, the lord or master as it were, of the line of Raghu, an ancestor of that warrior, and himself a celebrated hero and sovereign. Ráma is hence also termed Rághava (राघव), a regular derivative from Raghu, implying family descent. The exploits of the two heroes form the chief subject of another poem by our author, entitled Raghuvanśa (रघुवंश), or The race of Raghu.

Verse 85. We now begin the geographical part of the poem; which, as far as it can be made out through the difference of ancient and modern appellations, seems to be very accurately conceived. The two extreme points of the Cloud's progress are, the vicinity of Nagpore, as mentioned in the note on Verse 1, and the mountain Kailása, or rather the Himálaya range. During this course, the poet notices some of the most celebrated places, with the greater number of which we are still acquainted. In the first instance, we have here his direction due north from the mountain of Rámagiri; and we shall notice the other points as they occur.

Verse 87. Literally, the wives of the Siddhas. The Siddhas are originally human beings, but who, by devout abstraction, have attained superhuman powers, and a station apparently intermediate between men and gods. They tenat the upper regions of the air.

Verse 91. Each of the four quarters, and the four intermediate points of the compass, has, according to the Hindus, a regent or presiding deity. Each of these deities also has his male and female elephant. The names of them all are enumerated in the following verse of the Amara Kosha:

ऐरावतः

दिङ्नागानां पथि परिहरन् स्थूलहस्तावलेपान् ॥ १४ ॥
रत्नच्छायाव्यतिकर इव प्रेक्ष्यमेतत्पुरस्ता-
द्वल्मीकाग्रात् प्रभवति धनुःखण्डमाखण्डलस्य ॥
येन श्यामं वपुरतितरां कान्तिमालप्स्यते ते
बर्हेणेव स्फुरितरुचिना गोपवेषस्य विष्णोः ॥ १५ ॥

Now first their arrogance exchanged for shame,
Lost in thy bulk their long unrivalled fame.

Eastward, where various gems, with blending ray,
In Indra's bow o'er yonder hillock play,
And on thy shadowy form such radiance shed,
As Peacock's plumes around a Krishńa spread,
Direct thy course: to Málas smiling ground,
Where fragrant tillage breathes the fields around;

ANNOTATIONS.

ऐरावतः पुण्डरीको वामनः कुमुदोऽञ्जनः ।
पुष्पदन्तः सार्वभौमः सुप्रतीकश्च दिग्गजाः ॥

Airávata, Puńdaríka, Vámana, Kumuda, Anjana, Pushpadanta, Sárvvabhauma, and Supratíka, (are) the elephants of the sky.

Verse 95. A reference to the map will shew that it was necessary for the Cloud to begin the tour by travelling towards the east, in order to get round the lofty hills which in a manner form the eastern boundary of the Vindhya chain. It would otherwise have been requisite to have taken it across the most inaccessible part of those mountains, where the poet could not have accompanied it; and which would also have offended some peculiar notions entertained by the Hindus of the Vindhya hills, as we shall again have occasion to remark.

Verse 96. Indra's bow is the rainbow.

Verse 97. The body of Kṛishńa is represented of a dark blue colour; and the plumes of the peacock are frequently arranged upon the images of this deity. Allusion is especially made to Kṛishńa in his juvenile character, as a cow-herd in the groves of Vṛindávana.

Verse 99. It is not easy, after the lapse of ages, to ascertain precisely the site of several places

त्वय्यायत्तं कृषिफलमिति भ्रूविकारानभिज्ञैः
प्रीतिस्निग्धैर्जनपदवधूलोचनैः पीयमानः ॥
सद्यस्सीरोत्कषणसुरभिक्षेत्रमारुह्य मालं
किञ्चित् पश्चाद्व्रज लघुगतिः किञ्चिदेवोत्तरेण ॥ १६ ॥

Thy fertile gifts, which looks of love reward,
Where bright-eyed peasants tread the verdant sward.

Thence sailing north, and veering to the west,
On Ámrakúta's lofty ridges rest; 104

ANNOTATIONS.

places enumerated in the poem before us. The easterly progress of the Cloud, and the subsequent direction by which he is to reach the mountain Ámrakúta, prove that the place here mentioned must be somewhere in the immediate vicinity of Ruttunpoor, the chief town of the northern half of the province of Cheteesger'h, and described in Captain Blunt's tour, Asiatic Researches, Vol. vii., and also in that of Mr. Colebrooke, published in the Asiatic Annual Register for 1806. The only modern traces that can be found of it are in a place called Malda, a little to the north of Ruttunpoor. In Ptolemy's map, there is a town called Maleta; and situated, with respect to the Vindhya mountains, similarly with the Mála of our poet. I should have supposed that the Mála mentioned from the geography of the Puráńas by Mr. Wilford (Asiatic Researches, viii. 336) was the same with the place alluded to in the text of Kálidása: if, however, that gentleman is correct in applying the name to the Malbhoom of Midnapoor, it will be much further to the east than will do for our present purpose, and must be an entirely different place. There is little reason to think that either of these Málas are the country of the Malli, who are mentioned by Pliny; and who are more probably the same with the Μαλλοὶ of Arrian, and the inhabitants, as is stated by Major Rennell, of the province of Multan.

Verse 104. The course pointed out to the Cloud, and an allusion which follows to the vicinity of the Narmadá river, furnish us with reasons for supposing that the mountain here mentioned is that more commonly designated by the name of Omerkuntuk. The change of sound is not more violent than it is in a number of evident corruptions from the Śanskrit language, now current in the dialects of India. The term Ámrakúta means the Mango Peak, and refers to the abundance of mango-trees in the incumbent and surrounding forests. Should this

त्वामासारप्रशमितवनोपप्लवं साधु मूर्ध्ना
वक्ष्यत्यध्वश्रमपरिगतं सानुमानाम्रकूटः ॥
न क्षुद्रोऽपि प्रथमसुकृतापेक्षया संश्रयाय
प्राप्ते मित्रे भवति विमुखः किम्पुनर्यस्तथोच्चैः ॥ १७ ॥

Oft have thy showers the mountain's flames allayed,
Then fear not wearied to demand its aid.
Not e'en the basest, when a falling friend
Solicits help it once was his to lend, 108
The aid that gratitude exacts denies:
Much less shall noble minds the claim despise.

ANNOTATIONS.

this conjecture be correct, it will invalidate the derivation assigned with some ingenuity to the word Omerkuntuk, in a prefatory note to a pleasing little oriental poem published in England, called the Metamorphosis of Sona. The author of that note imagines the proper name to be Omer Khandaka; and he is happy in the affinity of the sound, though not in his definition of the sense, as "the district of Omer" is exceedingly unmeaning, and erroneous. Amara Khandaka might mean the "immortal portion," but I do not know of any reason for assigning such an epithet to the mountain in question.

Verse 107. The Hindus have been the object of much idle panegyric, and equally idle detraction. Some writers have invested them with every amiable attribute, and they have been deprived by others of the common virtues of humanity. Amongst the excellencies denied to them, gratitude has been always particularized; and there are many of the European residents in India who scarcely imagine that the natives of the country ever heard of such a sentiment. To them, and to all detractors on this head, the above verse is a satisfactory reply; and that no doubt of its tenor may remain, I add the literal translation of the original passage. "Even a low man, when his friend comes to him for assistance, will not turn away his face, in consideration of former kindness;—how, therefore, should the exalted act thus?"

D

छन्नोपान्तः परिणतफलद्योतिभिः काननाम्रै-
स्त्वय्यारूढे शिखरमचलः स्निग्धवेणीसवर्णे ॥
नूनं यास्यत्यमरमिथुनप्रेक्षणीयामवस्थां
मध्ये श्यामः स्तन इव भुवश्शेषविस्तारपाण्डुः ॥ १८ ॥

अध्वक्लान्तं प्रतिमुखगतं सानुमांश्चित्रकूट-
स्तुङ्गेन त्वां जलद शिरसा वक्ष्यति श्लाघमानः ॥
आसारेण त्वमपि शमयेस्तस्य नैदाघमग्निं
सद्भावार्द्रः फलति नचिरेणोपकारो महत्सु ॥ १९ ॥

When o'er the wooded mountain's towering head
Thy hovering shades like flowing tresses spread,
Its form shall shine with charms unknown before,
That heavenly hosts may gaze at, and adore;
This earth's round breast, bright swelling from the ground,
And with thy orb as with a nipple crowned.

Next bending downwards from thy lofty flight,
On Chitrakúta's humbler peak alight;
O'er the tall hill thy weariness forego,
And quenching rain-drops on its flames bestow;
For speedy fruits are certain to await
Assistance yielded to the good and great.

ANNOTATIONS.

Verse 117. The mountain here mentioned must be in the vicinity of Omerkuntuk, and part of the same range: the name signifies, "the variegated or wonderful peak," and is applied to a number of hills: the most famous hill of this name, as was mentioned in the first note, is situated in Bundelkund.

स्थित्वा तस्मिन् वनचरवधूभुक्तकुञ्जे मुहूर्त्तं
तोयोत्सर्गाद्रुततरगतिस्तत्परं वर्त्म तीर्णः ॥

Thence journeying onwards, Vindhya's ridgy chain,
And Reva's rill, that bathes its foot, attain; 124
Whose slender streams upon the brown hill's side,
Like painted streaks upon the dusky hide

ANNOTATIONS.

Verse 123. The Vindhya range of mountains holds a very distinguished station both in the mythology and geography of Hindustan: these points are both discussed at some length in the tour from Mirzapore to Nagpore, already cited; and, as in those passages which I have been able to investigate I find a perfectly accurate statement, I shall here transcribe the words of its author.

" Bind'h, in Sanskrit named Vind'hya, constitutes the limit between Hindustan and the Deccan. The most ancient Hindu authors assign it as the southern boundary of the region which they denominate Áryabhúma or Áryaverta. Modern authors, in like manner, make this the line which discriminates the northern from the southern nations of India. It reaches almost from the eastern to the western sea; and the highest part of the range deviates little from the line of the tropic. The mountainous tract, however, which retains the appellation, spreads much more widely: it meets the Ganges in several places towards the north; and the Godáveri is held to be its southern limit.

" Sanskrit etymologists deduce its name from a circumstance to which I have just now alluded: it is called Bind'hya, says the author of a Commentary on the Amercosh, because people think (ध्यायन्ति) the progress of the sun is obstructed (वैन्ध) by it. Suitably to this notion, the most elevated ridge of this tropical range of mountains is found to run from a point that lies between Chhota Nagpore and Palamu, to another that is situated in the vicinity of Ougein. But the course of the Nermadá river better indicates the direction of the principal range of the Vind'h hills. From Amracúta, where this river has its source, on the same spot with the Sone and the Hatsu, to the gulf of Cambaya, where it disembogues itself into the sea, the channel of the Nermadá is confined by a range of hills, or by a tract of elevated ground, in which numerous rivers take their rise; and by their subsequent course towards the Sone and Jamuna on one side, and towards the Tapti and Oodaver on the other, sufficiently indicate the superior elevation of that tract through which the Nermadá has forced its way.

The vast extent of this mountainous tract, contrasted with the small elevation of these hills, viewed

रेवां द्रक्ष्यस्युपलविषमे विन्ध्यपादे विशीर्णां
भक्तिच्छेदैरिव विरचितां भूतिमङ्गे गजस्य ॥ २० ॥

तस्यास्तिक्तैर्वनगजमदैर्वासितं वान्तवृष्टि-

Of the tall Elephant—in bright display,
Through stones and rocks wind slow their arduous way. 128

Here the soft dews thy path has lost resume,
And sip the gelid current's rich perfume,

ANNOTATIONS.

viewed from the plains of Hindustan, has furnished grounds for a legend to which the mythological writings of the Hindus often allude. Vind'hya having once prostrated himself before his spiritual guide, Agastya, still remains in that posture, by command of the holy personage. This humiliation is the punishment of his presumption, in emulating the lofty height of Himálaya and Meru. According to this legend, Vind'hya has one foot at Chunar; and hence the real name of that fortress is said to be Charanádri (चरणाद्रि): his other foot is, I think, placed by the same legend in the vicinity of Gayá: the vulgar, very inconsistently, suppose the head of the prostrate mountain near the temple of Vind'hya Vasini, four miles from Mirzapore."

Verse 124. The Revá is a name of the Narmadá river, which, as we have seen in the preceding note, rises from the mountain Ámrakúta or Omerkuntuk. It may be here observed, that the rivers are always personified by the Hindus, and are, in general, female personifications. Thus we have Gangá, the daughter of Jahnu; Yamuná, the daughter of the Sun; and Revá, or Narmadá, the daughter of Himála, as is said in the hymn translated from the Váyu Puráńa, and given by Captain Blunt, Asiatic Researches vii. 103. The names of the Narmadá river are thus stated in the Amara Kosha,

रेवा तु नर्म्मदा सोमोद्भवा मेकलकन्यका

"Revá, Nermadá, Sómódbhavá, and Mekala-Kanyaká;" which are explained by the best Commentators thus, "who flows, who delights, who is descended from the line of the moon, and who is the daughter of Mekala." The last term is applied either to the Vindhya mountain, or is considered to be the name of a Rishi or saint, and progenitor of the river-goddess. Tradition has assigned to this river a very Ovidian kind of tale; which is related in Captain Blunt's tour, and which has been repeated in verse, with much elegance and spirit, by the author of the Metamorphosis of Sona.

जम्बूकुञ्जप्रतिहतरयं तोयमादाय गच्छेः ॥
अन्तस्सारं घन तुलयितुं नानिलश्शक्ष्यति त्वां
रिक्तस्सर्वो भवति हि लघुः पूर्णतागौरवाय ॥ २१ ॥

Where the wild Elephant delights to shed
The juice exuding fragrant from his head. 132
Then swift proceed, nor shall the blast have force
To check with empty gusts thy ponderous course.

ANNOTATIONS.

Verse 131. The juice exuding fragrant from his head.] It is rather extraordinary that this juice which exudes from the temples of the elephant, especially in the season of rut, should have been unnoticed by modern writers on natural history, until the time of Cuvier (Regne animal), although mention of it is made by Strabo, from Megasthenes. The author of the Wild Sports of the East states, that "on each side of the elephant's temples there is an aperture about the size of a pin's head, whence an ichor exudes;" but he does not appear to have been aware of its nature. Indeed his descriptions, though entertaining, are frequently defective, owing to his extreme ignorance of the languages, the literature of which he so liberally devotes to the flames. In the Amara Kosha, this fluid is termed मदः and दानम् ; and the elephant, while it flows, is distinguished by the terms प्रभिन्नः, गर्ज्जितः मत्तः from the animal out of rut, or after the juice has ceased to exude, and which is then called उद्भ्रान्तः or निर्मदः. All these names are expressive of the circumstances. The exudation and fragrance of this fluid is frequently alluded to in Sanskrit poetry. Its scent is commonly compared to the odour of the sweetest flowers, and is then supposed to deceive and attract the bees. These circumstances occur in this passage from a work already referred to, the Rĭtu Sanhára:—

वनद्विपानां नवतोयदस्वनै-
र्मदान्वितानां स्वनतां मुहुर्मुहुः ।
कपोलदेशा विमलोत्पलप्रभा-
स्सभृङ्गयूथैर्मदवारिभिः श्रिताः ॥

Roars the wild Elephant inflamed with love,
And the deep sound reverberates from above;
His ample front, like some rich lotus, shews
Where sport the bees, and fragrant moisture flows.

नीपं दृष्ट्वा हरितकपिशं केशरैरर्द्धरूढै-
राविर्भूतप्रथममुकुलाः कन्दलीश्चानुकच्छम् ॥
दग्धारण्येष्वधिकसुरभिं गन्धमाघ्राय चोर्व्या-
श्शारङ्गास्ते जललवमुचस्सूचयिष्यन्ति मार्गम् ॥ २२ ॥

अम्भोविन्दुग्रहणरभसांश्चातकान् वीक्षमाणाः
श्रेणीभूताः परिगणनया निर्द्दिशन्तो वलाकाः ॥
त्वामासाद्य स्तनितसमये मानयिष्यन्ति सिद्धा-
स्सोत्कम्पानि प्रियसहचरीसम्भ्रमालिङ्गितानि ॥ २३ ॥

उत्पश्यामि द्रुतमपि सखे मत्प्रियार्थं यियासोः

Reviving nature bounteous shall dispense,
To cheer thy journey, every charm of sense;
Blossoms, with blended green and russet hue,
And opening buds, shall smile upon thy view.
Earth's blazing woods in incense shall arise,
And warbling birds with music fill the skies.

Respectful Demigods shall curious count
The chattering Storks, in lengthening order mount;
Shall mark the Chátakas, who, in thy train,
Expect impatiently the dropping rain.
And, when thy muttering thunders speak thee near,
Shall clasp their brides, half ecstasy, half fear.

Ah! much I dread the long-protracted way,
Where charms so numerous spring to tempt delay:

कालक्षेपं ककुभसुरभौ पर्व्वते पर्व्वते ते ॥
शुक्लापाङ्गैस्सजलनयनैः स्वागतीकृत्य केकाः
प्रत्युद्यातः कथमपि भवान् गन्तुमाशु व्यवस्येत् ॥ २४ ॥

Will not the frequent hill retard thy flight,
Nor flowery plain persuade prolonged delight?
Or can the Peacock's animated hail,
The bird with lucid eyes, to lure thee fail? 152

ANNOTATIONS.

Verse 151. Or can the Peacock's animated hail?] The wild peacock is exceedingly abundant in many parts of Hindustan, and is especially found in marshy places. The habits of this bird are, in a great measure, aquatic; and the setting in of the rains is the season in which they pair. The peacock is therefore always introduced in the description of cloudy or rainy weather, together with the Cranes and Chátakas, whom we have already had occasion to notice. Thus, in a little poem descriptive of the rainy season &c., entitled Ghatakarpara (घटकर्पर), the author says, addressing his mistress—

नवाम्बुमत्ताः शिखिनो नदन्ति मेघागमे कुन्दसमानदन्ति ॥

O thou, whose teeth enamelled vie
With smiling Kunda's pearly ray,
Hear how the Peacock's amorous cry
Salutes the dark and cloudy day!

And again, in one of the Śatakas or Centos of Bhartṛi Hari, where he is describing the same season—

शिखिकुलकलकेका एव रम्या वनान्ताः
सुखिनमसुखिनं वा सर्व्वमुत्कण्ठयन्ति ।

When smiling forests, whence the tuneful cries
Of clustering pea-fowls shrill and frequent rise;
Teach tender feelings to each human breast,
And charm alike the happy or distressed.

पाण्डुच्छायोपवनवृतयः केतकैः सूचिभिन्नै-
र्नीडारम्भे गृहबलिभुजामाकुलग्रामचैत्याः ॥
त्वय्यासन्ने फलपरिणतिश्यामजम्बूवनान्ता-

Lo! where awhile the Swans reluctant cower,
Daśárńa's fields await the coming shower.
Then shall their groves diffuse profounder gloom,
And brighter buds the deepening shade illume; 156
Then shall the ancient tree, whose branches wear
The marks of village reverence and care,

ANNOTATIONS.

Verse 154. Daśárńa's fields await the coming shower.] No traces of this name are to be found in modern maps: it is enumerated in Major Wilford's lists from the Puráńas, Asiatic Researches, vol. viii. amongst the countries situated behind the Vindhya mountains; and corresponds, according to him, with the Dosarene of Ptolemy and the Periplus. Ptolemy's map has also a Dosara and Dosaronis Fluvium; and in the Pauránik list of rivers, there is also a Dosarna river, which is said to rise from the mountain Chitrakúṭa. It may possibly correspond, at least in part, with the modern district of Cheteesger'h, as the etymology of both words refers to similar circumstances. Cheteesger'h is so named from its being supposed to comprise Thirty-six forts; and according to Bharata, the Commentator on our text, Daśárńa is derived from Daśa (दश) Ten, and Rĭna (ऋण), a strong hold or Durga, the Droog of the Peninsula, and thence means the district of the Ten citadels.

Verse 157. Then shall the ancient tree, &c.] A number of trees receive particular veneration from the Hindus; as the Indian fig, the Holy fig-tree, the Myrobalan trees, &c. In most villages there is at least one of these, which is considered particularly sacred, and is carefully kept and watered by the villagers, is hung occasionally with garlands, and receives the Prańám or veneratory inclination of the head, or even offerings and libations. The birds mentioned in the text by the epithet गृहबलिभुज् are the Vakas or Cranes. The term signifies "who eats the food of his female;" गृह commonly a house, meaning, in this compound, a wife. At the season of pairing, it is said that the female of this bird assists in feeding the male; and the same circumstance is stated with respect to the crow and the sparrow, whence the same epithet is applied to them also.

सम्पत्स्यन्ते कतिपयदिनस्थायिहंसा दशार्णाः ॥ २५ ॥

तेषां दिक्षु प्रथितविदिशालक्षणां राजधानीं
गत्वा सद्यः फलमतिमहत् कामुकत्वस्य लब्धा ॥
तीरोपान्तस्तनितसुभगं पास्यसि स्वादुयुक्तं
सभ्रूभङ्गं मुखमिव पयो वेत्रवत्याश्चलोर्म्मि ॥ २६ ॥

नीचैराख्यं गिरिमधिवसेस्तत्र विश्रामहेतो-
स्त्वत्सम्पर्कात् पुलकितमिव प्रौढपुष्पैः कदम्बैः ॥

Shake through each leaf, as birds profanely wrest
The reverend boughs to form the rising nest.

Where royal Vidiśa confers renown
Thy warmest wish shall fruit delightful crown:
There, Vetravati's stream ambrosial laves
A gentle bank, with mildly murmuring waves;
And there, her rippling brow and polished face
Invite thy smiles, and sue for thy embrace.

Next, o'er the lesser hills thy flight suspend,
And growth erect to drooping flowerets lend;

ANNOTATIONS.

Verse 161. Where royal Vidiśa confers renown.] Vidiśa is described as the capital of the district of Daśárńa. It appears to be the modern Bhilsah, in the province of Malwa. It is still a place of some note; and is well known in India for the superior quality of the tobacco raised in its vicinity.

Verse 163. The Vetravati is the modern Betwah. It rises on the north side of the Vindhya chain; and, pursuing a north-easterly course of 340 miles, traverses the province of Malwa and the south-west corner of Allahabad, and falls into the Jumna below Kalpee. In the early part of its course, it passes through Bhilsa or Vidiśa.

यः पण्यस्त्रीरतिपरिमलोद्गारिभिर्नागराणा-
मुद्दामानि प्रथयति शिलावेश्मभिर्यौवनानि ॥ २७ ॥

विश्रान्तस्सन् व्रज नगनदीतीरजातानि सिञ्च-

While sweeter fragrance breathes from each recess,
Than rich perfumes the hireling wanton's dress.

On Naga Nadi's banks thy waters shed,
And raise the feeble jasmin's languid head; 172

ANNOTATIONS.

Verse 167. Next o'er the lesser hills thy flight suspend.] The term in the text, नीचैराख्यं गिरिं, is explained by the Commentators, to signify either the hill named Níchais, a mountainous range, of little note, or of little elevation. It is of no great moment; but perhaps the latter, which meaning we select, is the most satisfactory.

Verse 168. And growth erect to drooping flowerets lend.] This passage, more literally rendered, is, "That hill which with upright flowers is like the body with its hair on end." The erection of the hairs of the body is, with the Hindus, constantly supposed to be the effect of pleasure or delight.

Verse 171. On Naga Nadi's banks.] Some of the Commentators notice various readings of the name of this river; which occurs as given in the translation, Naga Nadí (नगनदी), 'the mountain stream;' Nava Nadí (नवनदी), 'the new river;' and Vana Nadí (वननदी), 'the forest river.' It is probably one amongst a number of small streams falling from the Vindhya range of hills; and, indeed, the whole province of Malwa abounds in water; so that, as is stated in the Ayeen Akbery, "you cannot travel two or three cose without meeting with streams of good water, whose banks are shaded by the wild-willow and other trees, and decorated with the hyacinth and other beautiful and odoriferous flowers." Gladwin's Translation, vol. ii.—I have given the preference to the Naga Nadí as above, from finding a river west of the Betwah, which we have crossed, named the Parbatty; and which, rising in the Vindhya chain, runs north-west, till it joins another called, in Arrowsmith's Map, the Sepra; and the two together fall into the Chumbul. The word Parbatty, or Párvatí, means, 'sprung from the mountains;' and Naga Nadí, as I have mentioned, bears a similar import; so that they possibly are synonyms of the same stream.

नुद्यानानां नवजलकणैर्यूथिकाजालकानि ॥
गण्डस्वेदापनयनरुजा क्लान्तकर्णोत्पलानां
छायादानात् क्षणपरिचितः पुष्पलावीमुखानाम् ॥ २८ ॥

वक्रः पन्था यदपि भवतः प्रस्थितस्योत्तराशां
सौधोत्सङ्गप्रणयविमुखो मा च भूरुज्जयिन्याः ॥

Grant for a while thy interposing shroud,
To where those damsels woo the friendly Cloud;
As, while the garland's flowery stores they seek,
The scorching sunbeams singe the tender cheek,
The ear-hung lotus fades: and vain they chase,
Fatigued and faint, the drops that dew the face.

What though to northern climes thy journey lay,
Consent to track a shortly devious way;
To fair Ujjayiní's palaces and pride,
And beauteous daughters, turn awhile aside.

ANNOTATIONS.

Verse 175. As, while the garland's flowery stores they seek.] The use of garlands in the decoration of the houses and temples of the Hindus, and of flowers in their offerings and festivals, furnishes employment to a particular tribe or caste, the Málakáras or wreath-makers. The females of this class are here alluded to.

Verse 181. Ujjayiní, or the modern Oujein, is supposed to have been the residence of our poet, and the capital of his celebrated patron, Vikramáditya. Few cities, perhaps, can boast of a more continuous reputation; as it has been a place of great note, from the earliest periods of Hindu tradition down to the present day. It is now in the possession of the family of Scindiah, and is the capital of his territories. A full and highly-interesting account of it is to be found in the Sixth Volume of the Asiatic Researches, in the Narrative of a Journey from Agra to this city, by the late Dr. Hunter,—a gentleman, the activity of whose mind was only equalled by the accuracy of his judgment, and the extensiveness of whose acquirements was only paralleled by the unwearied continuance of his exertions.

विद्युद्दामस्फुरणचकितैस्तत्र पौराङ्गनानां
लोलापाङ्गैर्यदि न रमसे लोचनैर्वञ्चितो ऽसि ॥ २९ ॥

वीचिक्षोभस्तनितविहगश्रेणिकाञ्चीगुणायाः
संसर्पन्त्याः स्खलितसुभगं दर्शितावर्त्तनाभेः ॥
निर्विन्ध्यायाः पथि भव रसाभ्यन्तरं सन्निपत्य

Those glancing eyes, those lightning looks unseen,
Dark are thy days, and thou in vain hast been. 184

Diverging thither now the road proceeds,
Where eddying waters fair Nirvindhya leads,
Who speaks the language amorous maids devise,
The lore of signs, the eloquence of eyes; 188

ANNOTATIONS.

Verse 184. Dark are thy days.] The expression of the poet is simply, "If you do not enjoy "the glances, &c., you are defrauded" (वञ्चितो ऽसि), and the Commentators explain it by adding, "of the object of your life." That is, if you have not seen these beauties, you might as well have been blind, or not have existed at all. This compliment is rather hyperbolical; but we are acquainted with it in Europe: and the Italian proverb, "He who has not seen Rome has not seen any thing," conveys a similar idea.

Verse 186. Fair Nirvindhya leads.] This stream has not been found by name in the maps; but a number of small rivers occur between the Parbatty and the river mentioned below, the Sipra, one of which must be the Nirvindhya of the poet. The four following lines, descriptive of the female personification of the current, are englished rather with respect to the sense than the words, the plainness of which might perhaps offend European fastidiousness. There is not, however, any one of Kálidása's river-ladies who behaves so indecorously as several of Drayton's similar personifications; and there is not one of them possessed of speech at all, to say nothing of such speech as is made use of by the HAYLE, and other like "lusty nymphs," of that author's Poly-olbion.

स्त्रीणामाद्यं प्रणयवचनं विभ्रमो हि प्रियेषु ॥ ३० ॥

वेणीभूतप्रतनुसलिला तामतीतस्य सिन्धुः
पाण्डुच्छाया तटरुहतरुभ्रंशिभिः शीर्णपर्णैः ॥
सौभाग्यं ते सुभग विरहावस्थया व्यञ्जयन्ती
कार्श्यं येन त्यजति विधिना स त्वयैवोपपाद्यः ॥ ३१ ॥

प्राप्यावन्तीमुदयनकथाकोविदग्रामवृद्धां

And seeks, with lavish beauty, to arrest
Thy course, and woo thee to her bridal breast.

The torrent passed, behold the Sindhu glide,
As though the hair-band bound the slender tide;
Bleached with the withered foliage, that the breeze
Has showered rude from overhanging trees:
To thee she looks for succour, to restore
Her lagging waters, and her leafy shore.
Behold the city whose immortal fame
Glows in Avanti's or Viśála's name!

ANNOTATIONS.

Verse 191. Behold the Sindhu glide.] This is a stream also, with which the maps are not acquainted by name. As, however, it is the nearest river to Oujein, it may probably be the same with that now called Ságurmuttee. The river having been diminished by the preceding hot weather, the poet compares it to a long single braid of hair; and, conformably to the personification of it as a female, he supposes the braid to have been bound, in consequence of the absence of the Cloud, after the fashion in which the hair is worn by those women whose husbands are absent;—a custom we shall again be called upon to notice.

Verse 196. The synonyms of Oujein are thus enumerated in the Vocabulary of Hemachandra:

उज्जयिनी स्याद्विशालाऽवन्ती पुष्पकरण्डिनी ।

Ujjayiní, Viśálá, Avanti, and Pushpakarańdiní.

पूर्वोद्दिष्टामनुसर पुरीं श्रीविशालां विशालाम् ॥
स्वल्पीभूते सुचरितफले स्वर्गिणां गां गतानां
शेषैः पुण्यैर्हृतमिव दिवः कान्तिमत् खण्डमेकम् ॥ ३२ ॥

Renowned for deeds that worth and love inspire,
And bards to paint them with poetic fire; 200
The fairest portion of celestial birth,
Of Indra's paradise transferred to earth;
The last reward to acts of virtue given;
The only recompence then left to Heaven. 204

ANNOTATIONS.

Verse 199. Renowned for deeds &c.] I have here taken some liberty with the text, the literal translation of which is "famous for the story of Udayana, and the number of its learned men." The story of Udayana, or Vatsarája, as he is also named, is thus told concisely, by the Commentators on the poem:—Pradyota was a sovereign of Oujein, who had a daughter named Vásavadattá, and whom he intended to bestow in marriage upon a king of the name of Sanjaya. In the mean time, the princess sees the figure of Vatsarája, sovereign of Kusha Dwípa, in a dream, and becomes enamoured of him. She contrives to inform him of her love, and he carries her off from her father and his rival. The same story is alluded to in the Málati Mádhava, a drama by Bhavabhúti; but neither in that, nor in the Commentary on the Megha Dúta, is mention made of the author, or of the work in which it is related. Mr. Colebrooke, in his learned Essay on Sanskrit and Prákrit Prosody, in the Tenth Volume of the Asiatic Researches, has stated, that the allusion by Bhavabhúti was unsupported by other authority; not having, perhaps, noticed the similar allusion in this poem. He has also given an abstract of the Vásavadattá of Subandhu; a tale which corresponds, in many points, with that of Udayana, as here explained. Udayana is also the hero of part of the Kathá Sarit Ságara; and his marriage with Vásavadattá is there related in nearly a similar manner as that just described. The story was evidently popular; and the text might be rendered Ujjayin, "great or illustrious by the number of those skilled in the tale of Udayana."

Verse 204. The only recompence then left to Heaven.] To understand this properly, it is necessary to be acquainted with some of the Hindu notions regarding a future state. The highest

दीर्घीकुर्वन् पटुमदकलं कूजितं सारसानां
प्रत्यूषेषु स्फुटितकमलामोदमैत्रीकषायः ॥

Here, as the early Zephyrs waft along,
In swelling harmony, the woodland song;
They scatter sweetness from the fragrant flower
That joyful opens to the morning hour. 208

ANNOTATIONS.

highest kind of happiness is absorption into the divine essence, or the return of that portion of spirit which is combined with the attributes of humanity, to its original source. This happiness, according to the philosopher, is to be attained only by the most perfect abstraction from the world, and freedom from passion, even while in a state of terrestrial existence: but there are certain places, which, in the popular creed, are invested with so much sanctity, as to entitle all who die within their precincts to final absorption or annihilation. One of these is Oujein, or Avantí; and they are all enumerated in this verse:

अयोध्या मथुरा माया काशी काञ्ची अवन्तिका।
पुरी द्वारावती चैव सप्तैता मोक्षदायिकाः ॥

" Ayodhyá, Mathurá, Máyá, Káśí, Kánchí, Avantiká, and the city Dwárávatí, are the seven " places which grant eternal happiness."

Besides this ultimate felicity, the Hindus have several minor degrees of happiness; amongst which is the enjoyment of Indra's Swarga, or, in fact, of a Muhammadan paradise. The degree and duration of the pleasures of this paradise are proportioned to the merits of those admitted to it; and "they, who have enjoyed this lofty region of Swarga, but whose virtue is exhausted, revisit the habitation of mortals." The case now alluded to seems, however, to be something different from that so described by Sir William Jones. It appears, by the explanation of the Commentators, that the exhausted pleasures of Swarga had proved insufficient for the recompence of certain acts of austerity, which, however, were not such as to merit final emancipation: the divine persons had therefore to seek elsewhere for the balance of their reward; and for that purpose they returned to Earth, bringing with them the fairest portion of Swarga, in which they continued to live in the discharge of pious duties till the whole account was settled, and their liberated spirits were re-united with the great, uniform, and primeval essence. The portion of Swarga thus brought to Earth was the city Avantí; whose superior sanctity and divine privileges are here alluded to, and thus explained by the poet.

यत्र स्त्रीणां हरति सुरतग्लानिमङ्गानुकूल-
स्सिप्रावातः प्रियतम इव प्रार्थनाचाटुकारः ॥ ३३ ॥

जालोद्गीर्णैरुपचितवपुः केशसंस्कारधूपै-
र्बन्धुप्रीत्या भवनशिखिभिर्दत्तनृत्योपहारः ॥

With friendly zeal they sport around the maid
Who early courts their vivifying aid;
And, cool from Sipra's gelid waves, embrace
Each languid limb and enervated grace. 212

Here should thy spirit with thy toils decay,
Rest from the labours of the wearying way:
Round every house the flowery fragrance spreads;
O'er every floor the painted footstep treads; 216

ANNOTATIONS.

Verse 211. The Siprá is the river upon the banks of which Oujein stands, and which is called Sipparah in the maps. In Arrowsmith, however, there is another stream with a similar name, the Siprá, which appears to be a continuation of the Sagarmuttee, considerably to the north-east of Oujein. There can be no doubt of the position of the river mentioned by the poet.

Verse 216. The painted footstep.] Staining the soles of the feet with a red colour, derived from the Mehndee, the Lac, &c., is a favourite practice of the Hindu toilet. It is thus elegantly alluded to in the Ode to one of the Female Personifications of Music, the Rágini Asauveree:

The rose hath humbly bowed to meet,
With glowing lips, her hallowed feet,
And lent them all its bloom.

Hindu Odes, by John David Paterson, Esq., published in the New Series of Gladwin's Oriental Miscellany, Calcutta.

हर्म्येष्वस्याः कुसुमसुरभिष्वध्वखिन्नान्तरात्मा
त्यक्त्वा खेदं ललितवनितापादरागाङ्कितेषु ॥ ३४ ॥

भर्तुः कण्ठच्छविरिति गणैस्सादरं वीक्ष्यमाणः
पुण्यं यायास्त्रिभुवनगुरोर्धाम चण्डेश्वरस्य ॥

Breathed through each casement, swell the scented air,
Soft odours shaken from dishevelled hair;
Pleased on each terrace, dancing with delight,
The friendly Peacock hails thy grateful flight:
Delay then! certain in Ujjayin to find
All that restores the frame, or cheers the mind.

Hence, with new zeal, to Śiva homage pay,
The god whom earth and hell and heaven obey:
The choir who tend his holy fane shall view
With awe, in thee, his neck's celestial blue:

ANNOTATIONS.

Verse 223. The Commentators have thought proper, in explaining this verse and the preceding, to transpose the order of the explanations;—I do not see for what reason, and have therefore conformed to the text.

Verse 224. The god whom earth and hell and heaven obey.] "Lord of the three worlds" is the expression of the original text: the worlds are, Swarga or heaven, Pátála or hell, and Bhúmi or the earth.

Verse 226. With awe, in thee, his neck's celestial blue.] The dark blue of the Cloud is compared to the colour of the neck of Śiva, which became of this hue upon his swallowing the poison produced at the churning of the ocean. The story is thus related in Wilkins's Translation of an Episode of the Mahábhárat, affixed to his Bhagavad Gítá:—"As they continued to churn the ocean more than enough, that deadly poison issued from its bed, burning like a raging fire; whose dreadful fumes in a moment spread throughout the world, confounding the three regions of the universe with its mortal stench, until Seev, at the word of Brahmá, swallowed

the

धूतोद्यानं कुवलयरजोगन्धिभिर्गन्धवत्या-
स्तोयक्रीडाविरतयुवतिस्नानतिक्तैर्मरुद्भिः ॥ ३५ ॥

अप्यन्यस्मिन् जलधर महाकालमासाद्य काले
स्थातव्यं ते नयनविषयं यावदभ्येति भानुः ॥
कुर्वन् सन्ध्याबलिपटहतां शूलिनः श्लाघनीया-

Soft through the rustling grove the fragrant gale
Shall sweets from Gandhavati's fount exhale;
Where with rich dust the lotus-blossoms teem,
And youthful beauties frolic in the stream.

Here, till the sun has vanished in the west,
Till evening brings its sacred ritual, rest;—
Then reap the recompence of holy prayer,
Like drums thy thunders echoing in the air.
They who, with burning feet and aching arms,
With wanton gestures and emblazoned charms,

ANNOTATIONS.

the fatal drug, to save mankind; which remaining in the throat of that sovereign Dew of magic form, from that time he was called Neel-kant, because his throat was stained blue."

Verse 232. Till evening brings its sacred ritual, rest.] There are three daily and essential ceremonies performed by the Brahmans, termed Sandhyás (सन्ध्या), either from the word Sandhi (सन्धि), 'junction,' because they take place at the joinings of the day as it were, that is, at dawn, noon, and twilight: or as the term is otherwise derived from सम् 'with,' and ध्यै, 'to meditate religiously.' When the ceremonies of the Sandhyá are of a public nature, they comprehend the ringing of bells, blowing the conch, beating a tabor, &c.; and this kind of sound the Cloud is directed by the Yaksha to excite, as an act of devotion.

Verse 235. They who, with burning feet and aching arms.] The female attendants upon the idol.

मामन्द्राणां फलमविकलं लप्स्यसे गर्ज्जितानाम् ॥ ३६ ॥

पादन्यासक्कणितरसनास्तत्र लीलावधूतै-
रत्नच्छायाखचितवलिभिश्चामरैः क्लान्तहस्ताः ॥

In Mahádeva's fane the measure tread,
Or wave the gorgeous chowrie o'er his head,
Shall turn on thee the grateful-speaking eye,
Whose glances gleam, like bees, along the sky,
As from thy presence, showers benign and sweet
Cool the parched earth, and soothe their tender feet.

ANNOTATIONS.

Verse 238. The gorgeous chowrie.] The Chowrie, or more properly Chounri (چونري), is a brush of Peacock's feathers, or the tail of a particular kind of cow, &c., set in a handle of such materials as suit the fancy or the means of the proprietor. It is used for a fan, or to whisk off flies and other insects; and this piece of attention is always paid by the Hindus to the figures of their gods.

Verse 240. Whose glances gleam, like bees, along the sky.] Although this allusion may be new to European imagery, it is just and pleasing. The consequence of the glance is well conveyed by the sting of the bee, while its poetically radiating nature is not unaptly compared to the long flight of a line of these insects. The lengthened light of a glance is familiar to us; for Shakspeare speaks of "eyes streaming through the airy region": and the continuous flight of bees was noticed so long back as the time of Homer, who describes them as proceeding in branches, a circumstance which his translator, Pope, has omitted:—

> Βοτρυδὸν δὲ πέτονται ἐπ' ἄνθεσιν εἰαρινοῖσιν.
>
> Branching, they fly abroad o'er vernal flowers;

Or, as in Pope,

> Clust'ring, in heaps on heaps, the driving bees &c.

Verse 242. And soothe their tender feet.] It is to be recollected that these ladies are dancing bare-footed: divesting the feet of the shoes is a mark of reverence or respect paid to sacred places, such as the interior or vestibule of a temple, which has been from the remotest times practised in the East, as we know from the authority of Scripture.

वेश्यास्त्वत्तो नखपदसुखान् प्राप्य वर्षाग्रविन्दू-

Nay, more,—Bhaváni shall herself approve,
And pay thy services with looks of love; 244

ANNOTATIONS.

Verse 243. Bhaváni shall herself approve.] Bhaváni is one of the many names of the consort of Śiva. The reason of her satisfaction, and indeed the whole of this passage, although familiar to a Hindu, and although much amplified in the translation, requires a little explanation, to be rendered intelligible to the English reader. Śiva is supposed to be dancing at the performance of the evening Sandhyá, and to have assumed as his cloak the bloody skin of an elephant formerly belonging to an Asura destroyed by him. As this is no very seemly ornament, Bhaváni is delighted to find it supplied by the Cloud; which being of a dusky red, through the reflexion of the China roses now abundant, and being skirted, as it overhangs a forest, by the projecting branches of trees, resembles the elephant hide in colour, and its dangling limbs as well as in its bulk, and is mistaken for it by Śiva in his religious enthusiasm. The office performed by the Cloud has often been assigned to it in the West: thus, Horace, Ode II. Book I.:

Nube candentes humeros amictus,
Augur Apollo.——

Or come Apollo, versed in fate, and shroud
Thy shining shoulders with a veiling cloud.

So Milton, in his Penseroso, speaking of the Morning, describes it as

Kerchief'd in a comely cloud.

Lee invests sentiments of the mind with a similar garb, and has—

For true Repentance never comes to late;
As soon as born, she makes herself a shroud,
The weeping mantle of a fleecy cloud.

And a Poet of later day, but of no inferior name, has made a very fine use of this figure:

I've known her long, of worth most excellent;
But in the day of woe she ever rose
Upon the mind with added majesty;
As the dark mountain more sublimely towers,
Mantled in clouds and storm. Miss Baillie's De Montfort.

The

नामोक्ष्यन्ति त्वयि मधुकरश्रेणिदीर्घान् कटाक्षान् ॥ ३७ ॥

पश्चादुच्चैर्भुजतरु वनं मण्डलेनाभिलीन-
स्सान्ध्यं तेजः प्रतिनवजपापुष्परक्तं दधानः ॥
नृत्यारम्भे हर पशुपतेरार्द्रनागाजिनेच्छां
शान्तोद्वेगस्तिमितनयनं दृष्टभक्तिर्भवान्या ॥ ३८ ॥

When, as her Śiva's twilight rites begin,
And he would clothe him in the reeking skin,
He deems thy form the sanguinary hide,
And casts his elephant attire aside;
For at his shoulders, like a dusky robe,
Mantling, impends thy vast and shadowy globe;
Where ample forests, stretched its skirts below,
Projecting trees like dangling limbs bestow;
And vermil roses, fiercely blooming, shed
Their rich reflected glow, their blood-resembling red.

ANNOTATIONS.

The action, the elephant skin, and other attributes of Śiva, are well described in a passage cited by Mr. Colebrooke, in his Essay on Sanskrit Prosody, from the Drama of Bhavabhúti, though there assigned to a form of his consort Durgá:

प्रचलितकरिकृत्तिपर्यन्तचञ्चन्नखाघातभिन्नेन्दुनिस्यन्दमानामृत-
श्च्योतजीवत्कपालावलीमुक्तचण्डाट्टहासत्रसद्भूरिभूतप्रवृत्तस्तुतिः

The elephant hide that robes thee, to thy steps
Swings to and fro; the whirling talons rend
The crescent on thy brow; from the torn orb
The trickling nectar falls; and every scull
That gems thy necklace laughs with horrid life.
Attendant spirits tremble and applaud.

गच्छन्तीनां रमणवसतिं योषितां तत्र रात्रौ
रुद्धालोके नरपतिपथे सूचिभेद्यैस्तमोभिः ॥
सौदामिन्या कनकनिकषच्छायया दर्शयोर्वीं
तोयोत्सर्गस्तनितमुखरो मा च भूर्विक्लवास्ताः ॥ ३९ ॥

तां कस्याञ्चिद्भवनवडभौ सुप्तपारावतायां
नीत्वा रात्रिं चिरविलसनात् खिन्नविद्युत्कलत्रः ॥

Amidst the darkness palpable, that shrouds,
Deep as the touchstone's gloom, the night with clouds,
With glittering lines of yellow lightning break,
And frequent trace in heaven the golden streak:
To those fond fair who tread the royal way,
The path their doubtful feet explore betray,
Those thunders hushed, whose shower-foreboding sound
Would check their ardour, and their hopes confound.

On some cool terrace, where the turtle-dove
In gentlest accents breathes connubial love,
Repose awhile; or plead your amorous vows
Through the long night, the lightning for your spouse.

ANNOTATIONS.

Verse 255. Amidst the darkness palpable, that shrouds.] So Milton's celebrated expression,

> And through the palpable obscure find out
> His uncouth way.——

The literal interpretation of the original passage is, "the darkness that may be pierced with a needle."

दृष्टे सूर्य्ये पुनरपि भवान् वाहयेदध्वशेषं
मन्दायन्ते न खलु सुहृदामभ्युपेतार्थकृत्याः ॥ ४० ॥

तस्मिन् काले नयनसलिलं योषितां खण्डितानां
शान्तिं नेयं प्रणयिभिरतो वर्त्म भानोस्त्यजाशु ॥
प्रालेयास्रं कमलवदनात् सोऽपि हर्त्तुं नलिन्याः
प्रत्यावृत्तस्त्वयि कररुधि स्यादनल्पाभ्यसूयः ॥ ४१ ॥

गम्भीरायाः पयसि सरितश्चेतसीव प्रसन्ने
छायात्मापि प्रकृतिसुभगो लप्स्यते ते प्रवेशम् ॥

Your path retraced, resumed your promised flight,
When in the east the sun restores the light,
And shun his course; for with the dawning sky
The sorrowing wife dispels the tearful eye,
Her lord returned;—so comes the sun, to chase
The dewy tears that stain the Padma's face;
And ill his eager penitence will bear,
That thou shouldst check his progress through the air.

Now to Gambhíra's wave thy shadow flies,
And on the stream's pellucid surface lies,
Like some loved image faithfully imprest
Deep in the maiden's pure unsullied breast:

ANNOTATIONS.

Verse 275. Now to Gambhíra's wave.] This river, and the Gandhavatí in the vicinity of the temple of Śiva, which lately occurred, are probably amongst the numerous and nameless brooks with which the province of Malwa abounds.

तस्मादस्याः कुमुदविशदान्यर्हसि त्वं न धैर्या-
न्मोघीकर्त्तुं चटुलसफरोद्वर्त्तनप्रेक्षितानि ॥ ४२ ॥

And vain thy struggles to escape her wiles,
Or disappoint those sweetly treacherous smiles,
Which glistening Sapharas insidious dart,
Bright as the lotus, at thy vanquished heart.

ANNOTATIONS.

Verse 281. Which glistening Sapharas.] The Saphara is described as a small white glistening fish; which darting rapidly through the water, is not unaptly compared to the twinkling glances of a sparkling eye. Assigning the attributes of female beauty to a stream, ceases to be incongruous when we advert to its constant personification by the Hindus: and it is as philosophical as it is poetical, to affiance a River and a Cloud. The smiles of rivers, nay, of the Ocean itself, have often been distributed by poetical imagination: thus Lucretius, invoking Venus, says,

Tibi rident æquora ponti.
The ocean waves laugh on you:

for his late translator, Mr. Good, is very angry at the conversion of this laugh into a smile, as effected by less daring of his predecessors. Milton again gives to the Ocean, nose, as well as dimples:

Cheered with the grateful smell, old Ocean smiles,

And Metastasio, in his beautiful Ode to Venus, has,

E i flutti ridono
Nel mar placati.
The waves now placid play,
And laugh amidst the deep.

All these, however, as well as our author, are far surpassed by Drayton, in his Poly-olbion; where hill and dale, forest and river, are constantly described with male or female attributes. With respect to the streams, he is not satisfied with wedding them to various objects, but fairly subjects them to the pains of parturition. The instances are frequent; but we may be content with the following, especially as it is explained and defended by his very learned illustrator:—

When

तस्याः किञ्चित् करधृतमिव प्राप्तवानीरशाखं
हृत्वा नीलं सलिलवसनं मुक्तरोधोनितम्बम् ॥
प्रस्थानं ते कथमपि सखे लम्बमानस्य भावि
ज्ञातास्वादः पुलिनजघनां को विहातुं समर्थः ॥ ४३ ॥

त्वन्निस्यन्दोच्छ्वसितवसुधागन्धसम्पर्कपुण्य-

What breast so firm unmoved by female charms?
Not thine, my friend: for now her waving arms,
O'erhanging Bayas, in thy grasp enclosed,
Rent her cœrulean vest, and charms exposed,
Prove how successfully she tempts delay,
And wins thee loitering from the lengthening way.

Thence, satiate, lead along the gentle breeze
That bows the lofty summits of the trees;

ANNOTATIONS.

When Pool, quoth she, was young, a lusty sea-born lass,
Great Albion to this nymph an earnest suitor was,
And bare himself so well, and so in favour came,
That he in little time upon this lovely dame
Begot three maiden Isles, his darlings and delight.

"As Albion (son of Neptune), from whom that first name of this Britain was supposed, is well fitted to the fruitful bed of this Pool, thus personated as a sea-nymph, the plain truth (as words may certify your eyes, saving all impropriety of object) is, that in the Pool are seated three isles, Bruntsey, Fursey, and St. Helen's, in situation and magnitude as I name them. Nor is the fiction of begetting the Isles improper, seeing Greek antiquities tell us of divers in the Mediterranean and the Archipelagus; as, Rhodes, Delus, Hiera, the Echinades, and others which have been, as it were, brought forth out of the salt womb of Amphitrite." SELDEN'S Illustrations.

स्रोतोरन्ध्रध्वनितसुभगं दन्तिभिः पीयमानः ॥
नीचैर्वास्यत्युपजिगमिषोर्देवपूर्वं गिरिं ते
शीतो वायुः परिणमयिता काननोडुम्बराणाम् ॥ ४४ ॥

तत्र स्कन्दं नियतवसतिं पुष्पमेघीकृतात्मा
पुष्पासारैस्स्नपयतु भवान् व्योमगङ्गाजलार्द्रैः ॥

And pure with fragrance, that the earth in flowers
Repays profuse to fertilizing showers;
Vocal with sounds the elephants excite,
To Devagiri wings its welcome flight.

There change thy form, and showering roses shed,
Bathed in the dews of heaven, on Skanda's head;
Son of the Crescent's god, whom holy ire
Called from the flame of all-devouring fire,

ANNOTATIONS.

Verse 294. Devagiri is the mountain of the deity, and may perhaps be the same with a place called, in the map, Dewagur, situated south of the Chumbul, in the centre of the province of Malwa, and precisely in the line of the Cloud's progress; which, as we shall hereafter find, has been continued nearly due north from Oujein. This hill is the site of a temple of Kártikeya; which, as well as that of Śiva described above, we must suppose to have enjoyed, in the days of antiquity, considerable reputation, or they would not have been so particularly specified in the poem.

Verse 296. Bathed in the dews of heaven.] "Moistened with the waters of the Mandákini," the celestial Ganges. Skanda, or Kártikeya, is the son of Śiva and Párvatí, and the Mars of Hindu mythology. There are various legends respecting his birth, one of which is presently noticed by the poet.

Verse 297. Several instances of the solitary production of offspring occur in the Hindu as well as in the Grecian mythology. Thus, as Pallas sprang from the brow of Jupiter, we have Skanda generated solely by the deity Śiva: Gangá springs from the head of the same deity, and Ganeśa is the self-born son of the goddess Párvatí. The miraculous birth of the warrior deity,

रक्षाहेतोर्नवशशिभृता वासवीनां चमूना-
मत्यादित्यं हुतवहमुखे सम्भृतं तद्धि तेजः ॥ ४५ ॥

ज्योतिर्लेखावलयि गलितं यस्य बर्हं भवानी
पुत्रप्रेम्णा कुवलयदलप्रापि कर्णे करोति ॥
धौतापाङ्गं हरशशिरुचा पावकेस्तं मयूरं
पश्चादद्रिग्रहणगुरुभिर्गर्जितैर्नर्तयेथाः ॥ ४६ ॥

To snatch the Lord of Swarga from despair,
And timely save the trembling hosts of air.

Next bid thy thunders o'er the mountain float,
And echoing caves repeat the pealing note;
Fit music for the bird, whose lucid eye
Gleams like the horned beauty of the sky;
Whose moulting plumes, to love maternal dear,
Lend brilliant pendants to Bhaváni's ear.

ANNOTATIONS.

deity, Skanda, was for the purpose of destroying Táraka, an Asur or demon, who, by the performance of continued and severe austerities, had acquired powers formidable to the gods. The eccentric genius of Southey has rendered it unnecessary, by his poem, 'The Curse of Keháma,' for me to explain the nature or results of these acts of devotion. The germ of Skanda was cast by Śiva into the flame of Agni, the god of fire; who, being unable to sustain the increasing burden, transferred it to the goddess Gangá: she accordingly was delivered of the deity, Skanda; who was afterwards received and reared, among thickets of the Śara reed (Saccharum Sara), by the six daughters of a king, named Krittiká; or, according to other legends, by the wives of seven great Rishis or Saints. In either case, they form in astronomy the asterism of the Pleiades. Upon his coming to maturity, Skanda encountered and killed the demon, who had filled the region of Indra with dismay:—

Emissumque imâ de sede Typhoëa terrâ,
Cœlitibus, fecisse metum.

आराध्यैनं शरवनभवं देवमुल्लङ्घिताध्वा
सिद्धद्वन्द्वैर्जलकणभयाद्वीणिभिर्दत्तमार्गः ॥
व्यालम्बेथास्सुरभितनयालम्भजां मानयिष्यन्
स्रोतोमूर्त्या भुवि परिणतां रन्तिदेवस्य कीर्त्तिम् ॥ ४७ ॥

To him whose youth in Śara thickets strayed,
Reared by the nymphs, thy adoration paid,
Resume thy road, and to the world proclaim
The glorious tale of Rantideva's fame,
Sprung from the blood of countless oxeń shed,
And a fair river through the regions spread.

ANNOTATIONS.

Verse 305 &c. Whose moulting plumes, to love maternal dear.] Skanda, or Kártikeya, is represented mounted upon a peacock; and Bhaváni we have already seen is the wife of Śiva, and half-mother to this deity. We have also noticed the frequency of the allusion to the delight the peacock is supposed to feel upon the appearance of cloudy and rainy weather.

Verse 310. Rantideva is the son of Sankriti, and sixth in descent from Bharata. Vishńu Puráńa, p. 450.

Verse 311. Sprung from the blood of countless oxen shed.] The sacrifice of the horse or of the cow, the गोमेधा or अश्वमेधा, appears to have been common in the earliest periods of the Hindu ritual. It has been conceived that the sacrifice was not real, but typical; and that the form of sacrificing only was performed upon the victim, after which it was set at liberty. The text of this passage, however, is unfavourable to such a notion, as the metamorphosis of the blood of the kine into a river certainly implies that blood was diffused. The expression of the original, literally rendered, is, "sprung from the blood of the daughters of Surabhi," that is, 'kine;' Surabhi being a celebrated cow produced at the churning of the ocean, and famed for granting to her votaries whatever they desired. "Daughter of Surabhi" is an expression of common occurrence, to denote the cow.

Verse 312. And a fair river through the regions spread.] The name of this river is not mentioned in the text of the poem, but is said by the Commentators to be the Charmanvatí; and such a name occurs in Major Wilford's lists, from the Puráńas, amongst those streams which seem to arise from the north-west portion of the Vindhya mountains. The modern appellation

त्वय्यादातुं जलमवनते शार्ङ्गिणो वर्णचौरे
तस्यास्सिन्धोः पृथुमपि तनुं दूरभावात् प्रवाहम् ॥
प्रेक्षिष्यन्ते गगनगतयो नूनमावर्ज्य दृष्टी-

Each lute-armed spirit from thy path retires,
Lest drops ungenial damp the tuneful wires.
Celestial couples, bending from the skies,
Turn on thy distant course their downward eyes,
And watch thee lessening in thy long descent,
To rob the river's scanty stores intent;
As clothed in sacred darkness not thine own,
Thine is the azure of the costly stone,

ANNOTATIONS.

appellation of the Charmanvatí is generally conceived to be the Chumbul, which corresponds with it in source and situation; and which, as it must have been traversed by the Cloud in its northerly course, would most probably have been described by the poet. It may be curious to trace the change of Charmanvatí into Chumbul; which seems very practicable, notwithstanding their present dissimilarity. Tavernier, describing the route from Surat to Agra by way of Brampore, calls this river the Chammelnadi; the possessive termination Vatí (वती) having been confounded with the Nadí (नदी) 'a river': Chammelnadi is, therefore, the Chammel river. Again, the addition Nadí being regarded as superfluous, it has been dropped altogether, and we have the Chammel, or Chambel. The word Chammel may readily be deduced from Charman; as, in the dialects of Hindustan, the letters N and L are constantly interchangeable, and careless pronunciation may easily convert Charmel into Chammel, or Chambel.

Verse 314. These two lines occur a little earlier in the Sanskrit; but as they seemed more connected with the two following, and to be rather awkward in their original position, they have been introduced here.

Verse 319. In sacred darkness not thine own.] Being of the same dark blue colour as Kṛishńa; a hue the poet charges the Cloud with having stolen.

रेकं मुक्तागुणमिव भुवः स्थूलमध्येन्द्रनीलम् ॥ ४८ ॥
तामुत्तीर्य्य व्रज परिचितभ्रूलताविभ्रमाणां
पक्ष्मोत्क्षेपादुपरि विलसत्कृष्णसारप्रभाणाम् ॥
कुन्दक्षेपानुगमधुकरश्रीजुषामात्मविम्बं
पात्रीकुर्व्वन् दशपुरवधूनेत्रकौतूहलानाम् ॥ ४९ ॥

A central sapphire in the loosened girth
Of scattering pearls, that strung the blooming earth.

The streamlet traversed, to the eager sight
Of Daśapura's fair impart delight;
Welcomed with looks that sparkling eyes bestow,
Whose arching brows like graceful creepers glow,
Whose upturned lashes to thy lofty way
The pearly ball and pupil dark display;
Such contrast as the lovely Kunda shows,
When the black bee sits pleased amidst her snows.

ANNOTATIONS.

Verse 321. A central sapphire &c.] This comparison, when understood, is happily imagined; but to understand it, we must suppose ourselves above the Cloud, and to be looking obliquely downwards upon its dark body; as shining drops of rain form a continuous line on either side of it, and connect it with the earth.

Verse 324. Daśapura, according to its etymology, should mean a district; that of the ten cities. It is said however, by the Commentators, to be the name of a city; and by one of them, Mallináth, to be that of the city of Rantideva: if he is correct, it may possibly be the modern Rintimpore or Rantampore; especially as that town, lying a little to the north of the Chumbul, and in the line from Oujein to Tahnesar, is consequently in the course of the Cloud's progress, and the probable position of Daśapura.

Verse 329. Such contrast as the lovely Kunda shews.] The Kunda (Jasminum pubescens) bears a beautiful white flower; and the large black bee being seated in the centre of its cup, they

ब्रह्मावर्त्तं जनपदमधश्छायया गाहमानः
क्षेत्रं क्षत्रप्रधनपिशुनं कौरवं तद् भजेथाः ॥
राजन्यानां शितशरशतैर्यत्र गाण्डीवधन्वा

Hence to the land of Brahma's favoured sons,
O'er Kuru's fatal field, thy journey runs.
With deepest glooms hang o'er the deadly plain,
Dewed with the blood of mighty warriors slain.
There Arjun's wrath opposing armies felt,
And countless arrows strong Gándíva dealt,

ANNOTATIONS.

they afford a very delicate and truly poetical resemblance to the dark iris, and white ball of a full black eye.

Verse 331. Hence to the land of Brahmá's favoured sons.] Brahmávartta (ब्रह्मावर्त्त) is the abode of Brahmá, or the holy land of the Hindus. It is thus described by Menu, ii. 17:

सरस्वतीदृषद्वत्योर्देवनद्योर्यदन्तरम् ।
तं देवनिर्मितं देशं ब्रह्मावर्त्तं प्रचक्षते ॥

"Between the two divine rivers, Saraswatí and Drishadwatí, lies the tract of land which the sages have named Brahmávartta, because it was frequented by the gods."

Verse 332. Kuru-Kshetra (कुरुक्षेत्र), the Field of the Kurus, is the scene of the celebrated battle between them and the Pańdus, which forms the subject of the Mahábhárata. It lies a little to the south-east of Tahnesar, and is still a place of note and pilgrimage. It is not far from Panniput, the seat of another celebrated engagement, that between the assembled Princes of Hindustan, and the combined strength of the Marhattas. This part of the country, indeed, presenting few obstacles to the movement of large armies, has in every period of the history of Hindustan been the theatre of contention.

Verse 335. Arjun was the friend and pupil of Krishńa, and the third of the Pańdava Princes. He has been long ago introduced to European readers, especially in Sir Charles Wilkins's able translation of the Bhaguvad-Gítá; and appears, in the opening of that poem, in a very amiable light:

अहोवत महत् पापं कर्त्तुं व्यवसिता वयम् ।
यद्राज्यसुखलोभेन हन्तुं स्वजनमुद्यताः ॥ ४४ ॥

यदि

धारापातैस्त्वमिव कमलान्यभ्यषिञ्चन्मुखानि ॥ ५० ॥

हित्वा हालामभिमतरसां रेवतीलोचनाङ्कां
बन्धुप्रीत्या समरविमुखो लाङ्गली याः सिषेवे ॥
कृत्वा तासामभिगममपां सौम्य सारस्वतीना-

Thick as thy drops, that, in the pelting shower,
Incessant hurtle round the shrinking flower.

O'er Saraswatí's waters wing your course,
And inward prove their purifying force;
Most holy, since, oppressed with heaviest grief,
The ploughshare's mighty Lord here sought relief;

ANNOTATIONS.

यदि मामप्रतीकारमशस्त्रं शस्त्रपाणयः ।
धार्तराष्ट्रा रणे हन्युस्तन्मे क्षेमतरं भवेत् ॥ ४५ ॥

"Alas! that for the lust of the enjoyments of dominion we stand here ready to murder the "kindred of our own blood. I would rather patiently suffer that the sons of Dhṛitaráshṫra, "with their weapons in their hands, should come upon me, and, unopposed, kill me un- "guarded in the field."

Verse 336. As the horses and swords of chivalry received particular names, so the weapons of the Hindu knights have been similarly honoured. Gáńdíva is the bow of Arjuna.

Verse 339. The Saraswatí, or, as it is corruptedly called, the Sursooty, falls from the southern portion of the Himálaya mountains, and runs into the great desert, where it is lost in the sands. It flows a little to the north-west of Kuru-kshetra; and though rather out of the line of the Cloud's progress, not sufficiently so to prevent the introduction into the poem of a stream so celebrated and so holy.

Verse 342. We have here the reason why the waters of the Saraswatí are objects of religious veneration. Balaráma is the eldest brother of Kṛishńa. He is called (लाङ्गली) Lángalí, (हलभृत्) Halabhṛit, &c., from his being armed with a ploughshare; which he is said to have employed

मन्तःशुद्धस्त्वमपि भविता वर्णमात्रेण कृष्णः ॥ ५१ ॥

तस्माद्गच्छेरनुकनखलं शैलराजावतीर्णां

No longer quaffed the wine cup with his wife,
But mournèd in solitude o'er kindred strife. 344

Thy journey next o'er Kanakhala bends,
Where Jahnu's daughter from the hills descends;

ANNOTATIONS.

employed as bills were formerly used, for pulling his enemies down from their horses, &c., which enabled him then to dispatch them with his club. Although Kṛishńa took an active part in the warfare between the Kurus and Páńdus, Balaráma refused to join either party; and retired into voluntary seclusion, filled with grief at the nature of the contest: 'deserting,' the poet says, 'his favourite liquor marked by the eyes of Revatí;'—that is, emulating their brightness as she shared the revels of her husband. Vishńu Puráńa, p. 510, 604.

Verse 345. The name is Kalakhala in the original, but it more properly is as given above. The meaning of the word, agreeably to a forced etymology, is thus explained in the Gangá-dwára Máhátmya section of the Skanda Puráńa:

खलः को नात्र मुक्तिं वै भजते तत्र मज्जनात् ।
अतः कनखलं तीर्थं नाम्ना चक्रुर्मुनीश्वराः ॥

"What man (कः) so wicked (खल) as not to obtain (न) future happiness from bathing there? Thence the holy sages have called this Tírtha, by the name of Kanakhala."

It also occurs in this passage of the Hari Vanśa portion of the Mahábhárata:

गङ्गाद्वारं कनखलं सोमो वै यत्र संस्थितः ॥

"Gangádwára, Kanakhala, and where the moon impends:"

and, in both instances, is applied to the place where the Ganges descends into the low ground of Hindustán. The name is still retained; as appears from the testimony of an impartial witness, Lieut. Webb, in his Survey of the Sources of the Ganges; a survey which has essentially improved the geography of those regions:—"The party arrived at Haridwára, and encamped at the village of Kanakhala" (Kankhal), on the west bank of the Ganges, at the distance of about two miles from the fair." Asiatic Researches, xi. 449. The Ganges does not now descend at Kankhal; and it is a question for geologists to solve, whether the Ganges has,

जह्नोः कन्यां सगरतनयस्वर्गसोपानपङ्क्तिम् ॥

Whose sacred waters, to Bhagírath given,
Conveyed the sons of Sagara to heaven. 348

ANNOTATIONS.

has, in the course of nineteen centuries, so corroded the skirts of the mountain, as to have thrown back the gorge through which she passes, a distance of two miles. See note on a view of Kankhal, Oriental Portfolio.

Verse 346. Where Jahnu's daughter from the hills descends.] Jahnu's daughter is Gangá, or the Ganges; which river, "after forcing its way through an extensive tract of mountainous country, here first enters on the plains." It is rather extraordinary that Kálidása should have omitted the name of Haridwára (Hurdwár), and preferred Kanakhala, especially as the former occurs in the Puráńas, in the Skanda Puráńa, as mentioned in the note, page 450, vol. xi. of the Researches; and in this passage from the Matsya Puráńa, cited in the Puráńa Sarvaswa:

सर्व्वत्र सुलभा गङ्गा त्रिषु स्थानेषु दुर्लभा ।
हरिद्वारे प्रयागे च गङ्गासागरसङ्गमे ॥

"The Ganges is everywhere easy of access, except in three places, Haridwára, Prayága, and her junction with the sea." Jahnu is the name of a sage, who, upon being disturbed in his devotions by the passage of the river, drank up its waters. Upon relenting, however, he allowed the stream to re-issue from his ear; and the affinity of Gangá to the saint arises from this second birth.

Verse 348. Conveyed the sons of Sagara to heaven.] The Ganges, according to the legend, was brought from heaven, by the religious rites of Bhagíratha, the great-grandson of Sagar; who, as well as that king, had engaged in a long series of acts of austerity, for the purpose of procuring the descent of the river to wash the ashes of Sagar's 60,000 sons. The youths had been reduced to this state by the indignation of Kapila, a saint, whose devotions they had disturbed in their eager quest of the horse that was to be the victim of an Áswamedha by their father. Their misfortunes did not, however, cease with their existence; as their admission to Swarga depended, according to the instructions of Garuda, upon the use of the water of the Ganges in the administration of their funeral rites. At this period the Ganges watered the plains of heaven alone; and it was no easy undertaking to induce her to resign those for an humble and earthly course. Sagara, his son Ansuman, and grandson Dilípa, died without being able to effect the descent of the heavenly stream: but his great-grandson, Bhagíratha, was more fortunate; and his long-continued austerities were rewarded by

गौरीवक्त्रभ्रुकुटिरचनां या विहस्यैव फेनै-
श्शम्भोः केशग्रहणमकरोदिन्दुलग्नोर्मिहस्ता ॥ ५२ ॥

तस्याः पातुं सुरगज इव व्योम्नि पूर्वार्द्धलम्बी
त्वं चेदच्छस्फटिकविशदं तर्कयेस्तिर्य्यगम्भः ॥
संसर्पन्त्यास्सपदि भवतः स्रोतसि च्छायया ऽसौ

She, who with smiling waves disportive strayed
Through Śambhu's locks, and with his tresses played;
Unheeding, as she flowed delighted down,
The gathering storm of Gaurí's jealous frown.

Should her clear current tempt thy thirsty lip,
And thou inclining bend the stream to sip;
Thy form, like Indra's Elephant, displayed,
Shall clothe the crystal waves with deepest shade;

ANNOTATIONS.

by the fall of the Ganges, the bathing of the ashes of his ancestors with the holy water, and the establishment of them in the enjoyments of Swarga. The whole story is told in the First Book of the Rámáyaña, from the 32d to the 35th section.

Verse 349. She, who with smiling waves disportive strayed.] The earth being unable to bear the sudden descent of so great a river as the Ganges, Śiva was induced, at the intercession of Bhagíratha, to interpose his sacred head. Accordingly, Gangá first alighted on the head of the deity, and remained for a considerable period wandering amongst the tresses of his long and entangled hair, to the extreme jealousy and displeasure, according to Kálidása, of the goddess Gaurí or Párvatí, Śiva's consort.

Verse 355. Thy form, like Indra's Elephant.] We have already noticed that presiding deities are attached to the various points of the compass, and that each of these deities is furnished with a male and female Elephant. Amongst these, the most distinguished is Airávata, the Elephant of Indra, in his capacity of Regent of the East.

स्यादस्थानोपगतयमुनासङ्गमेनाभिरामा ॥ ५३ ॥

आसीनानां सुरभितशिलं नाभिगन्धैर्मृगाणां
तस्या एव प्रभवमचलं प्राप्य गौरं तुषारैः ॥
वक्ष्यस्यध्वश्रमविनयने तस्य शृङ्गे निषण्ण-
श्शोभां शुभ्रत्रिनयनवृषोत्खातपङ्कोपमेयाम् ॥ ५४ ॥

With sacred glooms the darkening waves shall glide,
As where the Jumna mixes with the tide.
As Śiva's Bull upon his sacred neck,
Amidst his ermine, owns some sable speck;
So shall thy shade upon the mountain show,
Whose sides are silvered with eternal snow;
Where Gungá leads her purifying waves,
And the Musk Deer spring frequent from the caves.

ANNOTATIONS.

Verse 358. As where the Jumna mingles with the tide.] The waters of the Jumna, or Yamuná, are described as much darker than those of the Ganges at the point of their confluence, from the circumstances of the stream being less shallow and less discoloured with clay or sand. Occasionally, indeed, the waters of the Ganges there are so white from the diffusion of earthy particles, that, according to the creed of the natives, the river flows with milk. The confluence of rivers always forms a sacred spot in India: but the meeting of the Ganges and Jumna at Prayága or Allahabad, from the sanctity of both the currents, and from the supposed subterraneous addition of the Saraswatí, is a place of distinguished holiness.

Verse 359. As Śiva's Bull upon his sacred neck.] The Bull is the vehicle of Śiva, and the animal of the god is always painted of a milk-white colour.

Verse 364. And the Musk Deer spring frequent from the caves.] This animal is what is called the Thibet Musk; "but its favourite residence is among the lofty Himalley (Himálaya) mountains, which divide Tartary from Hindustán." See the best account of the Musk Deer yet published, in Gladwin's Oriental Miscellany, Calcutta 1798, accompanied with accurate drawings by Mr. Home, of the figure, teeth, hoofs, &c.

तं चेद्वायौ सरति सरलस्कन्धसङ्घट्टजन्मा
बाधेतोल्काक्षयितचमरीबालभारो दवाग्निः ॥

From writhing boughs should forest flames arise,
Whose breath the air, and brand the Yak supplies;

ANNOTATIONS.

Verse 365. Should forest flames arise.] The conflagration of the woods in India is of frequent occurrence; and the causes of it are here described by the poet. The intertwining branches of the Saral (Pinus longifolia), of the Bambu, and other trees, being set in motion by the wind, their mutual friction engenders flame. This spread abroad by the air, and, according to the poet, by the thick tails of the Yak of Tartary or Bos Grunniens (from which Chowries are made), readily communicates to the surrounding foliage, dried up by the heat of the sun, and exceedingly inflammable. The burning of a forest is so well described in the Ritu Sanhára, that I cannot avoid citing the passage, although its length perhaps requires an apology:

पटुतरवनदाहात् प्लुष्टशष्पप्ररोहाः
परुषपवनवेगात् क्षिप्तसंशुष्कपर्णाः ॥
दिनकरपरितापात् क्षीणतोयाः समन्ताद्
विदधति भयमुच्चैर्वीक्ष्यमाणा वनान्ताः ॥ २२ ॥

विकचनवकुसुम्भस्वच्छसिन्दूरभासा
परुषपवनवेगोद्भूतवेगेन तूर्णम् ॥
तरुविटपलताग्र्यालिङ्गनव्याकुलेन
दिशि दिशि परिदग्धा भूमयः पावकेन ॥ २३ ॥

ध्वनति पवनविद्धः पर्वतानां दरीषु
स्फुटति पटुनिनादः शुष्कवंशस्थलीषु ॥
प्रसरति तृणमध्ये लब्धवृद्धिः क्षणेन
क्षपयति मृगवर्गं प्रान्तलग्नो दवाग्निः ॥ २४ ॥

बहुतर इव जातः शाल्मलीनां वनेषु
स्फुरति कनकगौरः कोटरेषु द्रुमाणाम् ॥
परिणतदलशाखादुत्पतत्याशु वृक्षाद्
भ्रमति पवनधूतः सर्वतोऽग्निर्वनान्ते ॥ २५ ॥

Which,

अर्हस्येनं शमयितुमलं वारिधारासहस्रै-
रापन्नार्त्तिप्रशमनफलाः सम्पदो ह्युत्तमानाम् ॥ ५५ ॥

ये त्वां मुक्तध्वनिमसहनाः स्वाङ्गभङ्गाय तस्मिन्
दर्पोत्सेकादुपरि शरभा लङ्घयिष्यन्त्यलङ्घ्यम् ॥

Instant afford the aid 'tis thine to lend,
And with a thousand friendly streams descend.
Of all the fruits that fortune yields, the best
Is still the power to succour the distrest.
Shame is the fruit of actions indiscreet,
And vain presumption ends but in defeat.

ANNOTATIONS.

Which, omitting a few repetitions and excrescences, may be thus translated:

The forest flames—the foliage, sear and dry,
Bursts in a blaze beneath the torrid sky.
Fanned by the gale, the fires resplendent grow,
Brighter than blooming Safflower's vermil glow;
Brighter than Minium's fierceness, as they wind
Around the branch, or shoot athwart the rind:
Play through the leaves, along the trunk ascend,
And o'er the top in tapering radiance end.
The crackling Bambu rushing flames surround,
Roar through the rocks, and through the caves resound.
The dry blade fuel to their rage supplies,
And instant flame along the herbage flies,
Involves the forest tenants in its sphere,
And in its rapid course outstrips the deer.
Like palest gold the towering ray aspires,
And wafting gusts diffuse the wasting fires:
Wide fly the sparks, the burning branches fall,
And one relentless blaze envelopes all.

तान् कुर्वीथास्तुमुलकरकावृष्टिहासावकीर्णान्
के वा न स्युः परिभवपदं निष्फलारम्भयत्नाः ॥ ५६ ॥

तत्र व्यक्तं दृषदि चरणन्यासमर्द्धेन्दुमौले-
श्शश्वत् सिद्धैरुपचितबलिं भक्तिनम्रः परीयाः ॥

So shall the Śarabhas, who thee oppose,
Themselves to pain and infamy expose;
When round their heads, amidst the lowering sky,
White as a brilliant smile, thy hailstones fly.

Next to the mountain, with the foot imprest
Of him who wears the crescent for his crest,

ANNOTATIONS.

Verse 373. The Śarabha is a fabulous animal, described as possessing eight legs, and of a fierce untractable nature. It is supposed to haunt these mountains especially.

Verse 376. White as a brilliant smile.] It is remarkable that a laugh or smile is always compared to objects of a white colour, by Hindu writers.

Verse 377. Next to the mountain, with the foot imprest.] The fancied or artificial print of some saint or deity on hills or detached stones is a common occurrence in the creeds of the East. The idea is not confined to the inhabitants of Hindustán; but is asserted similarly by those of Nepal, Ceylon, and Ava; as may be seen in Turner's Journey to Nepal, Symes's Embassy to Ava, &c. The Mussulmans also have the same notion with respect to many of the Prophets; for they believe that the marks of Adam's feet remain on a mountain in the centre of Ceylon; and that those of Abraham were impressed upon a stone which was formerly at Mecca, and which he had used as a temporary scaffold in constructing the upper part of the primary Kaaba. A number of similar stories may be found in Mirkhond, and other Mohammedan authors. The Himálaya mountains are the scene of most of Śiva's adventures, his religious abstraction, his love, marriage, &c.; and the place here mentioned may have some connexion with the Ghát, and neighbouring hill at Haridwára, mentioned in Capt. Raper's account of the survey of the Ganges, by the name of Haraka Pairi, 'the foot of Hara or Śiva.'

यस्मिन् दृष्टे करणविगमादूर्ध्वमुद्धूतपापाः
कल्पन्ते ऽस्य स्थिरगणपदप्राप्तये श्रद्दधानाः ॥ ५७ ॥

Devoutly pass, and with religious glow
Around the spot in pious circles go:
For there have Saints the sacred altar raised,
And there eternal offerings have blazed,
And blest the faithful worshippers; for they
The stain of sin with life shall cast away,
And, after death, a glad admittance gain
To Śiva's glorious and immortal train.

ANNOTATIONS.

Verse 380. Around the spot in pious circles go.] Circumambulating a venerable object, or person, is a usual mark of profound respect. Thus, in Sakuntalá, Kanwa thus addresses his foster-daughter, on the eve of her departure:

वत्से इतः सद्यो हुताग्नीन् प्रदक्षिणीकुरुष्व ।

"My best beloved, come and walk with me round the sacrificial fire."

And again, in the Rámáyańa, we have the same ceremony described thus:

जनकस्य वचः श्रुत्वा पाणीन् पाणिभिरस्पृशन् ।
चत्वारस्ते चतुर्णां वशिष्ठस्य मते स्थिताः ॥
अग्निं प्रदक्षिणं कृत्वा वेदिं राजानमेव च ।
ऋषींश्चापि महात्मानः सहभार्य्या रघूद्वहाः ॥

"Hearing the words of Janaka, the four supporters of Raghu's race, previously placed according to the direction of Vaśishtha, took the hands of the four damsels within theirs, and, with their spouses, circumambulated the fire, the altar, the king, and the sages."

Rámáyańa, with Translation, 1, 60, 37.

A somewhat similar practice seems to have been in use amongst the Celtic nations. The Highland leech, who is called to the aid of Waverley, "would not proceed to any operation until he had perambulated his couch three times, moving from east to west, according to the course of the sun." And Sir Walter Scott observes, in a Note, that "the Highlanders will still make the 'deasil'" (the circumambulation, or 'pra-dakshińa') "around those whom they wish well to."

शब्दायन्ते मधुरमनिलैः कीचकाः पूर्य्यमाणाः
संरक्ताभिस्त्रिपुरविजयो गीयते किन्नरीभिः ॥
निर्ह्रादी ते मुरज इव चेत् कन्दरेषु ध्वनिः स्यात्
सङ्गीतार्थो ननु पशुपतेस्तत्र भावी समग्रः ॥ ५८ ॥

प्रालेयाद्रेरुपतटमतिक्रम्य तांस्तान् विशेषान्

Here wake the chorus:—bid the thunder's sound,
Deep and reiterated, roll around,
Loud as a hundred drums;—while softer strains
The swelling gale breathes sweetly through the canes;
And from the lovely songsters of the skies,
Hymns to the victor of Tripura rise.

Thence to the snow-clad hills thy course direct,
And Krauncha's celebrated pass select;

ANNOTATIONS.

Verse 391. The lovely songsters of the skies] are the females of the Kinnaras, or demigods, attendant upon Kuvera, and the musicians of Swarga.

Verse 392. Hymns to the victor of Tripura rise.] Tripura is the name of a city, or rather, as its etymology implies, three cities collectively: these formed the domain of a celebrated Demon, or Asur, destroyed by Śiva, and were reduced to ashes by that Deity. According to the Commentators, we have here a full and complete concert in honour of Mahádeva.

Verse 394. And Krauncha's celebrated pass select.] I have not been able to make any thing of this pass or hole (क्रौञ्चरन्ध्र). The original text states it to be on the very skirt (उपतट) of the snowy mountain; and calls it also हंसद्वार, 'The gate of the geese,' who fly annually this way to the Mánasarovara lake. Krauncha is described as a mountain, in the Mahábhárat; and, being personified, is there called the son of Mainaka. A mountain also called Krauncha Meru occurs in Mr. Wilford's lists, amongst those mountains situated in the north. It must lie at some distance from the plains; and perhaps the Poet, by using the term उपतट, implies its relative situation with the loftiest part of the range or proper snow-clad mountains.

हंसद्वारं भृगुपतियशोवर्त्म यत्क्रौञ्चरन्ध्रम् ॥
तेनोदीचीं दिशमनुसरेस्तिर्य्यगायामशोभी
श्यामः पादो बलिनियमनाभ्युद्यतस्येव विष्णोः ॥ ५९ ॥

That pass the swans in annual flight explore;
And erst a Hero's mighty arrows tore.
Winding thy way due north through the defile,
Thy form compressed, with borrowed grace shall smile:
The sable foot that Bali marked with dread,
A god triumphant o'er creation spread.

ANNOTATIONS.

Verse 396. And erst a Hero's mighty arrows tore.] The Krauncha pass, or defile, in the Krauncha mountain, is said to have been made by the arrows of Bhṛigupati, or Paraśuráma, who was educated by Śiva on Mount Kailása, and who thus opened himself a passage from the mountains upon the occasion of his travelling southwards to destroy the Kshatriya or military race. Paraśuráma is an Avatár, or descent of Vishńu, in the person of the son of the Saint Jamadagni; and this Saint being also descended from the celebrated sage Bhṛigu, his son is named Bhṛigupati, or, Chief of that race. See Legend of Paraśuráma, Vishńu Puráńa, p. 401. The fissure in the Krauncha mountain is, in the Váyu and Vámana Puráńas, ascribed to Kártikeya. Ibid, p. 169, note 10.

Verse 399. The sable foot that Bali marked with dread.] The story of Bali and the Vámana, or dwarf Avatár, was first told by Sonnerat, and has since been frequently repeated. As the former is a good specimen of the style in which Hindu legends were narrated by European travellers in the last century, it may be here inserted. "The fifth incarnation was in a Bramin dwarf, under the name of Vamen: it was wrought to restrain the pride of the giant Bely. The latter, after having conquered the gods, expelled them from Sorgon: he was generous, true to his word, compassionate, and charitable. Vichenou, under the form of a very little Bramin, presented himself before him while he was sacrificing, and asked him for three paces of land to build a hut. Bely ridiculed the apparent imbecility of the dwarf, in telling him that he ought not to limit his demand to a bequest so trifling;—that his generosity could bestow a much larger donation of land. Vamen answered, that being of so small a stature, what he asked was more than sufficient. The prince immediately granted his request; and,

गत्वा चोर्द्ध्वं दशमुखभुजोच्छ्वासितप्रस्थसन्धेः

Ascended thence, a transient period rest,
Renowned Kailása's venerated guest.

ANNOTATIONS.

and, to ratify his donation, poured water into his right hand; which was no sooner done, than the dwarf grew so prodigiously, that his body filled the universe! He measured the earth with one pace, and the heavens with another; and then summoned Bely to give him his word for the third. The prince then recognised Vichenou, adored him, and presented his head to him: but the god, satisfied with his submission, sent him to govern the Pandalon; and permitted him to return every year to the earth, the day of the full moon, in the month of November."

SONNERAT's Voyages in the East Indies, Calcutta edition, vol. I. p. 22.

Verse 402. Kailása's venerated guest.] Kailása, as it here appears, a part of the Himálaya range, is in fable a mountain of costly gems or of crystal, the site of Kuvera's capital, and the favourite haunt of Śiva. I shall borrow, from the notes to Southey's 'Curse of Kehama,' a description of it from Baldæus, curious enough in itself, but still more so for its strange medley of accuracy and incorrectness, and its uncouth transformation and commixture of the Sanskrit names. "The residence of Ixora (Íśwara or ईश्वर) is upon the silver mount Kalaja (Kailása or कैलास), to the south of the famous mountain Mahameru, being a most delicious place, planted with all sorts of trees, that bear fruit all the year round. The roses and other flowers send forth a most odoriferous scent; and the pond at the foot of the mount is enclosed with pleasant walks of trees, that afford an agreeable shade; whilst the peacocks and divers other birds entertain the ear with their harmonious noise, as the beautiful women do the eyes. The circumjacent woods are inhabited by a certain people called Munis or Rixis (Rishis or ऋषि), who, avoiding the conversation of others, spend their time in offering daily sacrifices to their god.

"It is observable, that though these Pagans are generally black themselves, they do represent these Rixis to be of a fair complexion, with long white beards, and long garments hanging cross-ways, from about the neck down over the breast. They are in such high esteem among them, that they believe whom they bless are blessed, and whom they curse are cursed.

"Within the mountain lives another generation, called Jexaquinnera (Yaksha or यक्ष, and Kinnara or किन्नर), and Quendra (Indra or इन्द्र), who are free from all trouble, and spend their days in continual contemplation, praises, and prayers to god. Round about the mountain stand seven ladders, by which you ascend to a spacious plain, in the middle whereof is a bell of

कैलासस्य त्रिदशवनितादर्पणस्यातिथिः स्याः ॥
तुङ्गोच्छ्रायैः कुमुदविशदैर्यो वितत्य स्थितः खं
राशीभूतः प्रतिदिशमिव त्र्यम्बकस्याट्टहासः ॥ ६० ॥

That mount, whose sides with brightest lustre shine,
A polished mirror, worthy charms divine;
Whose base a Rávan from its centre wrung,
Shaken, not sundered, stable though unstrung;
Whose lofty peaks to distant realms in sight
Present a Śiva's smile, a lotus white.

ANNOTATIONS.

of silver and a square table, surrounded with nine precious stones of divers colours: upon this table lies a silver rose, called Tamarapua (?), which contains two women as bright and fair as a pearl: one is called Brigasiri (?), *i.e.* 'The lady of the mouth;' the other Tarasiri (?), *i.e.* 'The lady of the tongue:' because they praise God with the mouth and tongue. In the centre of this rose is the triangle of Quivelinga (Siva-linga); which, they say, is the permanent residence of God." BALDÆUS. The latter part of this description is quite new to the Pandits, and I suspect is rather Mohammedan than Hindu. Little is said of Kailása in authentic Hindu legend. See Vishńu Puráńa, p. 172.

Verse 406. Shaken, not sundered, stable though unstrung.] This alludes to a legend of Rávańa's having attempted to remove the mountain from its situation; although he did not succeed as well as Satan and his compeers, when,

"From their foundations loosening to and fro,
They plucked the seated hills."

He considerably unhinged its foundations. The story perhaps originates with the curious vibrating rock at Mahábalipuram; of which it may be said, as is observed by Selden of Mainamber, *i.e.* Ambrose's stone in Cornwall, not far from Penzance, that "it is so great, that many men's united strength cannot remove it, yet with one finger you may wag it."

Verse 407. Whose lofty peaks to distant realms in sight.] The lofty peaks of the Himálaya range of mountains are very justly stated by the poet to be visible to surrounding regions (प्रतिदिशम्). They are seen, in the south, from situations more remote than those in which any other peaks have been discerned; and the supposition of their exceeding even the Andes in elevation has been confirmed by recent inquiries.

उत्पश्यामि त्वयि तटगते स्निग्धभिन्नाञ्जनाभे
सद्यःकृत्तद्विरददशनच्छेदगौरस्य तस्य ॥
शोभामद्रेः स्तिमितनयनप्रेक्षणीयां भवित्री-
मंशन्यस्ते सति हलभृतो मेचके वाससीव ॥ ६१ ॥

And lo! those peaks, than ivory more clear,
When yet unstained the parted tusks appear,
Beam with new lustre, as around their head
Thy glossy glooms metallic darkness spread; 412
As shews a Halabhrita's sable vest,
More fair the pallid beauty of his breast.

ANNOTATIONS.

Verse 412. Thy glossy glooms metallic darkness spread.] The expression in the original (स्निग्धभिन्नाञ्जनाभे) may be rendered, "shining like glossy powdered antimony," a preparation used for darkening the eye-lashes or the edges of the eye-lids, a practice common to the females of the East. It is also explained to mean merely, "black divided antimony;" and the shining greyish-blue of the sulphuret of antimony, the substance alluded to, may often be observed in the hue of heavy clouds.

Verse 413. Halabhṛita is a name of Balaráma; and implies, as has been before explained, his use of a ploughshare as a weapon. He is represented of a white colour, clothed in a dark-blue vest; and is thus alluded to in the introduction to the Gíta Govinda of Jayadeva:

वहसि वपुषि विशदे वसनं जलदाभं हलहतिभीतिमिलितयमुनाभम् ॥
केशव धृतहलधररूप जय जगदीश हरे ॥

Thus translated by Sir William Jones, in his Essay on the Chronology of the Hindus: "Thou "bearest on thy bright body a mantle shining like a blue Cloud, or like the water of the "Yamuna tripping towards thee through fear of thy furrowing ploughshare, O Cesava! "assuming the form of Balaráma, be victorious O Heri! Lord of the Universe."

Verse 416. In sport may Gaurí with her Śiva stray.] I have already noticed that these mountains are the scene of Śiva's loves and sports: they may still be considered as his favourite haunts, for some traces of him seem to start up in every direction amongst them. See the late Travels to the Source of the Ganges, and Col. Hardwicke's Tour to Sirinagur.

हित्वा तस्मिन् भुजगवलयं शम्भुना दत्तहस्ता
क्रीडाशैले यदि च विहरेत् पादचारेण गौरी ॥
भङ्गीभक्त्या विरचितवपुः स्तम्भितान्तर्जलौघः
सोपानत्वं व्रज पदसुखस्पर्शमारोहणेषु ॥ ६२ ॥

तत्रावश्यं वलयकुलिशोद्घट्टनोद्गीर्णतोयं
नेष्यन्ति त्वां सुरयुवतयो यन्त्रधारागृहत्वम् ॥

Haply across thy long and mountain way
In sport may Gaurí with her Śiva stray;
Her serpent bracelet from her wrist displaced,
And in her arms the mighty god embraced.
Should thus it fortune, be it thine to lend
A path their holy footsteps may ascend;
Close in thy hollow form thy stores comprest,
While by the touch of feet celestial blest.

Then shall the nymphs of heaven, a giddy train,
Thy form an instrument of sport detain;
And with the lightning, round each wrist that gleams,
Shall set at liberty thy cooling streams.

ANNOTATIONS.

Verse 424. Thy form an instrument of sport.] Literally, "They shall take thee as being the abode of an artificial water-work"—a jet-d'eau, or shower-bath; or, according to some of the Commentators, a vessel for sprinkling water, either a common syringe or squirt, or the more elegant Asiatic apparatus in use for sprinkling perfumed waters, especially rose-water—a Gooláb-pásh.

Verse 425. And with the lightning, round each wrist that gleams.] The diamond and thunderbolt, according to Hindu notions, are of one substance, and are called by the same appellation (वज्र). As the fall of the thunderbolt is usually followed by rain, and may thus be

ताभ्यो मोक्षस्तव यदि सखे घर्म्मलब्धस्य न स्यात्
क्रीडालोलाः श्रवणपरुषैर्गर्जितैर्भाययेस्ताः ॥ ६३ ॥

हेमाम्भोजप्रसवि सलिलं मानसस्याददानः
कुर्व्वन् कामात् क्षणमुखपटप्रीतिमैरावतस्य ॥
धुन्वन् वातैस्सजलपृषतैः कल्पवृक्षांशुकानि

But should they seek thy journey to delay—
A grateful solace in the sultry day—
Speak harsh in thunder, and the nymphs shall fly
Alarmed, nor check thy progress through the sky.

Where bright the mountain's crystal glories break,
Explore the golden lotus-covered lake;
Imbibe the dews of Mánasa, and spread
A friendly veil round Airavata's head;

ANNOTATIONS.

be considered as its cause; the propinquity and the mutual friction of the same substance upon the wrists of our young ladies is, in like manner, supposed to occasion the dispersion of the fluid treasures of the Cloud.

Verse 433. Mánasa, Mánasarovara, or commonly Man-sarour, is a celebrated lake situated in the centre of the Himálaya mountains, and was long said to be the source of the Ganges and Brahmaputra rivers: with respect to the first of these, the statement has been found to be erroneous; and we have no positive proofs of its accuracy with regard to the latter. When the passage in the text was translated, the chief information regarding the latter was derived from the vague reports of Hindu Pilgrims. Since then, Mánasarovara was visited by that enterprising traveller, Moorcroft. He has not yet had a successor.

We here take leave of the geographical part of the poem, which is highly creditable to Kálidása's accuracy; and now come to the region of unmixed fable, the residence of Kuvera and his attendant demigods.

Verse 434. A friendly veil round Airavata's head.] Indra's Elephant, ut supra, verse 355.

च्छायाभिन्नस्फटिकविशदं निर्व्विशेस्तं नगेन्द्रम् ॥ ६४ ॥

तस्योत्सङ्गे प्रणयिन इव स्रस्तगङ्गादुकूलां
न त्वं दृष्ट्वा न पुनरलकां ज्ञास्यसे कामचारिन् ॥
या वः काले वहति सलिलोद्गारमुच्चैर्विमानै-
र्मुक्ताजालग्रथितमलकं कामिनीवाभ्रवृन्दम् ॥ ६५ ॥

विद्युत्वन्तं ललितवनितास्सेन्द्रचापं सचित्रा-
स्सङ्गीताय प्रहतमुरजाः स्निग्धगम्भीरघोषम् ।

Or, life dispensing, with the Zephyrs go,
Where heavenly trees with fainting blossoms blow.

Now on the mountain's side, like some dear friend,
Behold the city of the gods impend;
Thy goal behold, where Ganga's winding rill
Skirts like a costly train the sacred hill;
Where brilliant pearls descend in lucid showers,
And Clouds, like tresses, clothe her lofty towers.

There every palace with thy glory vies,
Whose soaring summits kiss the lofty skies;

ANNOTATIONS.

Verse 436. Where heavenly trees with fainting blossoms blow.] Literally, the Kalpa trees, one of the five kinds which flourish in Indra's heaven. They are thus enumerated in the Amara Kosha:

पञ्चैते देवतरवो मन्दारः पारिजातकः ।
सन्तानः कल्पवृक्षश्च पुंसि वा हरिचन्दनम् ॥

Verse 438. The city of the gods impend.] Alaká, the capital of Kuvera.

अन्तस्तोयं मणिमयभुवस्तुङ्गमभ्रंलिहाग्राः
प्रासादास्त्वां तुलयितुमलं यत्र तैस्तैर्विशेषैः ॥ ६६ ॥

हस्ते लीलाकमलमलकं बालकुन्दानुविद्धं
नीता लोध्रप्रसवरजसा पाण्डुतामाननश्रीः ॥

Whose beauteous inmates bright as lightning glare,
And tabors mock the thunders of the air;
The rainbow flickering gleams along the walls,
And glittering rain in sparkling diamonds falls.

There lovely triflers wanton through the day,
Dress all their care, and all their labour play;
One while, the fluttering Lotus fans the fair,
Or Kunda top-knots crown the jetty hair.

ANNOTATIONS.

Verse 449. I have availed myself of the aid of the Commentators to make out this passage rather more fully than it occurs in the original, and consequently more intelligibly to the English reader. The poet describes the toilet of the Yakshinís, or female Yakshas, through the six seasons of the year, by mentioning as the selected flowers, those peculiar to each period. Thus the Lotus blooms in Sarat or the sultry season, two months of our autumn; the Kunda (Jasminum pubescens) in Śiśira or the dewy season; the Lodh, a species of tree (Symplocos racemosa, Rox.), is in blossom in Hemanta or winter; the Kuruvaka (Gomphræna globosa) in Vasanta or spring; the Śirísha (Mimosa Śirísha) in the hot months, or Gríshma; and the Nípa or Kadamba (Nauclea Kadamba) at the setting in of the rains. It is to the Commentators also that I am indebted for the sole occupation of the goddesses being pleasure and dress. The fact is,

——To sing, to dance,
To dress, and troll the tongue, and roll the eye,

constitutes a very well-educated female, according to the customs of Hindustan. We cannot help, however, being pleased with the simplicity and propriety of taste which gives to the graceful ornaments of nature so prominent a part in the decoration of feminine beauty.

चूडापाशे नवकुरुवकं चारुकर्णे शिरीषं
सीमन्ते ऽपि त्वदुपगमजं यत्र नीपं वधूनाम् ॥ ६७ ॥

यस्यां यक्षास्सितमणिमयान्येत्य हर्म्यस्थलानि
ज्योतिश्छायाकुसुमरचितान्युत्तमस्त्रीसहायाः ॥
आसेवन्ते मधु रतिरसं कल्पवृक्षप्रसूतं
त्वद्गम्भीरध्वनिषु शनकैः पुष्करेष्वाहतेषु ॥ ६८ ॥

Now, o'er the cheek the Lodh's pale pollen shines,
Now midst their curls the Amaranth entwines.
These graces varying with the varying year,
Śirísha-blossoms deck the tender ear;
Or new Kadambas, with thy coming born,
The parted locks and polished front adorn.

Thus graced, they woo the Yakshas to their arms,
And gems, and wine, and music, aid their charms.
The strains divine with art celestial thrill,
And wines from grapes of heavenly growth distil.
The gems bestrew each terrace of delight,
Like stars that glitter through the shades of night.

ANNOTATIONS.

Verse 462. And wines from grapes of heavenly growth distil.] So MILTON, Paradise Lost, v. 426:

——In heaven, the trees
Of life ambrosial fruitage bear, and vines yield nectar.

And again, line 835:

——Rubied nectar flows,
Fruit of delicious vines, the growth of heaven.

Verse 464. Like stars that glitter through the shades of night.] Thus B. JONSON:

The starres that are the jewels of the night.

गत्युत्कम्पादलकपतितैर्यत्र मन्दारपुष्पैः
कूत्तच्छेदैः कनकनलिनैः कर्णविभ्रंशिभिश्च ॥
मुक्ताजालैस्स्तनपरिसरच्छिन्नसूत्रैश्च हारै-
र्नैशो मार्गस्सवितुरुदये सूच्यते कामिनीनाम् ॥ ६९ ॥

नीवीबन्धोच्छ्वसितशिथिलं यत्र यक्षाङ्गनानां

There, when the Sun restores the rising day,
What deeds of love his tell-tale beams display!
The withered garlands on the pathway found;
The faded lotus prostrate on the ground;
The pearls, that bursting zones have taught to roam,
Speak of fond maids, and wanderers from home.

Here filled with modest fears, the Yaksha's bride
Her charms from passion's eagerness would hide;

ANNOTATIONS.

Verse 470. Speak of fond maids, and wanderers from home.] I have already mentioned that the Hindus always send the lady to seek her lover, and they usually add a very reasonable degree of ardour and impatience. Our poet, in another place, compares the female so engaged to a rapid current. Thus, in the Ritu Sanhára:

निपातयन्त्यः परितस्तटद्रुमान्
प्रवृद्धवेगैस्सलिलैरनिर्मलैः ।
स्त्रियः प्रकामा इव जातविभ्रमाः
प्रयान्ति नद्यस्त्वरितं पयोनिधिम् ॥

Fast flow the turbid torrents, as they sweep
The shelving valleys to rejoin the deep:
Impetuous as the maid whom passion warms,
And drives impatient to her lover's arms,
Along they bound with unresisted force,
And banks and trees demolish in their course.

वासः कामादनिभृतकरेष्वाक्षिपत्सु प्रियेषु ॥
अर्चिस्तुङ्गानभिमुखगतान् प्राप्य रत्नप्रदीपान्
ह्रीमूढानां भवति विफलप्रेरणा चूर्णमुष्टिः ॥ ७० ॥

नेत्रा नीतास्सततगतिना ये विमानाग्रभूमी-
रालेख्यानां सजलकणिका दोषमुत्पाद्य सद्यः ॥
शङ्कास्पृष्टा इव जलमुचस्त्वादृशा यत्र जालै-

The bold presumption of her lover's hands
To cast aside the loosened vest, withstands;
And, feeble to resist, bewildered turns
Where the rich lamp with lofty radiance burns;
And vainly whelms it with a fragrant cloud
Of scented dust, in hope the light to shroud.

The gale that blows eternally their guide,
High over Alaká the clouds divide
In parted masses, like the issuing smoke
Of incense by the lattice-meshes broke:
Scattered they float, as if dispersed by fear,
Or conscious guilt spoke retribution near;

ANNOTATIONS.

Verse 478. Of scented dust.] She casts upon it a handful of Chúrńa: which means not only any powdered or pounded substance, but especially aromatic powders; which we may suppose to constitute part of an Indian lady's toilet, as they did in the last century of those of Europe, when the toilet of a belle was equipped

With patches, powder-box, pulvil, perfumes.

धूमोद्गारानुकृतिनिपुणा जर्जरा निष्पतन्ति ॥ ७१ ॥

यत्र स्त्रीणां प्रियतमभुजोच्छ्वासितालिङ्गिताना-
मङ्गग्लानिं सुरतजनितां तन्तुजालावलम्बाः ॥
त्वत्संरोधापगमविशदैः प्रेरिताश्चन्द्रपादै-
र्व्यालुम्पन्ति स्फुटजललवस्यन्दिनश्चन्द्रकान्ताः ॥ ७२ ॥

मत्वा देवं धनपतिसखं यत्र साक्षाद्वसन्तं

Their just award for showers that lately soiled
Some painted floor, or gilded roof despoiled.

Ere yet thy coming yields opposing gloom,
The moon's white rays the smiling night illume,
And on the moon-gem concentrated fall,
That hangs in woven nets in every hall;
Whence cooling dews upon the fair descend,
And life renewed to languid nature lend.

What though while Śiva with the god of gold
Delights a friendly intercourse to hold;

ANNOTATIONS.

Verse 486. Some painted floor.] It is customary amongst the Hindus, upon festival occasions, to smooth and paint the ground on which worship is to be performed, or the assembly to be held. As this spot is generally in an open area within the walls of the house, a shower of rain is, of course very hostile to such decoration.

Verse 489. The moon-gem, or Chandrakánta (चन्द्रकान्त), which is supposed to absorb the rays of the moon, and to emit them again in the form of pure and cool moisture.

प्रायश्चापं न वहति भयान्मन्मथः षट्पदज्यम् ॥
सभ्रूभङ्गप्रहितनयनैः कामिलक्ष्येष्वमोघै-
स्तस्यारम्भश्चटुलवनिताविभ्रमैरेव सिद्धः ॥ ७३ ॥
अत्रागारं धनपतिगृहादुत्तरेणास्मदीयं

The Lord of Love, remembering former woe,
Wields not in Alaká his bee-strung bow,
Yet still he triumphs: for each maid supplies
The fatal bow with love-inspiring eyes;
And wanton glances emulate the dart,
That speeds unerring to the beating heart.

Northward from where Kuvera holds his state,
Where Indra's bow surmounts the arching gate;

ANNOTATIONS.

Verse 495. The Lord of Love, remembering former woe.] This alludes to the fate which befel the Hindu Cupid upon his assailing Śiva, whom, at the desire of the gods, he inflamed with the love of Párvatí. Śiva, in his wrath, reduced the little deity to ashes, by a flame from the eye in his forehead; and, although he was subsequently restored to animation, he is here supposed to remain in dread of his former enemy. The whole story is spiritedly told in Sir William Jones's Hymns to Camdeo and to Durgá.

Verse 499. And wanton glances emulate the dart.] The eye-darting arrows is an idea familiar to English poetry; as in these instances:

> Her eye darted contagious fire. — MILTON.
>
> Her eyes carried darts of fire,
> Feathered all with swift desire. — GREENE's "Never too late."
>
> I mote perceive how in her glancing sight
> Legions of loves with little wings did fly,
> Darting their deadly arrows fiery bright. — SPENSER. Sonnet 16.
>
> And those love-darting eyes shall roll no more. — POPE's Elegy.

दूराल्लक्ष्यं सुरपतिधनुश्चारुणा तोरणेन ॥
यस्योद्याने कृतकतनयः कान्तया वर्द्धितो मे
हस्तप्राप्यस्तवकनमितो बालमन्दारवृक्षः ॥ ७४ ॥

वापी चास्मिन् मरकतशिलाबद्धसोपानमार्गा
हैमैश्छन्ना कमलमुकुलैः स्निग्धवैदूर्य्यनालैः ॥
यस्यास्तोये कृतवसतयो मानसं सन्निकृष्टं
न ध्यास्यन्ति व्यपगतशुचस्त्वामपि प्रेक्ष्य हंसाः ॥ ७५ ॥

Where on rich boughs the clustering flower depends,
And low to earth the tall Mandára bends;
Pride of the grove, whose wants my fair supplies,
And nurtures like a child—my dwelling lies.

There is the fountain, emerald steps denote,
Where golden buds on stalks of coral float;
And for whose limpid waves the Swans forsake,
Pleased at thy sight, the mount-encircled lake.

ANNOTATIONS.

Verse 504. The tall Mandára.] The Coral-tree, Erythrina Indica.

Verse 506. And nurtures like a child.] Tender attachment to natural objects is one of the most pleasing features in the poetical compositions of the Hindus. It is very frequently expressed, and perhaps in few places with more beauty than in the drama of Sakuntalá, where, upon departing from the bower of her foster-father, she bids adieu to the plants she had carefully tended, and the orphan fawn she had reared. The whole of this scene must be read with pleasure; and may be classed with the departure of Goldsmith's village family from Auburn, and the farewell of Eve to the bowers of Paradise.

यस्यास्तीरे रचितशिखरः पेशलैरिन्द्रनीलैः
क्रीडाशैलः कनककदलीवेष्टनः प्रेक्षणीयः ॥
मद्गेहिन्याः प्रिय इति सखे चेतसा कातरेण
प्रेक्ष्योपान्तस्फुरिततडितं त्वां तमेव स्मरामि ॥ ७६ ॥

रक्ताशोकश्चलकिशलयः केशरस्तत्र कान्तः
प्रत्यासन्नः कुरुवकवृतेर्माधवीमण्डपस्य ॥

Soft from the pool ascends a shelving ground,
Where shades devoted to delight abound;
Where the cœrulean summit towers above
The golden circle of a plantain-grove:
Lamented haunts! which now in thee I view,
As glittering lightnings girt thy base of blue.

See where the clustering Mádhavi entwines,
And bright Kuruvaka the wreath confines;
Profuse, Aśoka sheds its radiant flower,
And budding Keśara adorns the bower:

ANNOTATIONS.

Verse 517. The Mádhavi entwines.] This Creeper (Gærtnera racemosa, or Banisteria Bengalensis) is often alluded to by the Poets, for its superior elegance, and the beauty of its red blossoms.

Verse 518. Kuruvaka is the crimson Amaranth. The Sanskrit name is also applied to a blue species of Barleria.

Verse 519. Profuse, Aśoka sheds its radiant flower.] Jonesia Aśoka; speaking of which, Sir William Jones says, "The vegetable world scarcely exhibits a richer sight than an Aśoka-tree in full bloom.

Verse 520. And budding Keśara.] A tree yielding a strong-smelling flower (Mimusops elengi).

एकस्सख्यास्तव सह मया वामपादाभिलाषी
काङ्क्षत्यन्यो वदनमदिरां दोहदच्छद्मनास्याः ॥ ७७ ॥

तन्मध्ये च स्फटिकफलका काञ्चनी वासयष्टि-
र्मूले बद्धा मणिभिरनतिप्रौढवंशप्रकाशैः ॥
तालैश्शिञ्जद्वलयसुभगैः कान्तया नर्त्तितो मे
यामध्यास्ते दिवसविगमे नीलकण्ठः सुहृद् वः ॥ ७८ ॥

These are my rivals; for the one would greet,
As I would willingly, my charmer's feet;
And, with my fondness, would the other sip
The grateful nectar of her honeyed lip.

A golden column, on a crystal base,
Begirt with jewels, rises o'er the place.
Here, when the evening twilight shades the skies,
The blue-necked Peacock to the summit flies,
And moves in graceful circles to the tone
My fair awakens from her tinkling zone.

ANNOTATIONS.

Verse 521. These are my rivals, &c.] These allusions refer to some particular notions of the Hindus respecting the Keśara and Aśoka, which plants are said to blossom upon being touched respectively by the face or foot of a female: the story is, probably, originally poetical.

Verse 528. The blue-necked Peacock to the summit flies.] The wild Peacock, although it lays its nest upon the ground, is said, by Captain Williamson, to roost constantly on the loftiest trees.

Verse 530. My fair awakens from her tinkling zone.] A girdle of small bells (क्षुद्रघण्टिका) is a favourite Hindu ornament; also silver circles at the ankles and wrists, which emit a ringing noise as the wearer moves.

L

एभिस्साधो हृदयनिहितैर्लक्षणैर्लक्षयेथाः
द्वारोपान्ते लिखितवपुषौ शङ्खपद्मौ च दृष्ट्वा ॥

These be thy guides—and faithfully preserve
The marks I give thee: or e'en more, observe, 532
Where painted emblems holy wealth design,
Kuvera's treasures—that abode is mine.

ANNOTATIONS.

Ver. 534. Kuvera's treasures.] Thick with sparkling oriental gems
The portal shone.—— Paradise Lost, B. iii. 507.

For such Kuvera's nine treasures are sometimes supposed to be. Rámásrama, commenting upon Amara, thus enumerates them, from the Śabdárńava:

पद्मो ऽस्त्रियां महापद्मः शङ्खो मकरकच्छपौ ।
मुकुन्दनन्दनीलाश्च खर्वश्च निधयो नव ॥

"The Padma, Mahápadma, Śankha, Makara, Kachhapa, Mukunda, Nanda, Níla, and Kharva, are the nine Nidhis." The Śabda Ratnávali also has the same reading. In Hemachandra, and the Śabda Mála, कुन्द is substituted for नन्द. Nidhi (निधि) is the generic name; but how it should be rendered into English, I am not prepared to say. Mr. Colebrooke calls the particular Nidhis, 'auriferous gems.' See his translation of the Amara Kosha. Some of the words bear the meanings of precious or holy things: thus, Padma is the Lotus; Śankha the shell or conch. Again, some of them imply large numbers; thus, Padma is 10,000 millions, and Mahápadma is 100,000 millions, &c.; but all of them are not received in either the one or the other acceptation. We may translate almost all into things: thus, a lotus, a large lotus, a shell, a certain fish, a tortoise, a crest, a mathematical figure used by the Jainas. Níla refers only to colour; but Kharva, the ninth, means a dwarf. Mr. Kindersley, translating through the medium of the Tamul, has called eight of Kuvera's gems, the coral, pearl, cat's-eye, emerald, diamond, sapphire, ruby, and topaz. The ninth he leaves undetermined. In Dr. Hunter's Dictionary, I find one only of the nine in the Hindoostanee Language, نيلم or نيل من Neelum or Neelmun, derived from नीलमणि 'a blue gem,' and interpreted the Sapphire. पद्मराग, Padma-colour, means a Ruby; and possibly the Padma may be the same: perhaps कच्छप, the tortoise, means tortoise-shell; and Makara may be an error for Maraka or Marakata, an Emerald, or it may imply the same stone from the green colour of a fish: these, however, are mere conjectures. Agreeably to the system of the Tantrikas, the Nidhis are personified,

मन्दच्छायं भवनमधुना मद्वियोगेन नूनं
सूर्य्यापाये न खलु कमलं पुष्यति स्वामभिख्याम् ॥ ७९ ॥

गत्वा सद्यः कलभतनुतां तत्परित्राणहेतोः
क्रीडाशैले प्रथमकथिते रम्यसानौ निषण्णः ॥
अर्हस्यन्तर्भवनपतितां कर्त्तुमल्पाल्पभासं
खद्योतालीविलसितनिभां विद्युदुन्मेषदृष्टिम् ॥ ८० ॥

Haply its honours are not now to boast,
Dimmed by my fate, and in my exile lost.
For when the sun withdraws his cheering rays,
Faint are the charms the Kamala displays.

To those loved scenes repaired, that awful size,
Like a young elephant, in haste disguise;
Lest terror seize my fair one, as thy form
Hangs o'er the hillock, and portends the storm.
Thence to the inner mansion bend thy sight,
Diffusing round a mild and quivering light;
As when, through evening shades, soft flashes play
Where the bright fire-fly wings his glittering way.

ANNOTATIONS.

personified, and upon certain occasions, as the worship of Lakshmí, the goddess of prosperity, &c., come in for a share of religious veneration. They have also their peculiar mantras, or mystical verses.

Verse 538. The Kamala is a name of the lotus.

Verse 546. Where the bright fire-fly wings his glittering way.] The fire-fly presents a very beautiful appearance, as its soft and twinkling light is contrasted with the deep shade of the bushes, in which it may be seen in great numbers during the wet season. The phæno-menon is common to the East and the West Indies; and it may be amusing to see the effect produced

तन्वी श्यामा शिखरदशना पक्वबिम्बाधरोष्ठी

There, in the fane, a beauteous creature stands,
The first best work of the Creator's hands; 548

ANNOTATIONS.

produced by it on different persons and at different periods. Moore, meeting with it in America, writes some elegant stanzas on the subject; and adds to the lightness of his verse, the solidity of prose in the authority of this note:—"The lively and varying illumination with which these fire-flies light up the woods at night gives quite an idea of enchantment. Puis ces mouches se developpant de l'obscurité de ces arbres, et s'approchant de nous, nous les voyions sur les orangers voisins, qu'ils mettoient tout en feu, nous rendant la vue de leurs beaux fruits, que la nuit avoit ravie, &c.—L'Histoire Des Antilles." See Moore's Odes and Epistles. We have now to hear the description of a Traveller of 1672, the learned and very devout Johannes Fryer, M.D.

"The next day, at twelve o'clock at noon, we struck into our old road at Moorbar, from whence, before, we were misguided: we packed hence by five in the afternoon, and left our burnt wood on the right-hand; but entered another, which made us better sport, deluding us with false flashes, that you would have thought the trees on a flame, and presently, as if untouched by fire, they retained their wonted verdure. The Coolies beheld the sight with horror and amazement, and were consulting to set me down and shift for themselves; whereof being informed, I cut two or three with my sword, and, by breathing a vein, let Shitan (the Devil) out, who was crept into their fancies; and led them, as they do a startling jade, to smell to what their wall-eyes represented amiss; where we found an host of flies, the subject both of our fear and wonder, which the sultry heat and moisture had generated into being, the certain prodromus of the ensuing rain, which followed us from the hills. This gave my thoughts the contemplation of that miraculous bush crowned with innocent flames that gave to Moses so pleasant and awful a prospect; the fire, that consumes every thing, seeming rather to dress than offend it."

Verse 548. The first best work of the Creator's hands.] Literally, the first creation of Brahmá: and 'first' may refer to time, or to degree: it most probably here means 'best.' So Milton, speaking of Eve:

"Oh, Fairest of creation! last and best
Of all God's works."—— Paradise Lost, B. ix. 896.

We now enter upon perhaps the most pleasing part of this elegant little poem, the description of the Yaksha's wife. I may perhaps come under the denomination of those who, according to

मध्ये क्षामा चकितहरिणीप्रेक्षणा निम्ननाभिः ॥
श्रोणीभारादलसगमना स्तोकनम्रा स्तनाभ्यां
या तत्र स्याद्युवतिविषये सृष्टिराद्यैव धातुः ॥ ८१ ॥

तां जानीयाः परिमितकथां जीवितं मे द्वितीयं

Whose slender limbs inadequately bear
A full-orbed bosom, and a weight of care;
Whose teeth like pearls, whose lips like Bimbas show,
And fawn-like eyes still tremble as they glow. 552

Lone as the widowed Chakravâki mourns,
Her faithful memory to her husband turns,

ANNOTATIONS.

to the illiberal and arrogant criticism of such a writer as a Mr. Pinkerton, prove, "That the climate of India, while it inflames the imagination, impairs the judgment;" when, standing in very little awe of such a poetical censor, I advance an opinion, that we have few specimens, either in classical or modern poetry, of more genuine tenderness or delicate feeling.

Verse 551. Whose lips like Bimbas show.] The Bimba (Bryonia grandis) bears a red fruit, to which the lip is very commonly compared.

Verse 553. The Chakravâki is the ruddy goose (Anas Casarca), more commonly known in India by the appellation, Brahmany Duck or Goose. These birds are always observed to fly in pairs during the day, but are supposed to remain separate during the night. In the Hindoostanee Philology of Messrs. Gilchrist and Roebuck, an amusing account of the popular belief on this subject is thus given: "This bird, in the poetry of the Hindus, is their turtle-
" dove, for constancy and connubial affection; with the singular circumstance of the pair being
" doomed for ever to nocturnal separation, for having offended one of the Hindu divinities
" (Munis or Saints), whence,

" Chukwa chukuee do june in mut maro ko,e
" Ye mare kurtar ke ruen bichora ho,e.

" Mark Heaven's decree, and man forbear
" To aim thy shafts, or puny thunder
" At these poor fowls, a hapless pair,
" Who pass the lonely nights asunder.

" If

दूरीभूते मयि सहचरे चक्रवाकीमिवैकाम् ॥
गाढोत्कण्ठां गुरुषु दिवसेष्वेषु गच्छत्सु बालां
जातां मन्ये शिशिरमथितां पद्मिनीं वान्यरूपाम् ॥ ८२ ॥

And sad, and silent, shalt thou find my wife,
Half of my soul, and partner of my life, 556
Nipped by chill sorrow, as the flowers enfold
Their shrinking petals from the withering cold.

ANNOTATIONS.

"If we believe popular tradition and assertions, the cause is so far confirmed by the effect "observable in the conduct of these birds to the present day, who are said to occupy the "opposite banks of a water or stream regularly every evening, and exclaim the live-long night "to each other, thus:

"Chuku,ee muen a,oon? Nuheen nuheen chukwa.—
"Chukwa muen a,oon? Nuheen nuheen chuku,ee,

"Say, shall I come, my dear, to thee?
"Ah no, indeed, that cannot be.—
"But may I wing my love to you?
"Nay chuck, alas! this will not do."

Verse 556. Half of my soul, and partner of my life.] So MILTON:

Part of my soul, I seek thee; and thee claim,
My other half.——

जीवितं मे द्वितीयम्, "My second existence," are the words of the original; and the other expression, "my half," is not more uncommon in Sanskrit than in Western poetry. Thus these tender, and, as Mrs. Malaprop thinks, profane expressions of endearment seem to have obtained a very extensive circulation. 'My life,' 'my soul,' are common to most of the European languages; and the most frequent epithet by which a mistress is addressed in Persian or Hindoostanee, جان, is of a similar import. Amongst the Romans, 'vita' and 'anima' were used in the same manner, or even in the temperate warmth of friendship; as Horace calls Virgil:

Animæ dimidium meæ!
Half of my soul!

And

नूनं तस्याः प्रबलरुदितोच्छूननेत्रं प्रियाया
निश्श्वासानामशिशिरतया भिन्नवर्णाधरौष्ठम् ॥
हस्ते न्यस्तं मुखमसकलव्यक्ति लम्बालकत्वा-
दिन्दोर्दैन्यं त्वदनुसरणक्लिष्टकान्तेर्बिभर्त्ति ॥ ८३ ॥

आलोके ते निपतति पुरे सा बलिव्याकुला वा

I view her now! Long weeping swells her eyes,
And those dear lips are dried by parching sighs. 560
Sad on her hand her pallid cheek declines,
And half unseen through veiling tresses shines;
As when a darkling night the moon enshrouds,
A few faint rays break straggling through the Clouds. 564

Now at thy sight I mark fresh sorrows flow,
And sacred sacrifice augments her woe.

ANNOTATIONS.

And Propertius, addressing his Mistress, calls her his Life:

Æratas rumpam, mea Vita, catenas.

I'll burst, my Life, the brazen chains.

We may suppose the Romans derived these pretty words from the Greeks; and indeed, as we learn from Juvenal, vi. 194, they were very fond of employing, though not in the most becoming manner, the original terms Ζωὴ καὶ ψυχὴ, the English translation of which has been given at some length by Mrs. Tighe, in her poem of Psyche; and, with some addition, by Lord Byron, in his Anglo-Greek song, the burthen of which is the old sentiment in a modern antique shape, or 'My Life, I love you,' in the Ζωή μου, σᾶς ἀγαπῶ, of the Greek of the Morea.

Verse 566. And sacred sacrifice augments her woe.] Thus Laodameia to Protesilaus, in Ovid:

Thura damus lacrymamque super.

We offer incense up, and add our tears.

The

मत्सादृश्यं विरहतनुताभावगम्यं लिखन्ती ॥
पृच्छन्ती वा मधुरवचनां सारिकां पञ्जरस्थां
कच्चिद्भर्तुः स्मरसि निभृते त्वं हि तस्य प्रियेति ॥ ८४ ॥

I mark her now with Fancy's aid retrace
This wasted figure and this haggard face.
Now from her favourite bird she seeks relief,
And tells the tuneful Sáriká her grief;
Mourns o'er the feather'd prisoner's kindred fate,
And fondly questions of its absent mate.

ANNOTATIONS.

The Commentators, however, are not agreed how to interpret this passage in the original text, बलिव्याकुला nor the expression निपतति पुरे, "She falls before thee": they seem, however, to conceive it means, that the approach of the Cloud reminding her of its being the period at which absent husbands usually return home, she recollects that the return of her own lord is proscribed; and therefore either falls in a swoon, or with excess of affliction. The sacrifice is to be performed to render the gods propitious, or it is a sacrifice called काकबलि, usually performed by women at the beginning of the rainy season. Some interpret पुरे "In the city," not "Before, in front."

Verse 570. The Sáriká (Grakula religiosa) is a small bird, better known by the name of Mainá? It is represented as a female, while the parrot is described as a male bird: and as these two have, in all Hindu tales, the faculty of human speech, they are constantly introduced, the one inveighing against the faults of the male sex, and the other exposing the defects of the female. They are thus represented in the fourth story of that entertaining collection, the Buetal Pucheesee:

मैना बोली कि पुरुष अधर्मी पापी दग़ाबाज़ स्त्रीहत्या करने वाले होते है। यिह सुनकर तोते ने कहा कि नारी भी दग़ाबाज़ झूठी बेवकुफ लालची हत्यारी होती है ॥

Ladies have always been distinguished for maintaining pet animals; and the fancy seems to have been equally prevalent in the East and West, and in ancient or modern times. The Swallow of Lesbia, 'Passer deliciæ meæ puellæ,' may rival the Sáriká of the wife of the Yaksha, and Bullfinch of Mrs. Throckmorton. See Cowper's Poems.

उत्सङ्गे वा मलिनवसने सौम्य निक्षिप्य वीणां
मद्गोत्राङ्कं विरचितपदं गेयमुद्गातुकामा ॥
तन्त्रीमार्द्रां नयनसलिलैस्सारयित्वा कथञ्चि-

In vain the lute for harmony is strung,
And round the robe-neglected shoulder slung;
And faltering accents strive to catch in vain
Our race's old commemorative strain:
The falling tear, that from reflection springs,
Corrodes incessantly the silvery strings;
Recurring woe still pressing on the heart,
The skilful hand forgets its grateful art,

ANNOTATIONS.

Verse 573. In vain the lute for harmony is strung.] The lute is here put for the Víṅá or Been, a stringed instrument of sacred origin, and high celebrity amongst the Hindus. In Bengul, however, players on this instrument are very rarely met with; and amongst the natives of this province, the English fiddle is its substitute. In the Játras, or dramatic performances still current amongst them, I have seen the entrance of Nárada, the traditionary inventor of the Víṅá, bearing, in its stead, a violin. The Víṅá is much the most harmonious and scientific of all the Hindu instruments of music. A description of it may be found in the First Volume of the Asiatic Researches.

Verse 574. "Robe-neglected" is here put for मलिनवसने, 'dirty clothes.' So Laodameia says:

> Et quâ possum squalore tuos imitare labores, &c.
>
> And with my squalid vesture ape thy toils.

Verse 576. Our race's old commemorative strain.] "The verse made in honour of my kindred": a circumstance that points out some affinity to the songs of the ancient minstrels and family bards.

भूयो भूयस्स्वयमपि कृतां मूर्छनां विस्मरन्ती ॥ ८५ ॥

शेषान् मासान् गमनदिवसस्थापितस्यावधेर्वा
विन्यस्यन्ती भुवि गणनया देहलीमुक्तपुष्पैः ॥
संयोगं वा हृदयनिहितारम्भमासादयन्ती
प्रायेणैते रमणविरहे ह्यङ्गनानां विनोदाः ॥ ८६ ॥

सव्यापारामहनि न तथा पीडयेन्मद्वियोगः
शङ्के रात्रौ गुरुतरशुचं निर्विनोदां सखीं ते ॥
मत्सन्देशैस्सुखयितुमलं पश्य साध्वीं निशीथे
तामुन्निद्रामवनिशयनां सन्नवातायनस्थः ॥ ८७ ॥

And, idly wandering, strikes no measured tone,
But wakes a sad wild warbling of its own.

At times, such solace animates her mind
As widowed wives in cheerless absence find;
She counts the flowers, now faded on the floor,
That graced with monthly piety the door.
Thence reckons up the period, since from home,
And far from her, was I compelled to roam;
And deeming, fond, my term of exile run,
Conceives my homeward journey is begun.

ANNOTATIONS.

Verse 586. That graced with monthly piety the door.] The Hindus pay a species of adoration to many inanimate objects. Amongst others, the door-way, or door-post, receives such homage as is rendered by hanging up a flower or a garland there once a month.

आधिक्षामां विरहशयने सन्निकीर्णैकपार्श्वां
प्राचीमूले तनुमिव कलामात्रशेषां हिमांशोः ॥
नीता रात्रिः क्षणमिव मया सार्द्धमिच्छारतैर्या
तामेवोष्णैर्विरहजनितैरश्रुभिर्यापयन्तीम् ॥ ८८ ॥

निःश्वासेनाधरकिशलयक्लेशिना विक्षिपन्तीं
शुद्धस्नानात् परुषमलकं नूनमागण्डलम्बम् ॥
मत्संयोगः क्षणमपि भवेत् स्वप्नजो ऽपीतिनिद्रा-

Lightened by tasks like these, the day proceeds;
But much I dread a bitterer night succeeds,
When thou shalt view her on the earth's cold breast,
Or lonely couch of separation rest,
Disturbed by tears those pallid cheeks that burn,
And visions of her dearer half's return.
Now seeking sleep, a husband to restore;
And waking now, his absence to deplore;
Deprived of slumber by returning woes,
Or mocked by idle phantoms of repose;
Till her slight form, consumed by ceaseless pain,
Shews like the moon, fast hastening to its wane.
Crisp from the purifying wave, her hair
Conceals the charms, no more her pleasing care;

ANNOTATIONS.

Verse 591. In this, and some of the following passages, considerable liberty has been taken with the order of the original.

माकांक्षन्तीं नयनसलिलोत्पीडरुद्धावकाशाम् ॥ ८९ ॥

आद्ये बद्धा विरहदिवसे या शिखा दाम हित्वा
शापस्यान्ते विगलितशुचा या मयोद्वेष्टनीया ॥
स्पर्शक्लिष्टामयमितनखेनासकृत् सारयन्तीं
गण्डाभोगात् कठिनविषमामेकवेणीं करेण ॥ ९० ॥

पादानिन्दोरमृतशिशिरान् जालमार्गप्रविष्टान्
पूर्वप्रीत्या गतमभिमुखं सन्निवृत्तं तथैव ॥

And, with neglected nails, her fingers chase,
Fatigued, the tresses wandering o'er her face.

Firm winds the fillet, as it first was wove,
When fate relentless forced me from my love;
And never flowery wreaths, nor costly pearls,
Must hope to decorate the fettered curls;
Loosed by no hand, until, the law divine
Accomplished, that delighted hand is mine.

Dull as the flower when clouds through æther sweep,
Not wholly waking, nor resigned to sleep,
Her heavy eyelids languidly unclose
To where the moon its silvery radiance throws

ANNOTATIONS.

Verse 607. Firm winds the fillet, as it first was wove.] The Veńi is a braid into which the long hair of the Hindustani women is collected, when they have lost their husbands. The dancing-girls also wear their hair in this manner.

Verse 616. To where the moon.] The moon is supposed to be the reservoir of amṛita or ambrosia, and to furnish the gods and manes with the supply. "It is replenished from the sun,

चक्षुः खेदात् सलिलगुरुभिः पक्ष्मभिश्छादयन्तीं
साभ्रे ऽह्नीव स्थलकमलिनीं न प्रबुद्धां न सुप्ताम् ॥ ९१ ॥

सा सन्न्यस्ताभरणमबला कोमलं धारयन्ती
शय्योत्सङ्गे निहितमसकृद्दुःखदुःखेन गात्रम् ॥
त्वामप्यश्रुं जललवमयं मोचयिष्यत्यवश्यं
प्रायः सर्व्वो भवति करुणावृत्तिरार्द्रान्तरात्मा ॥ ९२ ॥

जाने सख्यास्तव मयि मनस्सम्भृतस्नेहमस्मा-
दित्यम्भूतां प्रथमविरहे तामहं तर्कयामि ॥

Mild through the chamber: once a welcome light;
Avoided now, and hateful to her sight.

Those charms that glittering ornaments oppress,
Those restless slumbers that proclaim distress,
That slender figure worn by grief severe,
Shall surely gain thy sympathizing tear.
For the soft breast is swift to overflow,
In moist compassion, at the claims of woe.

The same fond wife as when compelled to part,
Her love was mine, I still possess her heart.
Her well-known faith this confidence affords,
Nor vain conceit suggests unmeaning words.

ANNOTATIONS.

sun, during the fortnight of the increase. On the full moon, the gods adore that planet for one night; and for the first day, all of them, together with the Pitṛis and Ṛishis, drink one kalá or digit daily, until the ambrosia is exhausted." Váyu Puráńa.

वाचालं मां न खलु सुभगम्मन्यभावः करोति
प्रत्यक्षं ते निखिलमचिराद्भ्रातरुक्तं मया यत् ॥ ९३ ॥

रुद्धापाङ्गप्रसरमलकैरञ्जनस्नेहशून्यं
प्रत्यादेशादपि च मधुनो विस्मृतभ्रूविलासम् ॥
त्वय्यासन्ने नयनमुपरि स्पन्दि शङ्के मृगाक्ष्या
मीनक्षोभाकुलकुवलयश्रीतुलामेष्यतीति ॥ ९४ ॥

वामश्चास्याः कररुहपदैर्मुच्यमानो मदीयै-
र्मुक्ताजालं चिरविरचितं त्याजितो दैवगत्या ॥

No boaster I! and time shall quickly teach,
With observation joined, how just my speech.

O'er her left limbs shall glad pulsations play,
And signs auspicious indicate the way;
And like the lotus trembling on the tide,
While its deep roots the sportive fish divide,

ANNOTATIONS.

Verse 631. O'er her left limbs shall glad pulsations play.] Palpitations in the left limbs, and a throbbing in the left eye, are here described as auspicious omens, when occurring in the female: in the male, the right side is the auspicious side, corresponding with the ideas of the Greeks, thus described by Potter:—

"The third sort of internal omens were the Παλμοὶ or Παλμικὰ οἰωνίσματα, so called ἀπὸ τοῦ πάλλειν, 'from palpitating.' Such were the palpitations of the heart, the eye, or any of the muscles, called, in Latin, 'saltationes,' and βόμβος, or 'a ringing in the ears,' which in the right ear was a lucky omen: so also was the palpitation of the right eye, as Theocritus telleth us:

'Αλλέται ὄφθαλμός μοι ὀ δεξιός.

My right eye twinkles."

सम्भोगान्ते मम समुचितो हस्तसंवाहनानां
यास्यत्यूरुः कनककदलीस्तम्भगौरश्चलत्वम् ॥ ९५ ॥

तस्मिन् काले जलद यदि सा लब्धनिद्रासुखा स्यात्
तच्चासीनः स्तनितविमुखो याममात्रं सहेथाः ॥
मा भूदस्याः प्रणयिनि मयि स्वप्नलब्धे कथञ्चित्
सद्यः कण्ठच्युतभुजलताग्रन्थि गाढोपगूढम् ॥ ९६ ॥

तामुत्थाप्य स्वजलकणिकाशीतलेनानिलेन
प्रत्याश्वस्तां सममभिनवैर्जालकैर्मालतीनाम् ॥
विद्युत्कम्पस्तिमितनयनां त्वत्सनाथे गवाक्षे

So tremulous throbs the eye's enchanting ball,
Loose o'er whose lids neglected tresses fall.

Soothed by expected bliss, should gentle sleep
O'er her soft limbs and frame exhausted creep,
Delay thy tidings, and suspend thy flight,
And watch in silent patience through the night.
Withhold thy thunders, lest the awful sound
Her slumber banish, and her dreams confound;
Where her fond arms, like winding shrubs, she flings
Around my neck, and to my bosom clings.

Behold her rising with the early morn,
Fair as the flower that opening buds adorn;
And strive to animate her drooping mind
With cooling rain-drops and refreshing wind;
Restrain thy lightnings, as her timid gaze
Shrinks from the bright intolerable blaze;

वक्तुं धीरस्तनितवचनैर्मानिनीं प्रक्रमेथाः ॥ ९७ ॥
भर्त्तुर्मित्रं प्रियमविधवे विद्धि मामम्बुवाहं
तत्सन्देशान्मनसि निहितादागतं त्वत्समीपम् ॥
यो वृन्दानि त्वरयति पथि श्राम्यतां प्रोषितानां
मन्द्रस्निग्धैर्ध्वनिभिरबलावेणिमोक्षोत्सुकानि ॥ ९८ ॥
इत्याख्याते पवनतनयं मैथिलीवोन्मुखी सा
त्वामुत्कण्ठोच्छ्वसितहृदया वीक्ष्य सम्भाष्य चैवम् ॥

And murmuring softly, gentle sounds prepare,
With words like these to raise her from despair:—

'Oh, wife adored! whose lord still lives for thee;
'Behold his friend and messenger in me;
'Who now approach thy beauteous presence, fraught
'With many a tender and consoling thought!
'Such tasks are mine:—where absent lovers stray,
'I speed the wanderer lightly on his way;
'And, with my thunders, teach his lagging mind
'New hopes the braid of absence to unbind.'

As beauteous Maithilí with glad surprise
Bent on the Son of air her opening eyes,
So my fair partner's pleased uplifted gaze
Thy friendly presence with delight surveys.

ANNOTATIONS.

Verse 660. 'The braid of absence' is the Veńi: see Note on Verse 607.

Verse 661. Maithilí is a name of Sítá, derived from Mithilá, the place of her nativity, and the modern Tirhut. The allusion relates to the discovery of her in Lanká, by Ráma's envoy, Hanumán, the Monkey chief, said to be the son of the Wind.

श्रोष्यत्यस्मात् परमवहिता सौम्य सीमन्तिनीनां
कान्तोदन्तः सुहृदुपगतस्सङ्गमात् किञ्चिदूनः ॥ ९९ ॥

तामायुष्मन् मम च वचनादात्मनश्चोपकर्त्तुं
ब्रूया एवं तव सहचरो रामगिर्य्याश्रमस्थः ॥
अव्यापन्नः कुशलमबले पृच्छति त्वां वियुक्तां

She smiles, she speaks, her misery foregoes,
And deep attention on thy words bestows;
For such dear tidings happiness impart,
Scarce less than mutual meeting to the heart. 668

Being, of years protracted, aid thy friend,
And with my words thine own suggestions blend!
Say thus: 'Thy lord o'er Ráma's mountain strays,
'Nor cares but those of absence blight his days. 672
'His only wish by me his friend to know,
'If he is blest with health, that thou art so:

ANNOTATIONS.

Verse 668. Scarce less than mutual meeting to the heart.] They have a proverb similar to this in the Hindustanee language, "A letter is half a meeting." The expression is common in the poetry of the Rekhta, and occurs thus in a Ghazal by Jirat:

کهتي هيں که مکتوب بهي هي نصف ملاقات

It also exists in the Arabic language; and is thus given in one of the Exercises of Captain Lockett's Translation of the Mi'at Ámil, and the Sharah Mi'at Ámil, or an Arabic Grammar and Commentary:

المُراسَلاتُ كما قِيْلَ نصْفُ المُلاقات

"Correspondence, they say, is half an interview."

N

भूतानां हि क्षयिषु करणेष्वाद्यमाश्वास्यमेतत् ॥ १०० ॥

अङ्गेनाङ्गं सुतनु तनुना गाढतप्तेन तप्तं
साश्रेणाश्रुद्रुतमविरतोत्कण्ठमुत्कण्ठितेन ॥
दीर्घोच्छ्वासं समधिकतरोच्छ्वासिना दूरवर्त्ती
सङ्कल्पैस्ते विशति विधिना वैरिणा रुद्धमार्गः ॥ १०१ ॥

शब्दाख्येयं यदपि किल ते यः सखीनां पुरस्तात्
कर्णे लोलः कथयितुमभूदाननस्पर्शलोभात् ॥

'For still this fear especially must wait
'On every creature of our passing state.

'What though to distance driven by wrath divine,
'Imagination joins his form with thine.
'Such as I view, is his emaciate frame;
'Such his regrets; his scorching pangs the same;
'To every sigh of thine his sigh replies,
'And tears responsive trickle from his eyes.

'By thee unheard, by those bright eyes unseen,
'Since fate resists, and regions intervene,
'To me the message of his love consigned
'Pourtrays the sufferings of his constant mind.

ANNOTATIONS.

Verse 675. For still this fear especially must wait.] It is to be recollected here, that even these heavenly Beings are of a perishable nature, and subject to the infirmities of existence. The whole are swept away at each Mahá-pralaya, or destruction of the Universe,

Which, like the baseless fabric of a vision,
Leaves not a wreck behind.

सो ऽतिक्रान्तः श्रवणविषयं लोचनाभ्यामदृश्य-
स्त्वामुत्कण्ठाविरचितपदं मन्मुखेनेदमाह ॥ १०२ ॥

श्यामास्वङ्गं चकितहरिणीप्रेक्षिते दृष्टिपातान्
गण्डच्छायं शशिनि शिखिनां वर्हभारेषु केशान् ॥
उत्पश्यामि प्रतनुषु नदीवीचिषु भ्रूविलासान्

'Oh! where he present, fondly would he seek,
'In secret whisper, that inviting cheek; 688
'Woo thee in close approach, his words to hear,
'And breathe these tender accents in thine ear.'

"Goddess beloved! how vainly I explore
"The world, to trace the semblance I adore. 692
"Thy graceful form the flexile tendril shews,
"And like thy locks the peacock's plumage glows;
"Mild as thy cheeks, the moon's new beams appear,
"And those soft eyes adorn the timid deer; 696

ANNOTATIONS.

Verse 695. Mild as thy cheeks, the moon's new beams appear.] Comparing a beautiful face to the moon has been supposed peculiar to Oriental Poets. Instances, however, may be found in English verse: perhaps that passage in Pope, where, speaking of an amiable female and the moon, he says, "Serene in virgin modesty she shines," may not be exactly in point, although the general idea is similar. Spenser, however, is sufficiently precise:

> Her spacious forehead, like the clearest moon,
> Whose full-grown orb begins now to be spent,
> Largely displayed in native silver shone,
> Giving wide room to beauty's regiment.

हन्तैकस्थं क्वचिदपि न ते चण्डि सादृश्यमस्ति ॥ १०३ ॥
त्वामालिख्य प्रणयकुपितां धातुरागैश्शिलाया-
मात्मानं ते चरणपतितं यावदिच्छामि कर्तुम् ॥
अस्रैस्तावन्मुहुरुपचितैर्दृष्टिरालुप्यते मे

"In rippling brooks thy curling brows I see,
"But only view combined these charms in thee.

"E'en in these wilds our unrelenting fate
"Proscribes the union, love and art create:
"When, with the colours that the rock supplies,
"O'er the rude stone thy pictured beauties rise,
"Fain would I think, once more we fondly meet,
"And seek to fall in homage at thy feet;—

ANNOTATIONS.

Verse 698. But only view combined these charms in thee.] This turn of the compliment, closely faithful to the original, conveys a high idea of the gallantry of a Hindu Bard; and as this gallantry cannot be the ten times repeated retail of romantic folly or chivalrous phrensy, it may be considered as the natural expression of unsophisticated tenderness. We have in these lines a complete description of beauty, agreeably to Hindu fancy; and I do not think the series of comparisons will much suffer by being contrasted with any similar series in classical or modern writers.

Verse 701. When, with the colours that the rock supplies.] "Having painted you with mineral colours" (धातुरागैः), that is, according to the Commentators, with 'red chalk,' &c. Our very limited acquaintance with the high land which is the scene of the Yaksha's exile prevents our specifying the mineral substances which he may be supposed to have employed. The expression in the text, however, is one of many circumstances that render it probable that the mountains which run across the northernmost part of the Peninsula are rich in the objects of mineralogical inquiry. We know that copper mines have been discovered in the eastern extremity of them, the ore of which is very productive. The Sálagrám stones, or Ammonites, are found in the Narmadá; and the several kinds of Makshicas, a class of ores not yet

क्रूरस्तस्मिन्नपि न सहते सङ्गमं नौ कृतान्तः ॥ १०४ ॥
धारासिक्तस्थलसुरभिणस्त्वन्मुखस्यास्य बाले
दूरीभूतं प्रतनुमपि मां पञ्चवाणः क्षिणोति ॥

" In vain ;—for envious tears my purpose blight,
" And veil the lovely image from my sight.

" Why should the god who wields the five-fold dart
" Direct his shafts at this afflicted heart ; 708

ANNOTATIONS.

yet investigated, are usually called नदीज and तापीज, or 'River-born,' and 'Tapti-born,' in reference to their being found in the course of the Tapti river.

Verse 707. Why should the god who wields the five-fold dart.] Kámadeva, the Hindu Cupid, is represented as the Eros of the Greeks, armed with a bow and arrows. These weapons are of peculiar construction, and most poetically formed. The bow is of sugar-cane ; the bow-string consists of a line of bees ; and the arrows are tipped each with a separate flower. The weapons and application of the allegory will be best explained by a verse in Sir William Jones's Hymn to this deity :

He bends the luscious cane, and twists the string,
With bees how sweet, but, ah ! how keen their sting !
He with five flowrets tips the ruthless darts,
Which through five senses pierce enraptured hearts.
Strong Chumpa, rich in odorous gold ;
Warm Arka, nursed in heavenly mould ;
Dry Nagesar, in silver smiling ;
Hot Kriticum, our sense beguiling ;
And last, to kindle fierce the scorching flame,
Love shaft, which gods bright Bela name.

In the Romaunt of the Rose there is something of a similar allegory : Cupid is armed with "ten brode arrows ;" of which, "five were shaven well and dight," and of a nature to produce virtuous attachment ; while the other five, "also black as fiend in hell," were 'Pride,' 'Villaine,' &c., and of pernicious properties.

घर्म्मान्ते ऽस्मिन् विगणय कथं वासराणि व्रजेयु-
र्दिक्संसक्तप्रविततघनव्यस्तसूर्य्यातपानि ॥ १०५ ॥
मामाकाशप्रणिहितभुजं निर्दयाश्लेषहेतो-
र्लब्धायास्ते कथमपि मया स्वप्नसन्दर्शनेषु ॥
पश्यन्तीनां न खलु बहुशो न स्थलीदेवतानां
मुक्तास्थूलास्तरुकिशलयेष्वश्रुलेशाः पतन्ति ॥ १०६ ॥
भित्त्वा सद्यः किशलयपुटान् देवदारुद्रुमाणां
ये तत्क्षीरस्रुतिसुरभयो दक्षिणेन प्रवृत्ताः ॥

" Nor spare to agonize an aching breast,
" By sultry suns and banishment oppressed?
" Oh, that these heavy hours would swiftly fly,
" And lead a happier fate, and milder sky!

" Believe me, dearest, that my doom severe
" Obtains from heavenly eyes the frequent tear;
" And where the spirits of these groves attend
" The pitying drops in pearly showers descend,
" As oft in sleep they mark my outstretched arms,
" That clasp in blissful dreams thy fancied charms,
" Play through the air, and fold in fond embrace
" Impassive matter and etherial space.

" Soft and delightful to my senses blows
" The breeze that southward wafts Himálaya's snows,

ANNOTATIONS.

Verse 715. And where the spirits of these groves attend.] Sthalí Devatás are, literally, 'the deities of the soil;' so completely has Hindu, like Grecian faith, peopled inanimate nature.

आलिङ्ग्यन्ते गुणवति मया ते तुषाराद्रिवाताः
पूर्व्वं स्पृष्टं यदि किल भवेदङ्गमेभिस्तवेति ॥ १०७ ॥

सङ्क्षिप्येत क्षणमिव कथं दीर्घयामा त्रियामा
सर्व्वावस्थास्वहरपि कथं मन्दमन्दातपं स्यात् ॥
इत्थं चेतश्चटुलनयने दुर्ल्लभप्रार्थनं मे
गाढोष्णाभिः कृतमशरणं त्वद्वियोगव्यथाभिः ॥ १०८ ॥

नन्वात्मानं बहु विगणयन्नात्मना नावलम्बे
तत् कल्याणि त्वमपि सुतरां मा गमः कातरत्वम् ॥

" And rich impregnated with gums divine,
" Exuding fragrant from the shattered pine,
" Diffuses sweets to all, but most to me ;—
" Has it not touched ? does it not breathe of thee ?

" What are my tasks ?—to speed the lagging night,
" And urge impatiently the rising light :
" The light returned, I sicken at the ray,
" And shun as eagerly the shining day :
" Vain are my labours in this lonely state ;
" But fate proscribes, and we must bow to fate.

" Let then my firmness save thee from despair,
" Who trust myself, nor sink beneath my care :

ANNOTATIONS.

Verse 733. Let then my firmness save thee from despair.] We are scarcely prepared for this sudden fortitude of the Yaksha ; but it is not by any means unnatural. The task of consoling partners in affliction necessarily diverts the mind from its own distress.

Reference

कस्यात्यन्तं सुखमुपगतं दुःखमेकान्ततो वा
नीचैर्गच्छत्युपरि च दशा चक्रनेमिक्रमेण ॥ १०९ ॥

"Trust to futurity; for still we view
"The always wretched, always blest, are few: 736
"Life like a wheel's revolving orb, turns round,
"Now whirled in air, now dragged along the ground.

ANNOTATIONS.

Reference to the principle is very frequent in the writings of the Hindus. The Átmana Bodha, or 'Knowledge of Spirit,' a small treatise which contains the ethical part of the Vedanta philosophy, and which has been translated and published by Dr. Taylor, concludes with this stanza:—

दिग्देशकालाद्यनपेक्ष्य सर्व्वगं
शीतादिहृन्नित्यसुखं निरञ्जनम् ।
यः स्वात्मतीर्थं भजते विनिष्क्रियः
सः सर्व्ववित् सर्व्वगतो ऽमृतो भवेत्

"He who has made the pilgrimage of his own spirit, a pilgrimage in which there is no concern respecting situation, place, or time; which is everywhere; in which neither cold nor heat are experienced; which bestows perpetual happiness and freedom from sorrow; he is without action, knows all things, pervades all things, and obtains eternal beatitude."

A fine passage inculcating the same feeling occurs in Menu; ch. viii. 84, where the legislator exhorts a witness to speak the truth:—

आत्मैव ह्यात्मनः साक्षी गतिरात्मा तथात्मनः ।
मा ऽवमंस्थाः स्वमात्मानं नृणां साक्षिणमुत्तमम् ॥

"The soul itself is its own witness; the soul itself is its own refuge: offend not thy conscious soul, the supreme internal witness of men." Sir WILLIAM JONES's Translation.

Verse 737.] Plutarch, in his 'Consolation to Apollonius,' has a similar idea, in similar words:

Τροχοῦ [γὰρ] περιστείχοντος, ἄλλοθ' ἡ τέρα
Ἁψὶς ὕπερθε γίγνετ', ἄλλοθ' ἡ τέρα.

The wheel of Life is ever on the round,
While one side's up, the other's on the ground.

शापान्तो मे भुजगशयनादुत्थिते शार्ङ्गपाणौ
मासानेतान् गमय चतुरो लोचने मीलयित्वा ॥
पश्चादावां विरहगुणितं तं तमात्माभिलाषं
निर्वेक्ष्यावः परिणतशरच्चन्द्रिकासु क्षपासु ॥ ११० ॥

भूयश्चापि त्वमसि शयने कण्ठलग्ना पुरा मे
निद्रां गत्वा किमपि रुदती सत्वरं विप्रबुद्धा ॥
सान्तर्हासं कथितमसकृत् पृच्छतश्च त्वया मे

" When from his serpent couch, that swims the deep,
" Śárangí rises from celestial sleep;
" When four more months, unmarked, have run their course;
" To us all gloom—the curse has lost its force:
" The grief from separation born expires,
" And Autumn's nights reward our chaste desires.

" Once more I view thee, as mine eyes unclose,
" Laid by my side, and lulled by soft repose;
" And now I mark thee startle from thy sleep,
" Loose thy enfolding arms, and wake to weep:
" My anxious love long vainly seeks reply;
" Till, as the smile relumes that lucid eye,

ANNOTATIONS.

Verse 740. The serpent couch is the great snake Ananta, upon which Vishńu, or, as he is here called, the Holder of the bow Śárnga (the horn-bow), reclines, during four months, from the 11th of Áshárha to the 11th of Kartik; or, as it has occurred in 1813 (the year in which the first edition was printed), from the 23d of June to the 26th of October. The sleep of Vishńu, during the four months of the periodical rains in Hindustan, seems to bear an emblematical relation to that season. It has been compared to the Egyptian Hieroglyphical account of the sleep of Horus, typical of the annual overflow of the Nile, by the late Mr. Paterson, in his ingenious Essay on the Origin of the Hindu Religion. Asiatic Researches, vol. viii.

दृष्टस्स्वप्ने कितव रमयन् कामपि त्वं मयेति ॥ १११ ॥

एतस्मान्मां कुशलिनमभिज्ञानदानाद्विदित्वा
मा कौलीनादसितनयने मय्यविश्वासिनी भूः ॥
स्नेहानाहुः किमपि विरहव्यापदस्ते ह्यभोग्या
इष्टे वस्तुन्युपचितरसाः प्रेमराशीभवन्ति ॥ ११२ ॥

कच्चित् सौम्य व्यवसितमिदं बन्धुकृत्यं त्वया मे
प्रत्यादेशान्न खलु भवतो धीरतां तर्कयामि ॥

"Thy arch avowal owns, that jealous fear
"Affrighted slumber, and aroused the tear.

"While thus, O goddess with the dark black eyes!
"My fond assurance confidence supplies,
"Let not the tales that idle tatlers bear,
"Subvert thy faith, nor teach thee to despair.
"True love, no time nor distance can destroy;
"And, independent of all present joy,
"It grows in absence, as renewed delight,
"Some dear memorials, some loved lines excite."

Such, vast Dispenser of the dews of heaven!
Such is my suit, and such thy promise given:
Fearless, upon thy friendship I rely,
Nor ask that promise, nor expect reply.

ANNOTATIONS.

Verse 764. Nor ask that promise nor expect reply.] We cannot help pausing here, to remark the ingenuity of the Poet in the conduct of his work. He sets out with excusing the apparent absurdity of the Yaksha's addressing himself to a Cloud as to a rational being, by

निश्शब्दो ऽपि प्रदिशसि जलं याचितश्चातकेभ्यः
प्रत्युक्तं हि प्रणयिषु सतामीप्सितार्थक्रियैव ॥ ११३ ॥

आश्वास्यैनां प्रथमविरहादुग्रशोकां सखीं मे
शैलादस्मात् त्रिणयनवृषोत्खातकूटान्निवृत्तः ।
साभिज्ञानप्रहितकुशलैस्तद्वचोभिर्ममापि
प्रातः कुन्दप्रसवशिथिलं जीवितं धारयेथाः ॥ ११४ ॥

To thee the thirsty Chátakas complain;
Thy only answer is the falling rain:
And still such answer from the good proceeds,
Who grant our wishes, not in words, but deeds.

Thy task performed, consoled the mourner's mind,
Haste thy return these solitudes to find:
Soar from the mountain, whose exalted brow
The horns of Śiva's bull majestic plough,
And, hither speeding, to my sorrowing heart,
Shrunk like the bud at dawn, relief impart,

ANNOTATIONS.

introducing a pleasing and natural sentiment: see Verse 32. The Cloud has now received his charge; and something is expected by way of reply, expressive either of refusal or assent. To have given the Cloud any thing like the faculty of speech, would have been straining probability overmuch; and we see in the above lines with what neatness Kálidása has extricated himself from the dilemma.

Verse 773. Thus Ovid, in his Tristia:—

Prospera sic vobis maneat Fortuna, nec unquam,
Contacti simili sorte, rogetis opem.

So may on thee propitious fortune wait,
Nor may'st thou need such aid, nor mourn so sad a fate!

एतत्कृत्वा प्रियसमुचितं प्रार्थनं चेतसो मे
सौहार्द्दाद्वा विधुर इति वा मय्यनुक्रोशबुद्ध्या ॥
इष्टान् देशान् विचर जलद प्रावृषा सम्भृतश्री-
र्मा भूदेवं क्वचिदपि न ते विद्युता विप्रयोगः ॥ ११५ ॥

श्रुत्वा वार्त्तां जलदकथितां तां धनेशो ऽपि सद्यः
शापस्यान्तं सदयहृदयस्संविधायास्तकोपः ॥
संयोज्यैतौ विगलितशुचौ दम्पती हृष्टचित्तौ
भोगानिष्टानविरतसुखं भोजयामास शश्वत् ॥ ११६ ॥

॥ इति श्रीकालीदासविरचितं मेघदूताभिधं महाकाव्यं सम्पूर्णम् ॥

With welcome news my woes tumultuous still,
And all my wishes tenderly fulfil!
Then, to whatever scenes invite thy way,
Waft thy rich stores, and grateful glooms convey;
And ne'er may destiny, like mine, divide
Thy brilliant spouse, the lightning, from thy side!

This said, he ceased:—the messenger of air
Conveyed to Alaká his wild despair.
The god of wealth, relenting, learnt his state,
And swift curtailed the limit of his fate;
Removed the curse, restored him to his wife,
And blest with ceaseless joy their everlasting life.

THE END.

A

VOCABULARY

(SANSKRIT AND ENGLISH)

OF THE

WORDS WHICH OCCUR IN THE FOREGOING PAGES.

AN EXPLANATION

OF THE

ABBREVIATIONS USED IN THIS VOCABULARY.

adj. .. adjective.
adv. .. adverb.
agt. .. a noun of agency, or verbal adjective.
átm. .. átmane-pada.
cl. .. class, or conjugation.
comp. .. composition.
compar. .. comparative.
du. .. dual.
ep. .. epithet, consisting for the most part of two or more words, and generally referrible to that class of compounds called Bahuvríhi.
f. .. feminine.
fut. .. future.
fut. p. p. .. future passive participle.
imp. .. imperative.
ind. .. indeclinable.
ind. p. p. .. indeclinable preter-participle.
indef. .. indefinite.
m. .. masculine.
m. f. .. masculine and feminine.
m. n. .. masculine and neuter.
n. .. neuter.
p. .. participle.
p. p. .. past, or passive participle.
par. .. parasmai-pada.
pass. .. passive voice.
pl. .. plural.
pot. .. potential.
pres. .. present.
pres. p. .. present participle.
pret. .. preterite.
prep. .. preposition.
pron. .. pronoun.
pronom. .. pronominal.
rel. .. relative.
s. .. substantive.
sin. .. singular.
1 *c.* .. 1st case, or nominative.
2 *c.* .. 2d case, or accusative.
3 *c.* .. 3d case, or instrumental.
4 *c.* .. 4th case, or dative.
5 *c.* .. 5th case, or ablative.
6 *c.* .. 6th case, or genitive.
7 *c.* .. 7th case, or locative.
8 *c.* .. 8th case, or vocative.
1 *cl.* .. 1st class, or conjugation.
2 *cl.* .. 2d class, &c,

VOCABULARY, SANSKRIT AND ENGLISH.

अ

अंश *s. m.* The shoulder.

अंशुक *s. n.* A leaf. **अंशुकानि** 2 *c. pl.*

अकरोत् 1 *pret. par. of* कृ 8 *cl.* Make.

अक्षत *p. p.* (*of* क्षण *with* अ) Unbroken. **अक्षतैः** 3 *c. pl. n.*

अग्नि *s. m.* Fire, heat. **अग्निः** 1 *c. sin.* **अग्निम्** 2 *c. sin.*

अग्र *s. n.* Top, summit, upper part, point, tip. **अग्रात्** 5 *c. sin.* **अग्राणि** 1 *c. pl. adj.* First, early. Chief, principal. Excellent, best.

अङ्क *s. n.* A mark, sign, note. **अङ्कात्** 5 *c. sin.*

अङ्कित *p. p.* (*of* अङ्कि) Marked, impressed. **अङ्कितम्** 2 *c. sin. m.* **अङ्कितेषु** 7 *c. pl. n.*

अङ्ग *s. n.* The body. A limb, member. **अङ्गम्** 1 *or* 2 *c. sin.* **अङ्गेन** 3 *c. sin.* **अङ्गे** 7 *c. sin.*

अङ्गना *s. f.* A woman. **अङ्गनाभिः** 3 *c. pl.* **अङ्गनानाम्** 6 *c. pl.*

अचल *s. m.* A mountain. **अचलः** 1 *c. sin.* **अचलम्** 2 *c. sin.*

अचिरात् *ind.* Shortly, in a little while.

अचेतन *adj.* Inanimate. **अचेतनेषु** 7 *c. pl. m.* or *n.*

अच्छ *adj.* Clear, transparent.

अजिन *s. n.* Skin, hide.

अञ्जन *s. n.* Collyrium, antimony, applied to the eyelashes to darken and improve them: a universal article of the Eastern toilet.

अट्टहास *s. m.* A loud laugh in which the teeth are all displayed. **अट्टहासः** 1 *c. sin.*

अतस् *ind.* Hence, on this account, therefore.

अति *prep.* Beyond, over. Very.

अतिक्रम्य *ind. p. p. of* क्रम् Pass, *with* अति Beyond. **अतिक्रान्त** *p. p.* Gone beyond. **अतिक्रान्तः** 1 *c. sin. m.*

अतितराम् *ind.* Much, excessively, exceedingly.

अतिथि *s. m.* A guest. **अतिथिः** 1 *c. sin.*

अतीत *p. p.* (*of* इ Go *with* अति Beyond,) Passed over, gone beyond. —**स्य** 6 *c. sin. m.*

अत्यन्त *adj.* Endless, uninterrupted. **अत्यन्तम्** 1 *c. sin. n.*

अत्यादित्य *adj.* Sun-surpassing, excelling the sun in brightness. **अत्यादित्यम्** 1 *c. sin. n.*

अत्र *ind.* Here.

अदृश्य *fut. p. p.* (*of* दृश *with* अ) Not to be seen. **अदृश्यः** 1 *c. sin. m.*

अद्रि *s. m.* A mountain. **अद्रेः** 6 *c. sin.* **अद्रौ** 7 *c. sin.*

अद्रिग्रहणगुरुभिः 3 *c. pl. n. ep. of* गर्जितैः (Augmented by the echoes of the mountain.)

अधम *adj.* Low, worthless. **अधमे** 7 *c. sin. m.*

अधर *s. m.* The lower lip. **अधरौष्ठ** The lower and upper lip, the lips.

अधस् *ind.* Down, downwards, below, beneath.

अधि *prep.* On, over, above, upon.

अधिक *adj.* Exceeding, excessive.

अधिकार *s. m.* Charge, office, post of authority.

अधिगुण *adj.* Excellent, virtuous, worthy. अधिगुणे 7 *c. sin. m.*

अधिवसेः *pot. par. of* वस 1 *cl.* Dwell, *with* अधि Settle, sit or perch upon.

अधीन *adj.* Dependent.

अधुना *ind.* Now, at present.

अध्यास्ते *pres. átm. of* आस 2 *cl.* Sit, *with* अधि.

अध्वन् *s. m.* A road.

अध्वश्रमविनयने *ep. of* शृङ्गे.

अन् *ind.* No, not, *un, in.*

अनतिप्रौढवंशप्रकाशैः *ep. of* मणिभिः.

अनपेक्ष्य *ind. p. p.* (*of* ईक्ष See, *with* अप *and* अन्) Not regarding; irrespective of.

अनभिज्ञ *adj.* Ignorant, unacquainted with. अनभिज्ञैः 3 *c. pl. n.*

अनभिलुलितज्याघाताङ्कात् *ep. of* मणिबन्धनात्.

अनल्प *adj.* Not a little.

अनिभृत *adj.* Bold, immodest.

अनिभृतकरेषु *ep. of* प्रियेषु.

अनिर्मल *adj.* Impure, turbid. अनिर्मलैः 3 *c. pl. n.*

अनिल *s. m.* Wind, breeze. अनिलः 1 *c. sin.* अनिलेन 3 *c. sin.* अनिलैः 3 *c. pl.*

अनु *prep.* After, like. Along.

अनुकच्छम् *ind.* Along the bank.

अनुकनखलम् *ind.* After Kanakhala.

अनुकूल *adj.* Favourable, propitious, kindly disposed, friendly. अनुकूलः 1 *c. sin. m.*

अनुकृति *s. f.* Imitation.

अनुक्रोश *s. m.* Tenderness, compassion.

अनुग *agt.* Following; settling upon.

अनुचर *s. m.* A follower, a servant. अनुचरः 1 *c. sin.*

अनुरूप *adj.* Fit, suitable. अनुरूपम् 2 *c. sin. m.*

अनुविद्ध *p. p.* (*of* विध Pierce, *with* अनु) Set, studded, interlaced, ornamented. अनुविद्धम् 1 *c. sin. n.*

अनुसर *imp. par. of* सृ 1 *cl.* Go, *with* अनु Follow, pursue, move onwards. अनुसरेः *pot.*

अनुसरण *s. n.* Interposal, interposition, intervention.

अन्त *s. m.* End, close, period, termination. अन्तः 1 *c. sin.* अन्तम् 2 *c. sin.* अन्ते 7 *c. sin.*

अन्तःशुद्ध *p. p.* (*of* शुध *with* अन्तर्) Pure within, purified inwardly. अन्तःशुद्धः 1 *c. sin. m.*

अन्तर् *and before certain consonants* अन्तः *or* अन्तस् *ind.* Within.

अन्तर *s. n.* Interval, intermediate space. अन्तरम् 1 *c. sin.*

अन्तरात्मन् *s. m.* The internal feelings, the heart or mind. अन्तरात्मा 1 *c. sin.*

अन्तर्भवन *s. n.* An inner apartment, the interior of a building.

अन्तर्बाष्पः *ep. of* अनुचरः (Suppressing his tears).

अन्तस्ताप *s. m.* Inward heat, burning pain or sorrow. अन्तस्तापात् 5 *c. sin.*

अन्तस्तोयम् *ep. of* त्वाम्.

अन्तस्सारम् *ep. of* त्वाम्.

अन्य *pronom.* Other, another. अन्यः 1 *c. sin. m.* अन्यस्मिन् 7 *c. sin. m.*

अन्यथा *ind.* Otherwise.

अन्यथावृत्ति *ep. of* चेतः (Altered, disturbed, subject to strong emotion).

अन्यरूप *adj.* Changed, altered. —पाम् 2 *c. sin. f.*

अन्वित *p. p.* (*of* इ Go, *with* अनु After) Possessed. अन्वितानाम् 6 *c. pl. m.*

अप् *s. f. pl. only,* Water. अपाम् 6 *c.*

अप *prep.* Off, from, away.

अपगम *s. m.* Departure, removal.

अपनयन *s. n.* A taking away, a removing.

अपरिगणयत् *pres. p. par. of* गण 10 *cl.* Reckon, count, calculate, *with* परि *and* अ. —यन् 1 *c. sin. m.*

अपाङ्ग *s. n.* The outer corner of the eye. अपाङ्गम् 1 *or* 2 *c. sin.* अपाङ्गैः 3 *c. pl.*

अपाङ्गप्रसर *s. m.* A side-glance, a leer.

अपाय *s. m.* Departure, withdrawment, disappearance. अपाये 7 *c. sin.*

अपि *ind.* Even, though, although. Also. Assuredly. Haply. *It sometimes implies,* Earnest interrogation or inquiry. *An expletive.*

अपेक्षा *s. f.* Regard, consideration. अपेक्षया 3 *c. sin.*

अप्रतीकार *adj.* Unresisting. —रम् 2 *c. sin. m.*

अबल *adj.* Weak, feeble.

अबला *s. f.* A woman. A wife. अबले 8 *c. sin.*

अभाव *s. m.* Non-existence, want, absence. अभावे 7 *c. sin.*

अभि *prep.* Over, above, upon. Against, before.

अभिख्या *s. f.* Beauty. Brilliancy. —ाम् 2 *c. sin.*

अभिगम *s. m.* A visit. अभिगमम् 2 *c. sin.*

अभिज्ञान *s. n.* A mark, sign, signal, or token whereby a thing or person is known.

अभिधा *s. f.* Name, title.

अभिनव *adj.* New, young. अभिनवैः 3 *c. pl. n.*

अभिमत *p. p.* (*of* मन *with* अभि) Wished, desired, approved, liked, relished.

अभिमतरसाम् *ep. of* हालाम्.

अभिमुख *adj.* Fronting. अभिमुखम् 1 *c. sin. n. used adverbially,* Facing, fronting, towards. अभिमुखगत Opposite, over against.

अभिराम *adj.* Beautiful. अभिरामा 1 *c. sin. f.*

अभिलाषिन् *agt.* Desirous, covetous, greedy. अभिलाषी 1 *c. sin. m.*

अभिलीन *p. p.* (*of* ली *with* अभि) Embraced; embracing; shrouding. अभिलीनः 1 *c. sin. m.*

अभिलुलित *p. p.* (*of* लुल Shake, *with* अभि) Playful, sportive, unsteady.

अभूत् 3 *pret. par. of* भू Be.

अभोग्य *fut. p. p.* (*of* भुज Enjoy, *with* अ) Not to be enjoyed. अभोग्याः 1 *c. pl. m.*

अभ्यन्तर *s. n.* Inner part, middle. —रम् 2 *c. sin.*

अभ्यषिञ्चत् 1 *pret. par. of* षिच 6 *cl.* Sprinkle, *with* अभि.

अभ्यसूय *adj.* Angry, vexed, impatient. अभ्यसूयः 1 *c. sin. m.*

अभ्युद्यत *p. p.* (*of* यम Restrain, *with* उत् *and* अभि) Prepared, exerting one's self. अभ्युद्यतस्य 6 *c. sin. m.*

अभ्युपेत *p. p.* (*of* इ Go, *with* उप *and* अभि) Promised, agreed.

अभ्युपेतार्थकृत्याः 1 *c. pl. m.* Pledged to the fulfilment of a request.

अभ्येति *pres. par. of* इ 2 *cl.* Go, *with* अभि Before. यावत् अभ्येति नयनविषयम् भानुः *may signify,* As long as the sun continues in sight, *i.e.* until sunset; *or,* until the sun comes into sight, *i.e.* until sunrise.

अभ्र *s. n.* A cloud.

अभ्रंलिह *agt.* Cloud-licking; who or what touches or sweeps the clouds.

अभ्रंलिहाग्राः *ep. of* प्रासादाः.

अमर *s. m.* A deity, an immortal.

अमरमिथुनप्रेक्षणीयाम् *ep. of* अवस्थाम्.

अमुम् 2 *c. sin. m.* (*of* अदस् *pron.*) This, that.

अमृत *adj.* Immortal. अमृतः 1 *c. sin. m.* *s. n.* Ambrosia, nectar, the liquor of immortality.

अमोघ *adj.* Not vain or fruitless, effectual. अमोघैः 3 *c. pl. m.*

अम्बु *s. n.* Water.

अम्बुवाह *s. m.* A cloud. अम्बुवाहम् 2 *c. sin.*

अम्भस् *s. n.* Water. अम्भः 2 *c. sin.*

अम्भोज *s. n.* A lotus.

अम्भोविन्दुग्रहणरभसान् *ep. of* चातकान्.

अयम् 1 *c. sin. m.* (*of* इदम् *pron.*) This.

अयमित *p. p.* (*of* यम *caus. form with* अ) Untrimmed, unpaired, unclipped.

अयमितनखेन *ep. of* करेण.

अरण्य *s. n.* A forest. **अरण्येषु** 7 *c. pl.*

अर्घ *s. m.* An oblation of various ingredients to a god or Brahman. **अर्घाय** 4 *c. sin.*

अर्घ्य *s. n.* A respectful oblation to gods or venerable men. **अर्घ्यम्** 1 *c. sin.*

अर्चिस् *s. m.* A flame.

अर्थ *s. m.* Thing, affair, matter, object. Subject matter. Request, suit. **अर्थः** 1 *c. sin.* **अर्थाः** 1 *c. pl.*

अर्थम् *ind.* For, for the sake, on account.

अर्थित्व *s. n.* Supplication, entreaty, the condition of a suppliant. **अर्थित्वम्** 2 *c. sin.*

अर्द्ध *s. n.* Half.

अर्द्धेन्दु *s. m.* A half moon, a crescent.

अर्द्धेन्दुमौलि *s. m.* Śiva, the god whose diadem is a half moon. **अर्द्धेन्दुमौलेः** 6 *c. sin.*

अर्हसि *pres. par.* (*of* अर्ह 1 *cl.* Deserve) Thou oughtest, or must. Wilt thou?

अलक *s. m. n.* A curl, lock, tress. **अलकम्** 1 *or* 2 *c. sin.* **अलकैः** 3 *c. pl.*

अलकत्व *s. n.* The state of a curl or tress. **अलकत्वात्** 5 *c. sin.*

अलका *s. f.* Name of a city, the capital of Kuvera. **अलकाम्** 2 *c. sin.*

अलकान्त *s. m.* A ringlet, the end of a curl.

अलङ्घ्य *fut p. p.* (*of* लघि *with* अ) Unsurmountable. **अलङ्घ्यम्** 2 *c. sin. m.*

अलम् *ind.* Enough, sufficient, able, competent, adequate, equal to; sufficiently, thoroughly.

अलस *adj.* Lazy, sluggish, slow, tardy.

अल्पाल्प *adj.* Very little.

अल्पाल्पभासम् *ep. of* हरितम्.

अव *prep.* Down.

अवकाश *s. m.* Opportunity, means, occasion.

अवकीर्ण *p. p.* (*of* कॄ *with* अव) Scattered. **अवकीर्णान्** 2 *c. pl. m.*

अवतीर्ण *p. p.* (*of* तॄ *with* अव) Descended. **अवतीर्णाम्** 2 *c. sin. f.*

अवधि *s. m.* Period, term, time. **अवधेः** 6 *c. sin.*

अवधूत *p. p.* (*of* धू *with* अव) Shaken, waved, brandished. **अवधूतैः** 3 *c. pl. n.*

अवनत *p. p.* (*of* णम *with* अव) Bending, stooping, bowed. **अवनते** 7 *c. sin. m.*

अवनि *s. f.* The earth, the ground.

अवनिशयनाम् *ep. of* साध्वीम्.

अवन्ती *s. f.* Name of a city. **अवन्तीम्** 2 *c. sin.*

अव मंस्थाः 3 *pret. átm. of* मन Honour, *with* अव Despise. *The augment dropped by virtue of the particle* मा.

अवलग्न *agt.* Hanging down. **अवलग्नाः** 1 *c. pl. m.*

अवलम्बिन् *agt.* Hanging down. **अवलम्बिनः** 1 *c. pl. m.*

अवलम्बे *pres. átm. of* लबि 1 *cl.* Hang, *with* अव Support.

अवलेप *s. m.* Arrogant pretension, pride. **अवलेपान्** 2 *c. pl.*

अवश्यम् *ind.* Certainly, necessarily, undoubtedly, inevitably.

अवस्था *s. f.* State, condition, circumstance. A part or hour of the day. **अवस्थाम्** 2 *c. sin.* **अवस्थया** 3 *c. sin.* **अवस्थासु** 7 *c. pl.*

अवहित *p. p.* (*of* धा *with* अव) Attentive, heedful.

अविकल *adj.* Full, complete. —**लम्** 2 *c. sin. n.*

अविधवा *s. f.* Not a widow. **अविधवे** 8 *c. sin.*

अविरत *p. p.* (*of* रम *with* वि *and* अ) Ceaseless, continual, incessant, uninterrupted.

अविरतोत्कण्ठम् *ep. of* अङ्गम्.

अविश्वासिन् *adj.* Distrustful. —नी 1 *c. sin. f.*

अविहत *p. p.* (*of* हन *with* वि *and* अ) Unobstructed, unimpeded.

अविहतगतिः *ep. of* त्वम् Understood.

अव्यापन्न *p. p.* (*of* पद *with* आ वि *and* अ) Not dead, not quite extinct, just alive. अव्यापन्नः 1 *c. sin. m.* अव्यापन्नाम् 2 *c. sin. f.*

अशरण *adj.* Destitute of refuge, defenceless, unsupported. अशरणम् 1 *c. sin. n.*

अशस्त्र *adj.* Unarmed. अशस्त्रम् 2 *c. sin. m.*

अशिशिर *adj.* Hot, scalding. अशिशिरैः 3 *c. pl. n.*

अशिशिरता *s. f.* Heat. अशिशिरतया 3 *c. sin.*

अशोक *s. m.* The Aśoka-tree. अशोकः 1 *c. sin.*

अश्र *s. n.* A tear. अश्रम् 2 *c. sin.* अश्रैः 3 *c. pl.*

अश्रु *s. m. n.* A tear. अश्रुम् 2 *c. sin.* अश्रुभिः 3 *c. pl.*

अश्रुद्रुतम् *ep. of* चक्षुम्.

अष्टाङ्ग *adj.* Eightfold.

असकल *adj.* Not total, partial.

असकलव्यक्ति 1 *c. sin. n. ep. of* मुखम्.

असकृत् *ind.* Not once, often, repeatedly, incessantly.

असहन *adj.* Impatient of, unable to endure. असहनाः 1 *c. pl. m.*

असि *pres. par. of* अस 2 *cl.* Be.

असित *adj.* Black (the reverse of white).

असितनयन *adj.* Black-eyed. असितनयने 8 *c. sin. f.*

असुखिन् *adj.* Unhappy. असुखिनम् 2 *c. sin. m.*

असौ 1 *c. sin. f.* (*of* अदस्) It, that.

अस्त *p. p.* (*of* अस) Removed, set aside.

अस्तकोपः *ep. of* धनेशः (Laid aside anger).

अस्तम् *ind.* Disappearance, setting, vanishing.

अस्ति *pres. par. of* अस 2 *cl.* Be.

अस्त्री *s. f.* Not the feminine gender, *i. e.* masculine or neuter. अस्त्रियाम् 7 *c. sin.*

अस्थान *s. n.* Out of place. (*Here it means,* Not at Prayága.)

अस्पृशन् 1 *pret. par. of* स्पृश 6 *cl.* Touch.

अस्मदीय *adj.* Belonging to me, my. अस्मदीयम् 1 *c. sin. n.*

अस्मात् 5 *c. sin. m. n. of* इदम् *pron.* This. From this, hence, on this account. अस्मिन् 7 *c. sin. m. n.* अस्य 6 *c. sin. m. n.* अस्याः 6 *c. sin. f.*

अहन् *s. n.* A day. अहः 1 *c. sin.* अहनि *or* अह्नि 7 *c. sin.*

अहम् 1 *c. sin. of* अस्मद् *pron.* I.

अहोबत *ind.* Alas!

आ

आ *prep.* To at, as far as, *governing the 5th case when prefixed to a noun.*

आकाङ्क्षत् *pres. p. par. of* काङ्क्ष 1 *cl. with* आ Long for, wish, desire. आकाङ्क्षन्तीम् 2 *c. sin. f.*

आकाश *s. m.* Air, atmosphere.

आकाशप्रणिहितभुजम् *ep. of* माम्.

आकुल *adj.* Crowded, filled to confusion, disturbed, disordered. Distressed. आकुलैः 3 *c. pl.*

आकुलग्रामचैत्याः *ep. of* दशार्णाः.

आक्षिपत् *pres. p. par. of* क्षिप *cl.* 6 Throw, *with* आ Catch at, grasp at. आक्षिपत्सु 7 *c. pl. m.*

आखण्डल *s. m.* Indra. आखण्डलस्य 6 *c. sin.*

आख्या *s. f.* Name, appellation.

आख्यात *p. p.* (*of* ख्या *with* आ) Said, spoken, declared, announced. आख्याते 7 *c. sin. n.*

आख्येय *fut. p. p. of the same verb.* आख्येयम् 2 *c. sin. n.*

आगत *p. p.* (*of* गम *with* आ) Come, arrived. आगतम् 2 *c. sin. m.* or *n.*

आगम *s. m.* Approach. आगमे 7 *c. sin.*

आगार *s. m.* A house, dwelling. —रम् 1 *c. sin.*

आघात *s. m.* A stroke, a blow.

आघ्राय *ind. p. p. of* घ्रा Smell, *with* आ.

आतप *s. m.* Sunshine.

आतपत्र *s. n.* A large umbrella, used in the East as a parasol.

आत्मन् *s. m.* Soul, self. आत्मा 1 *c. sin.* आत्मानम् 2 *c. sin.* आत्मना 3 *c. sin.* आत्मनः 6 *c. sin.*

आत्माभिलाष *s. m.* The soul's desire.

आददान *pres. p. átm. of* दा Give, *with* आ Take. आददानः 1 *c. sin. m.* आदातुम् *inf.* आदाय *ind. p. p.*

आदि *in comp.* Etcetera. आदेः 6 *c. sin.*

आद्य *adj.* First. आद्ये 7 *c. sin. m.* आद्या 1 *c. sin. f.* आद्यम् 1 *c. sin. n.*

आधान *s. n.* A taking, a receiving. Fructification, growth.

आधि *s. m.* Mental agony, anxiety.

आनन *s. n.* The face.

आपः 1 *c. pl. of* अप् *s. f.* Water.

आपन्न *p. p.* (*of* पद *with* आ) Unfortunate, afflicted.

आपन्नार्त्तिप्रशमनफलाः *ep. of* सम्पदः (Fruitful in relief to the pains of the afflicted).

आपृच्छस्व *imp. átm. of* प्रच्छ Ask, 6 *cl. with* आ Take leave of, bid adieu.

आबद्ध *p. p.* (*of* बन्ध *with* आ) Tied, bound.

आबद्धमालाः *ep. of* बलाकाः (Forming a wreath.)

आभरण *s. n.* Ornament.

आभा *s. f.* Beauty.

आभोग *s. m.* Prominence, protuberance, convexity. आभोगात् 5 *c. sin.*

आमन्द्र *adj.* Low, deep-toned (as the grumbling of thunder clouds). आमन्द्राणाम् 6 *c. pl. n.*

आमोक्ष्यन्ति 2*d fut. par. of* मुच Discharge, emit, dart, let loose, *with* आ.

आमोद *s. m.* A diffusive perfume, a strong scent.

आम्र *s. m.* The mango-tree. आम्रैः 3 *c. pl.*

आम्रकूट *s. m.* Mango-peak, name of a mountain. आम्रकूटः 1 *c. sin.*

आयत्त *p. p.* (*of* यत् *with* आ) Dependant. आयत्तम् 1 *c. sin. m.*

आयाम *s. m.* Length.

आयुष्मत् *adj.* Long-lived, *a friendly mode of address.* आयुष्मन् 8 *c. sin. m.*

आरम्भ *s. m.* A commencement, beginning, undertaking, enterprize, attempt, endeavour. आरम्भः 1 *c. sin.* आरम्भे 7 *c. sin.*

आराध्य *ind. p. p. of* राध Finish, *with* आ Worship, propitiate, gratify.

आरुह्य *ind. p. p. of* रुह *with* आ Mount, ascend, ride. आरूढ *p. p.* आरूढम् 2 *c. sin. m.* आरूढे 7 *c. sin. m.*

आरोहण *s. n.* Ascent. आरोहणेषु 7 *c. pl.*

आर्त्त *p. p. irreg.* (*of* ऋत Hate) Pained, afflicted. Disturbed, confounded. आर्त्ताः 1 *c. pl. m.*

आर्त्ति *s. f.* Pain, suffering.

आर्द्र *adj.* Wet, moist, bedewed. Reeking. Tender, soft. आर्द्रः 1 *c. sin. m.* आर्द्रैः 3 *c. pl. m.* आर्द्राः 2 *c. pl. f.*

आलप्स्यते 2*d fut. átm. of* लभ Gain, *with* आ, Receive, obtain.

आलम्बन *s. n.* A supporting, a sustaining.

आलम्भ *s. m.* Slaughter, killing. आलम्भजाम् 2 *c. sin. f.* Produced from the slaughter.

आलिख्य *ind. p. p. of* लिख Write, *with* आ Pourtray, delineate, sketch.

आलिङ्गन *s. n.* An embracing.

आलिङ्गित *p. p.* (*of* लिगि *with* आ) Embraced. आलिङ्गितानाम् 6 *c. pl.* *s. n.* An embrace.

आलिङ्गितानि 2 *c. pl.* आलिङ्ग्य *ind. p. p.* आलिङ्ग्यन्ते *pres. pass.*

आली *s. f.* A row, a line.

आलुप्यते *pres. pass. of* लुप Disturb, *with* आ Confuse, bedim.

आलेख्य *s. n.* A painting. आलेख्यानाम् 6 *c. pl.*

आलोक *s. m.* A seeing, looking: sight, view, aspect. आलोके 7 *c. sin.*

आवर्ज्य *ind. p. p. of* वृज 10 *cl.* Quit, *with* आ, Turn down slantwise.

आवर्त्त *s. m.* A whirlpool.

आवर्त्तिका *s. f.* A whirlpool.

आवली *s. f.* A row, string, necklace.

आवाम् 1 *c. du.* (*of* अस्मद् I) We both.

आविर्भूत *p. p.* (*of* भू *with* आविस् Manifest) Appeared, manifested, become visible.

आविर्भूतप्रथममुकुलाः *ep. of* कन्दलीः.

आशा *s. f.* Hope, desire. A quarter, region. आशाम् 2 *c. sin.*

आशाबन्ध *s. m.* Confidence, trust, expectation. आशाबन्धः 1 *c. sin.*

आशु *ind.* Quickly, speedily.

आश्रम *s. m.* A hermitage, the abode of retired saints or sages. आश्रमस्थ *agt.* A sojourner amongst hermitages.

आश्लिष्ट *p. p.* (*of* श्लिष Embrace, cling, *with* आ) Embraced. Embracing, clinging to. *Verbs characterized by the anubandha* ञि *may optionally use the passive participle in the sense of the present.*

आश्लिष्टसानुम् *ep. of* मेघम्.

आश्लेष *s. m.* Embracing, an embrace.

आश्वसत् *pres. p. par. of* श्वस् 2 *cl.* Breathe, *with* आ Revive, derive comfort. आश्वसन्त्यः 1 *c. pl. f.*

आश्वास्य *ind. p. p.* (*of* श्वस Breathe, *caus. form with* आ) Having consoled. *fut. p. p.* (*of* श्वस Breathe, *with* आ) To be breathed out or uttered. आश्वास्यम् 1 *c. sin. n.*

आषाढ *s. m.* The month Áshádha. आषाढस्य 6 *c. sin.*

आसन्न *p. p.* (*of* षद Sit, *with* आ) Near. आसन्ने 7 *c. sin. m.*

आसादयत् *pres. p. par.* (*of* षद Go, *caus. form with* आ) Obtaining, attaining, finding. आसादयन्ती 1 *c. sin. f.* आसाद्य *ind. p. p.* Having attained, reached, obtained, or received.

आसार *s. m.* A hard shower. आसारेण 3 *c. sin.* आसारैः 3 *c. pl.*

आसाराप्रशमितवनोपप्लवम् *ep. of* त्वाम्.

आसीन *pres. p. átm.* (*of* आस 2 *cl.*) Sitting, seated; lying. आसीनः 1 *c. sin. m.* आसीनानाम् 6 *c. pl. m.*

आसेवन्ते *pres. átm. of* षेव 1 *cl.* Serve, *with* आ Addict one's self.

आस्वाद *s. m.* Taste, flavour, enjoyment, sweets.

आह He says, आहुः They say. *See* ब्रू *in Gram.*

आहत *p. p. of* हन Strike, *with* आ. आहतेषु 7 *c. pl. n.*

इ

इच्छा *s. f.* Wish, will, desire. इच्छाम् 2 *c. sin.*

इच्छामि *pres. par. of* इष 1 *cl.* Wish.

इतः *ind.* Hither, this way.

इति *ind.* Thus. *A particle indicating words spoken, or thoughts entertained, expressed in the sentence immediately preceding it.*

इत्थम् *ind.* Thus, in this manner. इत्थम्भूत Being or become thus; thus circumstanced or employed. इत्थम्भूताम् 2 *c. sin. f.*

इदम् 1 *or* 2 *c. sin. n.* This.

इन्दु *s. m.* The moon. इन्दोः 6 *c. sin.*

इन्दुलग्नोर्मिहस्ता *ep. of* या.

इन्द्र *s. m.* Indra. *In comp.* Chiefest.

इन्द्रचाप *s. m.* Indra's bow, the rainbow.

इन्द्रनील *s. m.* The sapphire. इन्द्रनीलैः 3 *c. pl.*

इव *ind.* As, like, as it were.

इष्ट *p. p.* (*of* इष) Wished, desired, longed for. इष्टान् 2 *c. pl. m.*

ई

ईक्ष्यमाण *pres. p. p.* (*of* ईक्ष) Being beheld. ईक्ष्यमाणाः 1 *c. pl. m.*

ईप्सित *p. p.* (*of* आप *in desid. form,*) Wished, desired.

ईश *s. m.* A lord. ईश 8 *c. sin.*

ईश्वर *s. m.* A lord, chief. ईश्वराः 1 *c. pl.*

उ

उक्त *p. p.* (*of* वच) Said, spoken, asserted. उक्तम् 1 *c. sin. n.*

उग्रशोक *adj.* Sorely grieving. —काम् 2 *c. sin. f.*

उच्चैर्भुजतरु *ep. of* वनम् (Having trees like outstretched arms).

उच्चैस् *ind.* High, tall, lofty. Great, much.

उच्छिलीन्ध्र *s. n.* A mushroom.

उच्छिलीन्ध्रातपत्राम् *ep. of* महीम्.

उच्छून *adj.* Swollen.

उच्छ्राय *s. m.* Height, elevation. Summit, peak, ridge. उच्छ्रायः 1 *c. sin.* उच्छ्रायैः 3 *c. pl.*

उच्छ्वसित *p. p.* (*of* श्वस Breathe, *with* उत्) Heaving, beating. Blooming, enlivened, gladdened. Unfastened, untied. *s. n.* An undoing, an unfastening.

उच्छ्वास *s. m.* A sigh.

उच्छ्वासित *p. p.* (*of* श्वस Breathe, *caus. form with* उत्) Breathless, out of breath, Much, excessively. Loosened, disjointed.

उच्छ्वासिन् *agt.* Full of sighs, sighing. उच्छ्वासिना 3 *c. sin. n.*

उज्जयिनी *s. f.* The city Oujein. उज्जयिन्याः 6 *c. sin.*

उडुम्बर *s. m.* The glomerous fig-tree. उडुम्बराणाम् 6 *c. pl.*

उत् *or* उद् *prep.* Up. Off, from, out of.

उत्क *adj.* Desirous, eager, longing, wishing for. उत्काः 1 *c. pl. m.*

उत्कण्ठयन्ति *pres. par. of* कठि 10 *cl. with* उत् Inspire with tender emotions. उत्कण्ठित *p. p.* Distressed, sorrowful, regretting, wishing, sorrowing for. उत्कण्ठितेन 3 *c. sin. n.*

उत्कण्ठा *s. f.* Desire, regret, a languishing or pining after an absent object.

उत्कण्ठाविरचितपदम् *ep. of* इदम्.

उत्कण्ठोच्छ्वसितहृदया *ep. of* सा.

उत्कम्प *s. m.* Shake, tremor, agitation. उत्कम्पात् 5 *c. sin.*

उत्कर्षण *s. n.* A furrowing, a turning up with a plough.

उत्क्षेप *s. m.* A throwing, a tossing up. उत्क्षेपात् 5 *c. sin.*

उत्खात *p. p.* (*of* खन Dig, *with* उत्) Dug or scraped up.

उत्तर *pronom.* Northern. उत्तरेण *ind.* Northwards.

उत्तम *adj.* High, eminent, exalted, supreme, excellent. Beautiful. उत्तमानाम् 6 *c. pl. m.*

उत्तमस्त्रीसहायाः *ep. of* यक्षाः.

उत्तीर्य *ind. p. p.* (*of* तॄ Traverse, *with* उत्) Having crossed.

उत्थाप्य *ind. p. p.* (*of* स्था Stand, *caus. form with* उत्) Having made to arise, having roused.

उत्थित *p. p.* (*of* स्था *with* उत्) Arisen. उत्थिते 7 *c. sin. m.*

उत्पत *imp. par. of* पत 1 *cl.* Fall, *with* उत् Arise, ascend. उत्पतति *pres.*

उत्पल *s. n.* A blue lotus. A water-lily. उत्पलानाम् 6 *c. pl.*

उत्पश्यामि *pres. par. of* दृश 1 *cl.* See, *with* उत् View, behold, foresee, anticipate.

उत्पाद्य *ind. p. p.* (*of* पद Go, *caus. form with* उत्) Having caused or produced.

उत्पीड *s. m.* A gush.

उत्सङ्ग *s. m.* The haunch or part above the hip, the flank. The side or edge. उत्सङ्गे 7 *c. sin.*

उत्सर्ग *s. m.* Discharge, voidance. उत्सर्गात् 5 *c. sin.*

उत्सुक *adj.* Anxious, longing for. Zealously active for the accomplishment of a gratifying object. उत्सुकानि 2 *c. pl. n.*

उत्सेक *s. m.* Excess, overflow.

उदक् *ind.* Northern.

उदक *s. n.* Water. उदकेषु 7 *c. pl.*

उदङ्मुख *adj.* Facing the north. —खः 1 *c. sin. m.*

उदञ्च् *adj.* North, northern. उदीचीम् 2 *c. sin. f.*

उदन्त *s. m.* Tidings, intelligence. उदन्तः 1 *c. sin.*

उदय *s. m.* Rise, rising. उदये 7 *c. sin.*

उदयन *s. m.* Name of a king.

उद्गातुम् *inf. of* गै Sing, *with* उत्. उद्गातुकाम *adj.* Wishing to sing.

उद्गार *s. m.* A vomiting, or ejecting any thing from the mouth. Exhalation. उद्गारम् 2 *c. sin.*

उद्गारिन् *agt.* Ejecting any thing, as saliva; breathing out, sending forth in exhalations. उद्गारिभिः 3 *c. pl. n.*

उद्गीर्ण *p. p.* (*of* गॄ Swallow, *with* उत्) Ejected, cast forth. Breathed out, exhaled. उद्गीर्णैः 3 *c. pl. m.*

उद्गृहीत *p. p.* (*of* ग्रह Take, *with* उत्) Taken up, turned back, upraised.

उद्गृहीतालकान्ताः *ep. of* वनिताः.

उद्घट्टन *s. n.* Friction.

उद्दाम *adj.* Unbridled, excessive. उद्दामानि 2 *c. pl. n.*

उद्दिष्ट *p. p.* (*of* दिश *with* उत्) Mentioned, described. उद्दिष्टाम् 2 *c. sin. f.*

उद्धूत *p. p.* (*of* धू Shake, *with* उत्) Shaken off. Stirred up, stimulated.

उद्धूतपापाः *ep. of* श्रद्दधानाः (Shaken off their sins).

उद्यत *p. p.* (*of* यम *with* उत्) Ready, prepared. उद्यताः 1 *c. pl. m.*

उद्यान *s. n.* A garden, grove. उद्यानम् 2 *c. sin.* उद्याने 7 *c. sin.*

उद्भ्रंश *s. n.* A darting upwards.

उद्वह *s. m.* A son. उद्वहाः 1 *c. pl.*

उद्वेग *s. m.* Fear. Anxiety, distress, uneasiness.

उद्वेष्टनीय *fut. p. p.* (*of* वेष्ट Enclose, *with* उत्) To be unbound. उद्वेष्टनीया 1 *c. sin. f.*

उन्निद्र *adj.* Sleepless. उन्निद्राम् 2 *c. sin. f.*

उन्मुख *adj.* Looking upwards. उन्मुखी 1 *c. sin. f.* उन्मुखीभिः 3 *c. pl. f.*

उन्मेष *s. m.* A winking or twinkle of the eyes.

उप *prep.* By, near.

उपकर्तुम् *inf. of* कृ Do, *with* उप Aid.

उपकार *s. m.* Aid, assistance. उपकारः 1 *c. sin.*

उपगत *p. p.* (*of* गम Go, *with* उप) Gone near, encountered, met, mingling. Obtained. उपगतः 1 *c. sin. m.* उपगतम् 1 *c. sin. n.*

उपगम *s. m.* Approach. उपगमज *adj.* Born, or springing on the arrival. उपगमजम् 1 *c. sin. n.*

उपगूढ *p. p.* (*of* गुह *with* उप) Embraced. *s. n.* An embrace. उपगूढम् 1 *c. sin.*

उपचित *p. p.* (*of* चि Gather, *with* उप) Collected, assembled; increased, augmented, heaped. उपचितैः 3 *c. pl. n.*

उपचितबलिम् *ep. of* न्यासम्.

उपचितरसा: *ep. of* ते (Augmented in feeling).

उपचितवपु: *ep. of* त्वम्.

उपजिगमिषु *agt.* Desirous of going near. उपजिगमिषो: 6 *c. sin. m.*

उपतटम् *ind.* Near the skirt.

उपपाद्य *fut. p. p.* (*of* पद् Go, *with* उप) To be effected, done, shewn, or proved. उपपाद्य: 1 *c. sin. m.*

उपप्लव *s. m.* Disaster, calamity. उपप्लवम् 2 *c. sin.*

उपमेय *fut. p. p.* (*of* मा Measure, *with* उप) Comparable. उपमेयाम् 2 *c. sin. f.*

उपयुज्य *ind. p. p. of* युज Join, *with* उप Take (as meat or drink.)

उपरि *ind.* Up, upward, above.

उपल *s. m.* A rock, a stone.

उपवन *s. n.* A garden, a grove.

उपहार *s. m.* A complimentary gift, a present to a superior.

उपान्त *adj.* Near, close to. *s. n.* Side, skirt, base. उपान्ते 7 *c. sin.*

उपान्तस्फुरिततडित्वम् *ep. of* त्वाम्.

उपेक्षेत *pot. átm. of* ईक्ष 1 *cl.* See, *with* उप Leave, abandon.

उर्वी *s. f.* Earth, ground. उर्वीम् 2 *c. sin.* उर्व्या: 6 *c. sin.*

उल्का *s. f.* A spark of fire, a flame.

उल्काक्षपितचमरीवालभार: *ep. of* दवाग्नि: (Singed by its flames the bushy tails of the Yaks).

उल्लङ्घित *p. p.* (*of* लघि Go, *with* उत्) Passed over or beyond, advancing.

उल्लिङ्घिताध्वा *ep. of* त्वम् *understood.*

उष्ण *adj.* Hot, scorching, scalding. Sharp, acute. उष्णम् 2 *c. sin. m.* उष्णाभि: 3 *c. pl. f.* उष्णै: 3 *c. pl. n.*

ऊ

ऊन *adj.* Less. ऊन: 1 *c. sin. m.*

ऊरु *s. m.* The thigh. ऊरु: 1 *c. sin.*

ऊर्द्ध्वम् *ind.* Upwards; onwards, further.

ऊर्मि *or* ऊर्मी *s. f.* A wave. A current, the flowing of water.

ऋ

ऋतु *s. m.* A season.

ऋषि *s. m.* A sage. ऋषीन् 2 *c. pl.*

ए

एक *pronom.* One, a, a single. Lone, solitary. एक: 1 *c. sin. m.* एकम् 2 *c. sin. m.* or 1 *c. sin. n.* एकाम् 2 *c. sin. f.*

एकपत्नी *s. f.* A faithful wife, one devoted to her husband. एकपत्नीम् 2 *c. sin.*

एकस्थ *agt.* Standing together, combined, collected in one place. एकस्थम् 1 *c. sin. n.*

एकान्तत: *ind.* Solely, only, exclusively.

एतद् *pron.* This. एतद् 1 or 2 *c. sin. n.* एतस्मात् 5 *c. sin. n.* एतौ 2 *c. du. m.* एते 1 *c. pl. m.* एतान् 2 *c. pl. m.*

एत्य *ind. p. p.* (*of* इ Go, *with* आ) Having come or obtained.

एनम् 2 *c. sin. m. of* एतद् This. एनाम् 2 *c. sin. f.*

एभि: 3 *c. pl. m.* or *n. of* इदम् *pron.* This.

एव *ind.* Indeed, verily, truly. Likewise, also. Even, very, self-same.

एवम् *ind.* So, in like manner, thus.

एषु 7 *c. pl. m.* or *n. of* इदम् *pron.* This.

एष्यति 2 *fut. par. of* इ Go, attain.

ऐ

ऐरावत *s. m.* Indra's elephant.

ओ

ओघ *s. m.* Stream, flow. ओघ: 1 *c. sin.*

ओष्ठ *s. m.* The lip, especially the upper.

औ

औत्सुक्य *abs. s. n.* Perturbation. औत्सुक्यात् 5 *c. sin.*

क

कः 1 *c. sin. m. of* किम् Who? which? what?

ककुभ *s. m.* A kind of tree (Pentaptera Arjuna).

कच्चित् *ind.* Assuredly, certainly. *Also a particle of inquiry.*

कटाक्ष *s. m.* A glance. कटाक्षान् 2 *c. pl.*

कठिन *adj.* Hard, stiff.

कण *s. m.* A drop. कणैः 3 *c. pl.*

कणिका *s. f.* A droplet, an atom.

कण्ठ *s. m.* or *n.* The neck, the throat.

कण्ठच्छविः *ep. of* त्वम् *understood.*

कण्ठच्युतभुजलताग्रन्थि *ep. of* उपगूढम् (Having its knot of twining arms loosened from off (my) neck).

कतिचित् *ind.* Some, several.

कतिपय *ind.* How many? So many, several.

कतिपयदिनस्थायिहंसाः *ep. of* दशार्णाः.

कथञ्चित् *ind.* Somehow or other, by some means; by any means.

कथम् *ind.* How? in what manner?

कथमपि *ind.* Somehow or other, with difficulty; *referring, in verse* 3, *to* अन्तर्बाष्पः.

कथयत् *pres. p. par. of* कथ 10 *cl.* Say, tell, declare, explain, describe. कथयतः 6 *c. sin. m.* कथयितुम् *inf.*

कथा *s. f.* Talk, discourse, conversation.

कथित *p. p.* (*of* कथ) Mentioned, told, spoken of, declared, confessed. कथिते 7 *c. sin. m.* कथिताम् 2 *c. sin. f.* कथितम् 1 *c. sin. n.*

कदम्ब *s. m.* A plant, commonly Kadamba (Nauclea Kadamba). कदम्बैः 3 *c. pl.* 'The 'Kadamba flower, when full blown, is in'vested with projecting antheræ, like the erect 'bristles of the hedgehog. Delight, accord'ing to the Hindus, gives a bristling eleva'tion to the down of the body.' *Allusion is made to this in verse* 27.

कदली *s. f.* The plantain-tree.

कनक *s. n.* Gold.

कनककदलीवेष्टनः *ep. of* शैलः.

कनकनिकषच्छायया *ep. of* सौदामिन्या (Bright as a streak of gold on a touchstone).

कनकवलयभ्रंशरिक्तप्रकोष्ठः *ep. of* कामी.

कन्दर *s. m. n.* A cavern. कन्दरेषु 7 *c. pl.*

कन्दली *s. f.* The banana-tree. कन्दलीः 2 *c. pl.*

कन्या *s. f.* A daughter. कन्याम् 2 *c. sin.*

कपाल *s. m. n.* A scull.

कपिश *adj.* Brown, russet. कपिशम् 2 *c. sin. m.*

कपोल *s. m.* A cheek.

कमल *s. n.* A lotus. कमलानि 2 *c. pl.*

कमलवदन *s. n.* A lotus face, *i.e.* a lovely face.

कम्प *s. m.* Flash, glare (of lightning).

कर *s. m.* The hand. A ray of light, a beam of the sun or moon. करेण 3 *c. sin.* करेषु 7 *c. pl.*

करका *s. f.* Hail.

करण *s. n.* An organ of sense. The body. करणैः 3 *c. pl.* करणेषु 7 *c. pl.*

कररुध् *agt.* Ray-obstructing. कररुधि 7 *c. sin. m. n.*

कररुह *s. m.* A finger-nail.

करिन् *s. m.* An elephant.

करुणा *s. f.* Tenderness, pity, compassion.

करुणावृत्तिः *ep. of* अन्तरात्मा (Disposed to pity).

करोति *pres. par. of* कृ 8 *cl.* Make.

कर्ण *s. m.* The ear. कर्णे 7 *c. sin.*

कर्तुम् *inf. of* कृ Make.

कल *s. m.* A low or soft sound, as humming, buzzing, &c.

कलत्र *s. n.* A wife.

कलभ *s. m.* A young elephant.

कला *s. f.* A sixteenth of the moon's diameter, a digit.

कलामात्रशेषाम् *ep. of* तनुम्.

कल्प *s. m.* One of the trees of Swarga.

कल्पन्ते *pres. átm. of* क्लृप 1 *cl.* Be fitted or qualified.

कल्पित *p. p.* (*of* क्लृप) Made, prepared.

कल्पिताधीय *ep. of* तस्मै.

कल्याण *adj.* Happy, virtuous. कल्याणि 8 *c. sin. f.*

कश्चित् 1 *c. sin. m. of* किञ्चित् Some. A certain.

कषाय *adj.* Fragrant.

कस्य 6 *c. sin. m. of* किम् What?

कस्याञ्चित् 7 *c. sin. f. of* किञ्चित् Some.

काङ्क्षति *pres. par. of* काङ्क्ष 1 *cl.* Long for.

काञ्चन *adj.* Golden, of gold. काञ्चनी 1 *c. sin. f.*

काञ्ची *s. f.* A woman's zone or girdle.

कातर *adj.* Confused, disturbed, disordered. कातरेण 3 *c. sin. n.*

कातरत्व *s. n.* Perplexity, anxiety, despondency. कातरत्वम् 2 *c. sin.*

कानन *s. n.* A forest, a grove.

कान्त *p. p.* (*of* कम) Beautiful, elegant. कान्तः 1 *c. sin. m.* *s. m.* A husband.

कान्ता *s. f.* A wife, a mistress; any beloved or lovely woman. कान्तया 3 *c. sin.*

कान्ताविरहगुरुणा *ep. of* शापेन.

कान्ति *s. f.* Beauty, splendour, lustre. कान्तिम् 2 *c. sin.* कान्तेः 6 *c. sin.*

कान्तिमत् *adj.* Splendid. कान्तिमत् 1 *c. sin. n.*

काम *s. m.* Passion, desire. कामात् 5 *c. sin.* Willingly.

कामचारिन् *agt.* Going, or who goes where he pleases. कामचारिन् 8 *c. sin. m.*

कामपि 2 *c. sin. f. of* किमपि Some, a certain.

कामरूप *adj.* Assuming any form at pleasure. कामरूपम् 2 *c. sin. m.*

कामिन् *s. m.* A lover, an uxorious husband. An impassioned, fond, or wanton fellow. कामी 1 *c. sin. m.*

कामिनी *s. f.* A loving or affectionate woman. कामिनी 1 *c. sin.* कामिनीनाम् 6 *c. pl.*

कामुकत्व *s. n.* Desire. कामुकत्वस्य 6 *c. sin.*

कारण *s. n.* Cause, reason.

कार्श्य *s. n.* Leanness. कार्श्यम् 2 *c. sin.*

काल *s. m.* Time, season. काले 7 *c. sin.* काले काले From time to time (annually, at the rainy season).

कालीदास *s. m.* Servant of Kálí, a proper name.

काव्य *s. n.* A poem.

किंस्वित् *ind.* Hey! What!

किञ्चित् *pron. indef.* Something, somewhat, a little.

कितव *s. m.* A rogue, *used here as a term of endearment.* कितव 8 *c. sin.*

किन्नरी *s. f.* A female Kinnara or chorister of Swarga. किन्नरीभिः 3 *c. pl.*

किमपि *pron. indef.* Somewhat, a little.

किम्पुनर् *ind.* How much more? how therefore?

किल *ind.* Verily, assuredly. Probably, possibly, haply.

किशलय *s. m. n.* A young shoot. A sprout or bud (to which the lip of a mistress is compared). किशलयेषु 7 *c. pl.*

कीचक *s. m.* A bambu whistling or rattling in the wind. Any hollow bambu, reed, or cane. कीचकाः 1 *c. pl.*

कीर्त्ति *s. f.* Fame, renown, glory. कीर्त्तिम् 2 *c. sin.*

कुञ्ज *s. m.* A bower, an arbour. कुञ्जे 7 *c. sin.*

कुटज *s. m.* Name of a certain medicinal plant.

कुन्द *s. m. n.* A sort of jasmine.

कुन्दसमानदन्ती *s. f.* A woman whose teeth are like the jasmine. कुन्दसमानदन्ति 8 *c. sin.*

कुपित *p. p.* (*of* कुप) Incensed, angry, offended, jealous. कुपिताम् 2 *c. sin. f.*

कुमुद *s. n.* The white esculent water-lily.

कुरुबक *s. m.* The crimson amaranth. कुरुबकम् 1 *c. sin. n.* 'Names of plants generally 'become neuter, to signify the produce of the 'plant; viz. its blossoms and fruits: some 'add the root, and even the leaf.' Colebrooke's Translation of Amara Kosha.

कुरुबकवृतेः *ep. of* मधुपस्य.

कुरुष्व *imp. átm. of* कृ 8 *cl.* Make.

कुर्वत् *pres. p. par. of* कृ 8 *cl.* Do, make, perform. कुर्वन् 1 *c. sin. m.*

कुर्वीथाः *pot. átm. of* कृ 8 *cl.* Make.

कुल *s. n.* A herd, a flock of animals of the same species, a bevy. कुलैः 3 *c. pl.*

कुलिश *s. m. n.* A thunderbolt.

कुवलय *s. n.* Any water-lily. The blue lotus.

कुश *s. m.* Sacrificial grass.

कुशल *s. n.* Well-being, welfare, happiness. कुशलम् 2 *c. sin.* कुशलैः 3 *c. pl.* *adj.* Happy, well. Clever. Eloquent. Expert, skilful.

कुशलिन् *adj.* Happy, well. कुशलिनम् 2 *c. sin. m.*

कुसुम *s. n.* A flower. कुसुमैः 3 *c. pl.*

कुसुम्भ *s. n.* Safflower (Carthamus tinctorius).

कूजित *s. n.* The cry of a bird, cooing. कूजितम् 2 *c. sin.*

कूट *s. m.* The peak of a mountain. कूटात् 5 *c. sin.*

कृत *p. p.* (*of* कृ) Made, rendered. कृताम् 2 *c. sin. f.* कृतम् 1 *c. sin. n.*

कृतक *adj.* Artificial, factitious. Adopted.

कृतवसतयः *ep. of* हंसाः.

कृतान्त *s. m.* Destiny, *i.e.* the inevitable result of actions done in a past existence. कृतान्तः 1 *c. sin.*

कृत्त *p. p.* (*of* कृत) Cut, divided.

कृत्ति *s. f.* A hide, a skin.

कृत्य *s. n.* An act. कृत्यम् 1 *c. sin.*

कृत्या *s. f.* Act, action, doing.

कृत्वा *ind. p. p.* (*of* कृ) Having made, done, performed, fulfilled, or accomplished.

कृपण *adj.* Poor, indigent, deficient. कृपणाः 1 *c. pl. m.*

कृषि *s. f.* Husbandry, agriculture, cultivation of the soil.

कृष्ण *adj.* Black.

कृष्णसार *s. m.* The black antelope.

कॢप्त *p. p.* (*of* कॢप) Formed, fashioned, cut into shapes.

कॢप्तच्छेदैः *ep. of* पुष्पैः *or* नलिनैः.

के 1 *c. pl. m.* (*of* किम्) Who?

केका *s. f.* The cry of the peacock. केकाः 2 *c. pl.*

केतक *s. m.* A fragrant plant (Pandanus odoratissimus). केतकैः 3 *c. pl.*

केतकाधानहेतोः *ep. of* तस्य.

केश *s. m.* The hair. केशान् 2 *c. pl.*

केशर *s. m.* Name of a tree bearing a white strong-smelling flower. The filament of any vegetable. केशरः 1 *c. sin.* केशरैः 3 *c. pl.*

केशव *s. m.* A name of Vishńu or Krishńa.

कैलास *s. m.* The mountain Kailása. कैलासात् 5 *c. sin.* कैलासस्य 6 *c. sin.*

कोटर *s. m. n.* The hollow of a tree. कोटरेषु 7 *c. pl.*

कोमल *adj.* Soft, delicate. कोमलम् 2 *c. sin. n.*

कोविद *adj.* Learned, wise.

कौतूहल *s. n.* Curiosity. An eager glance. कौतूहलानाम् 6 *c. pl.*

कौरव *adj.* Related to, or named after Kuru, the common ancestor of the sons of Pándu and Dhritaráshtra. कौरवम् 2 *c. sin. n.*

कौलीन *s. n.* Evil report, detraction. कौलीनात् 5 *c. sin.*

क्रम *s. m.* Order, method, progress, course. क्रमेण 3 *c. sin.*

क्रिया *s. f.* A doing, performance.

क्रीडा *s. f.* Play, sport, pastime.

क्रूर *adj.* Cruel, pitiless, unrelenting.

क्रोध *s. m.* Anger.

क्रौञ्चरन्ध्र *s. n.* Krauncha pass, name of a place. क्रौञ्चरन्ध्रम् 2 *c. sin.*

क्लान्त *p. p.* (*of* क्लम्) Fatigued, wearied, aching. Faded, drooping. क्लान्तम् 2 *c. sin. m.*

क्लान्तहस्ताः *ep. of* वेश्याः.

क्लिष्ट *p. p.* (*of* क्लिश) Distressed, pained, hurt. Chafed, fretted. Impaired, obscured, bedimmed.

क्लिष्टकान्तेः *ep. of* इन्दोः.

क्लेशिन् *agt.* Paining, scorching, withering, blasting. क्लेशिना 3 *c. sin. m.*

क्व *ind.* Where? *The repetition of this adverb in verse* 5 *is to denote* difference, distance, disparity. *The first may be rendered by* Is not? *and the second, by* How then?

क्वचित् *ind.* Anywhere.

क्वणित *p. p.* (*of* क्वण) Sounded; jingling, rattling.

क्षण *s. m.* A moment. A measure of time equal to four minutes. क्षणम् *used adverbially,* For a moment, as a moment.

क्षत्र *s. m.* A man of the second, or military or regal class.

क्षपयति *pres. par. of* क्षै *caus. form,* Destroy, kill.

क्षपा *s. f.* Night. क्षपासु 7 *c. pl.*

क्षम *adj.* Able, adequate.

क्षय *s. m.* Loss, waste, destruction.

क्षयित *adj.* Wasted, consumed.

क्षयिन् *adj.* Frail, subject to decay. क्षयिषु 7 *c. pl. n.*

क्षाम *p. p. irreg.* (*of* क्षै) Wasted, emaciated. Slender. क्षामा 1 *c. sin. f.* क्षामाम् 2 *c. sin. f.*

क्षिणोति *pres. par. of* क्षि 5 *cl.* Wound.

क्षिप्त *p. p.* (*of* क्षिप) Scattered, driven about.

क्षीण *p. p.* (*of* क्षी) Wasted, diminished, shrunk, exhausted. क्षीणः 1 *c. sin. m.*

क्षीर *s. n.* Milk. क्षीरम् 1 *c. sin.*

क्षुद्र *adj.* Little, small. Mean, low. क्षुद्रः 1 *c. sin. m.*

क्षेत्र *s. n.* A field. क्षेत्रम् 1 *c. sin.*

क्षेप *s. m.* A throwing; a delaying, loitering, or passing away (of time). A clump of flowers. क्षेपम् 2 *c. sin.*

क्षेमतर *compar.* (*of* क्षेम Happy, well) Happier, better. क्षेमतरम् 1 *c. sin. n.*

क्षोभ *s. m.* Agitation, shaking, tossing about.

ख

ख *s. n.* Heaven, sky. खम् 2 *c. sin.* खे 7 *c. sin.*

खग *s. m.* A bird. खगाः 1 *c. pl.*

खचित *p. p.* (*of* खच) Set, inlaid.

खण्ड *s. n.* Part, portion. खण्डम् 1 *c. sin.*

खण्डिता *s. f.* A woman whose husband or lover has been guilty of infidelity. खण्डितानाम् 6 *c. pl.*

खद्योत *s. m.* A fire-fly (*from* ख Sky, *and* द्योत Illuminating).

खलु *ind.* Indeed, certainly, surely. *An expletive.*

खिन्न *p. p.* (*of* खिद) Wearied, distressed, exhausted. खिन्नः 1 *c. sin. m.*

खिन्नविद्युत्कलत्रः *ep. of* भवान्.

खेद *s. m.* Weariness, exhaustion; sorrow, affliction, distress. खेदम् 2 *c. sin.* खेदात् 5 *c. sin.*

ग

गगन *s. n.* (*also written* गगण) Sky.

गगनगतयः *ep. of* ते *understood.*

गङ्गा *s. f.* The Ganges.

गङ्गासागर *s. m.* Gangá ságar (name of a place).

गच्छत् *pres. p. par. of* गम् 1 *cl.* Go, pass. गच्छत्सु 7 *c. pl. m.* गच्छन्तीनाम् 6 *c. pl. f.* गच्छति *pres.* गच्छेः *pot.*

गज *s. m.* An elephant. गजः 1 *c. sin.* गजस्य 6 *c. sin.*

गण *s. m.* A troop of inferior deities, considered as Śiva's attendants, and under the especial superintendence of Gańeśa. गणैः 3 *c. pl.*

गणना *s. f.* Counting, numbering, enumeration. गणनया 3 *c. sin.*

गण्ड *s. m.* A cheek, especially the whole side of the face, including the temple.

गण्डस्वेदोपनयनरुजाक्लान्तकर्णोत्पलानाम् *ep. of* मुखानाम्.

गत *p. p.* (*of* गम) Gone, resorted, repaired; turned. गतः 1 *c. sin. m.* गतम् 2 *c. sin. m. n.* गते 7 *c. sin. m.* गतानाम् 6 *c. pl. m.*

गति *s. f.* A going, motion, march, progress. Course of events. Refuge, asylum. गतिः 1 *c. sin.* गत्या 3 *c. sin.*

गत्वा *ind. p. p. of* गम Go.

गन्तव्य *fut. p. p.* (*of* गम) To be gone to. गन्तव्या 1 *c. sin. f.* गन्तासि 1 *fut. par.* गन्तुम् *inf.*

गन्ध *s. m.* Smell, odour, perfume. गन्धम् 2 *c. sin.* गन्धैः 3 *c. pl.*

गन्धवती *s. f.* Name of a river. गन्धवत्याः 6 *c. sin.*

गन्धिन् *adj.* Fragrant, scented. गन्धिभिः 3 *c. pl. m.*

गमः (*after* मा) 3 *pret. par. of* गम Go.

गमन *s. n.* A going in general, moving, walking; departure.

गमय *imp. of* गम Go, *causal form.*

गमित *p. p.* (*of* गम *caus. form*) Made to go, sent, dismissed.

गमितमहिमा *ep. of* यक्षः.

गम्भीर *adj.* Deep; bass (as sound).

गम्भीरा *s. f.* Name of a river. गम्भीरायाः 6 *c. sin.*

गम्य *fut. p. p.* (*of* गम) To be gone to. गम्यम् 2 *c. sin. n.*

गर्जित *s. n.* The muttering of clouds, or rolling of distant thunder. गर्जितम् 2 *c. sin.* गर्जितैः 3 *c. pl.* गर्जितानाम् 6 *c. pl.*

गर्भ *s. m.* A fœtus, an embryo.

गर्भाधानक्षमपरिचयम् *ep. of* भवन्तम्.

गलित *p. p.* (*of* गल) Fallen, dropped, moulted. गलितम् 2 *c. sin. n.*

गवाक्ष *s. m.* An air-hole, loop-hole, a round window, a bull's eye. गवाक्षे *loc. sin.*

गाढ *adj.* Much, very, excessive. Heavy, oppressive. Firm, close.

गाण्डीव *s. m. n.* Gáńdiva, the bow of Arjuna.

गाण्डीवधन्वन् *s. m.* Armed with Gáńdiva, *i.e.* Arjuna. गाण्डीवधन्वा 1 *c. sin.*

गात्र *s. n.* The body. गात्रम् 2 *c. sin.*

गाहमान *pres. p. átm. of* गाह 1 *cl.* Overspread, envelope. गाहमानः 1 *c. sin. m.*

गिरि *s. m.* A mountain. गिरिम् 2 *c. sin.*

गीयते *pres. pass. of* गै Sing.

गुण *s. m.* A string. गुणम् 2 *c. sin.*

गुणवत् *adj.* Amiable, virtuous. गुणवति 8 *c. sin. f.*

गुणित *p. p. of* गुण Multiplied (arithmetically), increased, grown. गुणितम् 2 *c. sin. m.*

गुरु *adj.* Heavy, grievous, irksome, tedious. Oppressed; charged. Deep. गुरुणा 3 *c. sin. m.* गुरुभिः 3 *c. pl. n.* गुरुषु 7 *c. pl. m.* *s. m.* Any venerable personage, a sire, lord. गुरोः 6 *c. sin.*

गुरुतर *compar.* (*of* गुरु Heavy) Heavier, sorer.

गुरुतरशुचम् *ep. of* सखीम्.

गुह्यक *s. m.* A kind of demigod attendant upon Kuvera the deity of wealth, and guardian of his treasures. गुह्यकः 1 *c. sin.*

गृह *s. n.* A house, mansion. गृहात् 5 *c. sin.*

गृहबलिभुज् *s. m.* A kind of crane. A sparrow. A crow. गृहबलिभुजाम् 6 *c. pl.*

गेय *fut. p. p. of* गै Sing. *s. n.* A song. गेयम् 2 *c. sin.*

गेहिनी *s. f.* A wife. गेहिन्याः 6 *c. sin.*

गो *s. f.* The earth. गाम् 2 *c. sin.*

गोत्र *s. n.* Family, race, lineage.

गोप *s. m.* A herdsman. a cowherd.

गोपवेषस्य *ep. of* विष्णोः (Dressed as a herdsman).

गौर *adj.* White, hoary. Whitish, pale yellow. गौरः 1 *c. sin. m.* गौरम् 2 *c. sin. m.* गौरस्य 6 *c. sin. m.*

गौरव *s. n.* Weight, heaviness. गौरवाय 4 *c. sin.*

गौरी *s. f.* The goddess Gaurí, wife of Śiva.

ग्रथित *p. p.* (*of* ग्रन्थ) Strung. —म् 2 *c. sin. m. n.*

ग्रन्थि *s. m.* A knot.

ग्रहण *s. n.* A taking, laying hold of, seizing, seizure.

ग्राम *s. m.* A village, hamlet, an inhabited and unfortified place in the midst of fields and meadow land, where men of the servile class mostly reside, and where agriculture thrives. *In comp.* A multitude.

ग्लानि *s. f.* Langour, languidness. ग्लानिम् 2 *c. sin.*

घ

घण्टिका *s. f.* A bell.

घन *s. m.* A cloud. घन 8 *c. sin.*

घर्म *s. m.* Heat. The hot season.

घात *s. m.* A bruise, blow, stroke.

घोष *s. m.* Sound, noise. घोषम् 2 *c. sin.*

च

च *ind.* And, also. Both. *An expletive.*

चकित *p. p.* (*of* चक) Frightened, startled. Timid, timorous, fearful. चकितैः 3 *c. pl. n.* चकितचकितम् *n. used adverbially,* With great alarm.

चक्र *s. n.* A wheel.

चक्रवाकी *s. f.* The ruddy goose, commonly called, in India, the Brahmany duck or goose. चक्रवाकीम् 2 *c. sin.*

चक्रुः 2 *pret. par. of* कृ Make. चक्रे 2 *pret. átm.*

चक्षुस् *s. n.* The eye. चक्षुः 2 *c. sin.*

चञ्चत् *pres. p. par. of* चञ्च 1 *cl.* Dangle.

चटुल *adj.* Tremulous, rolling. Beautiful, lovely.

चण्ड *adj.* Fierce, violent.

चण्डा *s. f.* A name of the goddess Durgá, applied especially to her incarnation for the purpose of destroying Maheshásur. This exploit forms the subject of a section of the Márkańdeya Puráńa, and is particularly celebrated in Bengal at the Durga-púja, or festival held in honour of the goddess towards the close of the year (Oct.--Nov.).

चण्डी *s. f.* A passionate woman. A vixen, *a term of endearment.* चण्डि 8 *c. sin.*

चण्डेश्वर *s. m.* Chańdá's lord, *i. e.* Śiva.

चतुर् *num.* Four. चत्वारः 1 *c. pl. m.* चतुरः 2 *c. pl. m.* चतसृणाम् 6 *c. pl. f.*

चन्दन *s. m. n.* Sandal.

चन्द्रकान्त *s. m.* A fabulous gem, the moonstone, supposed to be formed of the congelation of the rays of the moon; a kind of crystal may perhaps be meant. चन्द्रकान्ताः 1 *c. pl.*

चन्द्रपाद *s. m.* A lunar ray. चन्द्रपादैः 3 *c. pl.*

चन्द्रिका *s. f.* Moonlight, a moonbeam. चन्द्रिकासु 7 *c. pl.*

चमरी *s. f.* A kind of deer, or rather the Bos grunniens, erroneously classed by the Hindu writers amongst the deer.

चमू *s. f.* A host. चमूनाम् 6 *c. pl.*

चरण *s. n.* A foot.

चल *adj.* Trembling, tremulous, wavy, undulary.

चलकिशलयः *ep. of* अशोकः *or* केशरः.

चलत्व *s. n.* Pulsation, a tremulous motion. चलत्वम् 2 *c. sin.*

चलोर्मि *ep. of* पयः.

चाटु *s. m.* Pleasing or grateful discourse, flattery.

चाटुकार *adj.* Complying with a request, humouring, complaisant. चाटुकारः 1 *c. sin. m.*

चातक *s. m.* A kind of cuckoo. चातकः 1 *c. sin.* —काः 1 *c. pl.* —कान् 2 *c. pl.* —केभ्यः 4 *c. pl.*

चाप *s. m.* A bow.

चामर *s. n.* A chowrie, the tail of the Bos grunniens, used to whisk off flies, also an emblem or insignia of princely rank. चामरैः 3 *c. pl.*

चारु *adj.* Pretty, elegant, beautiful. चारुणा 3 *c. sin. m. n.*

चाष *s. m.* The blue jay. चाषाः 1 *c. pl.*

चित्रकूट *s. m.* Name of a mountain. —कूटः 1 *c.*

चिर *adj.* Long. चिरम् *n.* A while, a long time.

चूडा *s. f.* A lock of hair on the crown of the head, a crest, a top-knot.

चूर्ण *s. m. n.* Aromatic powder, pounded sandal, &c.

चेत् *ind.* If.

चेतन *adj.* Living, animated.

चेतस् *s. n.* Mind, heart, soul, feelings. चेतः 1 *c. sin.* चेतसा 3 *c. sin.* चेतसः 6 *c. sin.* चेतसि 7 *c. sin.*

चैत्य *s. m.* A sacred tree, a religious fig-tree, &c., growing in a village or near it, and held in veneration by the villagers.

चौर *s. m.* A thief, robber, pilferer. चौरे 7 *c. sin.*

च्युत *p. p.* (*of* च्यु) Dropped, slipped, slidden.

छ

छद्मन् *s. n.* Plea, pretext. छद्मना 3 *c. sin.*

छन्न *p. p.* (*of* छद) Covered, clad. छन्ना 1 *c. sin. f.*

छन्नोपान्तः *ep. of* अचलः.

छवि *s. f.* Beauty, brilliancy, hue.

छादयत् *pres. p. par. of* छद 10 *cl.* Veil, cover, conceal. छादयन्तीम् 2 *c. sin. f.*

छाया *s. f.* Shade, shadow. Beauty, splendour, lustre, light, brilliancy, brilliant hue. Tint. A straight or continuous line. छायया 3 *c. sin.* *As the last member of a compound, it takes a short vowel, as,* गरुडच्छायम्. *See Wilson's grammar, page* 348.

छायात्मन् *s. m.* A reflected image, a shadow. छायात्मा 1 *c. sin.*

छायाभिन्न *adj.* Divided in radiance, reflecting light from various surfaces.

छिन्न *p. p.* (*of* छिद) Cut, snapped, broken.

छेद *s. m.* A cutting, segment, slice; a part, portion. Any distinguishing mark (as a streak, &c.) by which the face or person is decorated. छेदैः 3 *c. pl.*

ज

जगत् *s. n.* The world.

जघन *s. n.* The hip and loins.

जन *s. m.* A man, person; people, kindred. जनः 1 *c. sin.* जनम् 2 *c. sin.* जने 7 *c. sin.*

जनक *s. m.* Name of a king, sovereign of Mithilá, and father of Sítá.

जनकतनयास्नानपुण्योदकेषु *ep. of* आश्रमेषु.

जनपद *s. m.* Any inhabited country. जनपदम् 2 *c. sin.*

जनित *p. p.* (*of* जन *caus. form*) Produced, occasioned by. जनिताम् *acc. sin. f.* जनितैः 3 *c. pl. n.*

जन्मन् *s. n.* Birth, origin, production.

जम्बू *s. m.* The rose-apple.

जम्बूकुञ्जप्रतिहतरयम् *ep. of* तोयम्.

जय *imp. par. of* जि 1 *cl.* Conquer.

जर्ज्जर *adj.* Split, broken, divided into an infinitude of parts. जर्ज्जराः 1 *c. pl. m.*

जल *s. n.* Water. जलम् 2 *c. sin.*

जलद *s. m.* A cloud. जलद 8 *c. sin.*

जलदाभ *adj.* Bright as a cloud. जलदाभम् 2 *c. sin. n.*

जलधर *s. m.* A cloud. जलधर 8 *c. sin.*

जलमुच् *agt.* Water-shedding. A cloud. जलमुचः 1 *c. pl.*

जललवमुच् *agt.* Discharging drops of water. जललवमुचः 6 *c. sin. m.*

जवा *s. f.* The China rose.

जह्नु *s. m.* Name of a king or saint, son of Kuru. जह्नोः 6 *c.*

जात *p. p.* (*of* जन) Born, produced, sprung, grown, become, growing. जातः 1 *c. sin. m.* जातम् 2 *c. sin. m.* जाताम् 2 *c. sin. f.* जातानि 2 *c. pl. n.*

जातविभ्रमाः *ep. of* स्त्रियः (Precipitate).

जानामि *pres. par. of* ज्ञा 9 *cl.* Know. जानीयाः *pot.* जाने *pres. átm.*

जाया *s. f.* A wife. जायाम् 2 *c. sin.*

जाल *s. n.* A lattice, casement, window, eyelet, loophole. Net-work. A multitude. जालैः *ins. pl.*

जालक *s. n.* A bud, germ, unblown flower. जालकानि 2 *c. pl.* जालकैः 3 *c. pl.*

जीमूत *s. m.* A cloud. जीमूतेन 3 *c. sin.*

जीवत् *pres. p. par. of* जीव 1 *cl.* Come to life, revive.

जीवित *s. n.* Life, existence. जीवितम् 2 *c. sin.*

जुष् *agt. in comp.* Serving, sharing; possessing. जुषाम् 6 *c. pl.*

ज्ञात *p. p.* (*of* ज्ञा) Known, experienced.

ज्ञातास्वादः *ep. of* कः

ज्ञास्यसे 2*d fut. átm. of* ज्ञा Know.

ज्या *s. f.* A bowstring.

ज्योतिर्लेखावलयि *ep. of* बर्हम् (Studded with rows of stars.)

ज्योतिश्छायाकुसुमरचितानि *ep. of* स्थलानि.

ज्योतिस् *s. n.* A star. Fire, light.

त

तट *s. m. n.* Shore, bank, edge, margin, height, towering eminence.

तडित् *s. f.* Lightning.

तण्डुल *s. m.* Grain after threshing and winnowing, especially rice. तण्डुलाः 1 *c. pl.*

तत् *ind.* Therefore.

तत्पर *adj.* Diligent, closely attentive. तत्पराम् 2 *c. sin. f.*

तत्र *ind.* There.

तथा *ind.* Thus. So, in this manner, so much, likewise, in the same manner.

तथैव *ind.* So, even so, in the same manner.

तद् *pron.* He, she, it, that.

तदनु *ind.* After that, afterwards.

तनय *s. m.* A son. तनयः 1 *c. sin.* तनयम् 2 *c. sin.*

तनया *s. f.* A daughter.

तनु *s. f.* The body. तनुम् 2 *c. sin.* *adj.* Narrow, thin, slender, emaciated. तनुम् 2 *c. sin. m.* तनुना 3 *c. sin. n.*

तनुता *s. f.* Tenuity, thinness, extenuation, littleness, diminutiveness. तनुताम् 2 *c. sin.*

तन्तु *s. m.* A thread.

तन्तुजालावलम्बाः *ep. of* चन्द्रकान्ताः.

तन्त्री *s. f.* The wire or string of a lute. तन्त्रीः 2 *c. pl.*

तन्वी *s. f.* A thin, slender, delicate woman.

तप्त *p. p.* (*of* तप्) Inflamed, scorched by pain or sorrow. तप्तम् 2 *c. sin. n.* तप्तेन 3 *c. sin. n.*

तम् 2 *c. sin. m. of* तद्. तम् तम् This and that, all that, whatever.

तमस् *s. n.* Darkness, gloom. तमोभिः 3 *c. pl.*

तरु *s. m.* A tree. तरवः 1 *c. pl.* तरुषु 7 *c. pl.*

तर्कयामि *pres. par. of* तर्क 10 *cl.* Suspect, infer, suppose, conclude. Bethink one's self, have a mind. तर्कयेः *pot.*

तव 6 *c. sin. of* युष्मद् Thou.

तस्मात् 5 *c. sin. n. of* तद्. Therefore. तस्मिन् 7 *c. sin. m. n.* *For the doubling of the* न् *see Grammar.* तस्मै 4 *c. sin. m.* तस्य 6 *c. sin. m.* तस्याः 6 *c. sin. f.*

ताः 2 *c. pl. f. of* तद्. तान् 2 *c. pl. m.* तान् तान् These and those, many. ताभ्यः 5 *cl. pl. f.* ताम् 2 *c. sin. f.*

ताल *s. m.* A beating of time by clapping the hands together. तालैः 3 *c. pl.*

तावत् *ind.* So soon. Forthwith. Meanwhile, in the first place.

तासाम् 6 *c. pl. f. of* तद्.

तिक्त *adj.* Fragrant, spicy, aromatic. तिक्तैः 3 *c. pl. m.*

तिर्यञ्च् *adj.* Moving awry, meandering. Curved. तिर्यक् 2 *c. sin. n.*

तिल *s. m.* A plant bearing an oily seed, sesamum.

तीर *s. n.* Shore, bank, margin, brink. तीरे 7 *c. sin.*

तीरोपान्तस्तनितसुभगम् *ep. of* पयः.

तीर्ण *p. p.* (*of* तॄ) Traversed, passed, gone. तीर्णः 1 *c. sin. m.*

तीर्थ *s. n.* A holy place of pilgrimage. तीर्थम् 2 *c. sin.*

तुङ्ग *adj.* Lofty. तुङ्गम् 2 *c. sin. m.* तुङ्गेन 3 *c. sin. n.* तुङ्गान् 2 *c. pl. m.*

तुमुल *s. m.* A loud and confused noise, a clatter.

तुलयितुम् *inf. of* तुल 10 *cl.* Weigh, outweigh, counterpoise, equal, compete, vie.

तुला *s. f.* Resemblance, likeness. तुलाम् 2 *c. sin.*

तुषार *s. m.* Frost. Ice or snow. तुषारैः 3 *c. pl.*

तुषाराद्रि *s. m.* The Himálaya mountain.

तूर्णम् *ind.* Quick, swift, quickly.

तृण *s. n.* Grass.

तृषा *s. f.* Thirst.

ते 6 *c. sin. of* युष्मद् *and* 1 *c. pl. m. of* तद्.

तेजस् *s. n.* Splendour; radiance, glory, brilliancy. Male energy. तेजः 1 or 2 *c. sin.*

तेन 3 *c. sin. n. of* तद्. Therefore. तेषाम् 6 *c. pl. m.* तैः 3 *c. pl. m.* तैः तैः With these or those, with several or many.

तोय *s. n.* Water. तोयम् 2 *c. sin.* तोये 7 *c. sin.*

तोयद *s. m.* A cloud.

तोयोत्सर्गस्तनितमुखरः 1 *c. sin. m.* Noisy with rain and thunder.

तोरण *s. m. n.* The ornamented arch of a door or gateway. तोरणेन 3 *c. sin.*

त्यक्त्वा *ind. p. p. of* त्यज Leave, get rid of.

त्यज *imp. par. of* त्यज 1 *cl.* Quit, avoid, shun, get rid of. त्यजति *pres.* त्याजित *p. p. caus. form,* Made to quit. त्याजितः 1 *c. sin. m.*

त्रसत् *p. p. par.* (*of* त्रस 1 *cl.*) Fearing, starting with dread.

त्रिणयन *s. m.* Śiva (triocular).

त्रिणयनवृषोत्खातकूटात् *ep. of* शैलात्.

त्रिदश *s. m.* A god.

त्रिदशवनिता *s. f.* A goddess.

त्रिपुर *s. m.* Name of a demon.

त्रिभुवन *s. n.* The three worlds of heaven, earth, and hell.

त्रियामा *s. f.* Night, as consisting of three watches.

त्रिषु 7 *c. pl. n. of* त्रि *num.* Three.

त्र्यम्बक *s. m.* Śiva. त्र्यम्बकस्य 6 *c. sin.*

त्वत् *in compos. for* युष्मद्.

त्वत्तः *abl. sin. of* युष्मद्.

त्वत्प्रयाणानुरूपम् *ep. of* मार्गम्.

त्वद्गम्भीरध्वनिषु *ep. of* पुष्करेषु.

त्वन्निष्यन्दोच्छ्वसितवसुधागन्धसम्पर्कपुण्यः *ep. of* वायुः.

त्वम् 1 *c. sin. of* युष्मद् Thou. त्वाम् 2 *c. sin.* त्वया 3 *c. sin.* त्वयि 7 *c. sin.*

त्वरयति *pres. par. of* त्वर *caus. form,* Quicken, urge forward, accelerate.

त्वरितम् *p. p. sin. n. adverbially,* In haste, fast.

त्वादृश *adj.* Such as thee, like thyself. त्वादृशाः 1 *c. pl. m.*

द

दक्षिण *pronom.* South. दक्षिणेन Southwards.

दग्ध *p. p.* (*of* दह) Burned.

दत्त *p. p.* (*of* दा) Given.

दत्तनृत्योपहारः *ep. of* त्वम् *understood* (Complimented with a dance.)

दत्तमार्गः *ep. of* त्वम् (Given way to, having the road ceded.)

दत्तहस्ता *ep. of* गौरी (Handed, supported.)

दत्त्वा *ind. p. p.* (*of* दा) Having given.

ददर्श 2 *pret. par. of* दृश See.

दधान *pres. p. átm. of* धा 3 *cl.* Hold. Have, assume, possess. दधानः 1 *c. sin. m.*

दधि *s. n.* Curds.

दध्यौ 2 *pret. par. of* ध्यै Reflect, think, meditate.

दन्तिन् *s. m.* An elephant. दन्तिभिः 3 *c. pl.*

दम्पती 2 *c. du. of* दम्पति *s. m.* Husband and wife.

दयिता *s. f.* A cherished woman or wife.

दरी *s. f.* A cavern. दरीषु 7 *c. pl.*

दर्प *s. m.* Pride.

दर्पण *s. n.* A looking-glass, a mirror. दर्पणस्य 6 *c. sin.*

दर्शय *imp. par. of* दृश See, *caus. form.*

दर्शित *p. p.* (*of* दृश *caus. form*) Displayed, exposed to view.

दर्शितावर्त्तनाभेः *ep. of* निर्विन्ध्यायाः.

दल *s. m. n.* A leaf.

दव *s. m.* A wood, a forest.

दवाग्नि *s. m.* A wood on fire, the conflagration of a forest. दवाग्निः 1 *c. sin.*

दशन् *num.* Ten.

दशन *s. m. n.* A tusk.

दशपुर *s. m.* Name of a district or city.

दशमुख *s. m.* Name of the ten-faced giant Rávańa.

दशमुखभुजोच्छ्वासितप्रस्थसन्धेः *ep. of* कैलासस्य.

दशा *s. f.* State, condition (of mankind).

दशार्ण *s. m.* Name of a country. दशार्णाः 1 *c. pl.* *denoting* Its cultivated tracts or fields.

दान *s. n.* Giving; a gift. दानात् 5 *c. sin.*

दामन् *s. n.* A string, a cord. A chaplet, wreath or garland for the forehead. दाम 2 *c. sin.*

दायक *agt.* Giving, bestowing; a giver. दायिका 1 *c. sin. f.*

दाह *s. m.* A conflagration. दाहात् 5 *c. sin.*

दिक्संसक्तप्रविततघनव्यस्तसूर्यातपानि *ep. of* वासराणि.

दिङ्नाग *s. m.* An elephant of a quarter or point of the compass, one of eight attached to the north, north-east, &c. supporting the globe. दिङ्नागानाम् 6 *c. pl.*

दिन *s. m. n.* A day.

दिनकर *s. m.* The sun.

दिव् *s. f.* Heaven. दिवः 6 *c. sin.*

दिवस *s. m. n.* A day. दिवसे 7 *c. sin.* दिवसेषु 7 *c. pl.*

दिश् *s. f.* A region, quarter, space. दिशम् 2 *c. sin.* दिशि 7 *c. sin.* दिक्षु 7 *c. pl.*

दीर्घ *adj.* Long. दीर्घान् 2 *c. pl. m.* दीर्घीकुर्वन् 1 *c. sin. m.* Lengthening, prolonging.

दीर्घयामा *ep. of* त्रियामा.

दीर्घोच्छ्वासम् *ep. of* चक्रम्.

दुःख *s. n.* Misery, distress. दुःखम् 1 *c. sin.* दुःखदुःख Intense distress.

दुकूल *s. n.* Wove silk. Fine raiment.

दुर्लभ *adj.* Difficult of access, or attainment. दुर्लभा 1 *c. sin. f.*

दुर्लभप्रार्थनम् *ep. of* चेतः.

दूत *s. m.* A messenger.

दूर *adj.* Distant, far, remote. दूरात् 5 *c. sin. n.*

दूरबन्धुः *ep. of* अहम्.

दूरम् *sin. n. adverbially,* Far, to a distance.

दूरीभूत *adj.* Removed, afar off. दूरीभूतम् 2 *c. sin. m.* दूरीभूते 7 *c. sin. m.*

दूर्वा *s. f.* Bent grass, commonly *Dúb.*

दृषद् *s. f.* A stone, a rock. दृषदि 7 *c. sin.*

दृष्ट *p. p.* (*of* दृश्) Seen, viewed, beheld, regarded; appearing. दृष्टे 7 *c. sin. m. n.*

दृष्टभक्तिः *ep. of* त्वम् *understood* (Having thy service beheld).

दृष्टि *s. f.* A look, glance. Sight, seeing. The eye. दृष्टिः 1 *c. sin.* दृष्टिम् 2 *c. sin.* दृष्टीः 2 *c. pl.*

दृष्टिपात *s. m.* A look, a glance. —तान् 2 *c. pl.*

दृष्टोत्साहः *ep. of* त्वम् *understood.*

दृष्ट्वा *ind. p. p.* (*of* दृश्) Having seen.

देव *s. m.* A god. Śiva. देवम् 2 *c. sin.* देवानाम् 6 *c. pl.*

देवदारु *s. m.* A species of pine.

देवपूर्वम् *ep. of* गिरिम् (Preceded by Deva, having the word Deva prefixed).

देश *s. m.* Place, country. देशाः 1 *c. pl.* देशान् 2 *c. pl.*

देहली *s. f.* The threshold of a door, the lower part of the wooden frame of a door, or a raised terrace in front of it.

दैन्य *s. n.* Feebleness, weakness, a poor and pitiable state. दैन्यम् 2 *c. sin.*

दैव *s. n.* Destiny, fate, fortune.

दोष *s. m.* Spoil, damage, injury. दोषम् 2 *c. sin.*

दोहद *s. n.* A wish, a longing desire (particularly of a pregnant woman).

द्योतिन् *agt.* Shining. द्योतिभिः 3 *c. pl. m.*

द्रक्ष्यसि 2 *fut. par. of* दृश् See.

द्रुत *p. p.* (*of* द्रु) Dissolved, melted. Quick, swift. द्रुतम् 2 *c. sin. n. used adverbially,* Rapidly, quickly.

द्रुततर *compar.* (*of* द्रुत) Quicker, swifter.

द्रुम *s. m.* A tree. द्रुमान् 2 *c. pl.* द्रुमाणाम् 6 *c. pl.*

द्वन्द्व *s. n.* A pair. A couple of animals (male and female). द्वन्द्वैः 3 *c. pl.*

द्वार *s. n.* A door, gate, or rather the door or gateway; a passage, entrance. द्वारम् 2 *c. sin.*

द्वितीय *adj.* Second. द्वितीयम् 2 *c. sin. n.*

द्विरद *s. m.* An elephant (two-tusked).

ध

धनपति *s. m.* Kuvera, god of riches. धनपतेः 6 *c. sin.*

धनुःखण्ड *s. n.* A bow, the stick or horns of a bow. धनुःखण्डम् 1 *c. sin.*

धनुष् *s. n.* A bow.

धनेश *s. m.* Lord of wealth. धनेशः 1 *c. sin.*

धन्वन् *s. m. n.* A bow.

धातु *s. m.* A mineral, a fossil.

धातृ *s. m.* Brahmá, the creator. धातुः 6 *c. sin.*

धामन् *s. n.* A house, dwelling, abode. धाम 2 *c. sin.*

धारयत् *pres. p. par. of* धृ 10 *cl.* Bear, carry, have, possess, support, sustain. धारयन्ती 1 *c. sin. f.* धारयेथाः *pot.*

धारा *s. f.* A hard shower falling in large drops or hail.

धारिन् *agt.* Holding, containing. धारिणः 1 *c. pl. m.*

धार्त्तराष्ट्र *s. m.* A son of Dhṛitaráshtra. धार्त्तराष्ट्राः 1 *c. pl.*

धीर *adj.* Deep (as sound), grave.

धीरता *s. f.* Refusal. धीरताम् 2 *c. sin.*

धुन्वत् *pres. p. of* धु 5 *cl.* Shake. धुन्वन् 1 *c. sin. m.*

धूत *p. p.* (*of* धू) Shaken, agitated; fanned.

धूतोद्यानम् *ep. of* धाम.

धूप *s. m.* Fragrant powder. धूपैः 3 *c. pl.*

धूम *s. m.* Smoke, vapour.

धृत *p. p.* (*of* धृ) Held, worn, borne. धृतम् 2 *c. n.*

धैर्य्य *s. n.* Firmness, inflexibility. धैर्य्यात् 5 *c. sin.*

धौत *p. p. of* धाव White, bright, silvered, shining.

धौतापाङ्गम् *ep. of* मयूरम् (Whose eye vies in brightness).

ध्यास्यन्ति 2 *fut. par. of* ध्यै Think.

ध्वनति *pres. par. of* ध्वन 1 *cl.* Echo, reverberate.

ध्वनि *s. n.* Sound, noise. ध्वनिः 1 *c. sin.* ध्वनिम् 2 *c. sin.* ध्वनिभिः 3 *c. pl.*

ध्वनित *p. p.* (*of* ध्वन) Sounded, making a noise.

न

न *ind.* No, not, neither, nor. न न *imply an affirmative.*

नख *s. m.* A nail, claw. नखेन 3 *c. sin.*

नखपद *s. n.* A scratch; soreness (of feet) (*from* नख A nail, *and* पद A mark).

नग *s. m.* A mountain.

नगनदी *s. f.* Name of a river.

नगेन्द्र *s. m.* Chief of mountains, *i. e.* Kailása. नगेन्द्रम् 2 *c. sin.*

नचिरेण *ind.* Speedily, shortly.

नदति *and* नदन्ति *pres. par. of* णद 1 *cl.* Cry, utter a sound, sing.

नदी *s. f.* A river. नद्यः 1 *c. pl.*

ननु *ind.* Certainly, surely. *A particle of interrogation,* How? what? ननु न Do (I) not? can (I) not?

नभस् *s. n.* Sky, air. The month Śrávaṅa, the rains or rainy season. नभसि 7 *c. sin.*

नमित *p. p.* (*of* णम *caus. form*) Bowed, bent down. नमितः 1 *c. sin. m.*

नम्र *adj.* Bent, bowed, crooked, curved, inclined. नम्रः 1 *c. sin. m.* नम्रा 1 *c. sin. f.*

नयन *s. n.* The eye. नयनम् 1 *c. sin.* नयनैः 3 *c. pl.* (*for* नयनपातैः Glances).

नयनसलिल *s. n.* A tear. नयनसलिलम् 1 *c. sin.* नयनसलिलैः 3 *c. pl.*

नयनसलिलोत्पीडरुद्धावकाशाम् *ep. of* निद्राम्.

नरपति *s. m.* A king, a sovereign prince.

नरपतिपथ *s. m.* A royal road, forty cubits broad. नरपतिपथे 7 *c. sin.*

नर्त्तयेथाः *pot. par.* (*of* नृत Dance, *caus. form,*) नर्त्तित *p. p.* Made to dance. नर्त्तितः 1 *c. sin. m.*

नलिन *s. n.* A lotus or water-lily. नलिनैः 3 *c.*

नलिनी *s. f.* A lotus. नलिन्याः 6 *c. sin.*

नव *adj.* New, fresh.

नवन् *num. pl. only,* Nine. नव 1 *c.*

नवशशिभृत् *s. m.* Śiva (*from* नवशशिन् The

new moon, *and* भृत् Bearing). नवशशिभृता 3 *c. sin.*

नाग *s. m.* An elephant.

नागर *s. m.* A libertine. नागराणाम् 6 *c. pl.*

नाभि *s. m. f.* The navel. Musk. नाभिः 1 *c. sin.* नाभेः 6 *c. sin.*

नाम *ind.* By name, called, namely.

नामन् *s. n.* A name. नाम्ना 3 *c. sin.*

नाल *s. m. n.* A hollow or tubular stalk, the stalk of the water-lily, &c. नालैः 3 *c. pl.*

नि *prep.* In, *un.*

निःश्वास *s. m.* Breathing out, expiration, sighing. निःश्वासेन 3 *c. sin.*

निकष *s. m.* The touchstone.

निक्षिप्य *ind. p. p.* (*of* क्षिप Throw, *with* नि) Having placed or laid.

निखिल *adj.* All, entire, complete. निखिलम् 1 *c. sin. n.*

निचुल *s. m.* A plant, commonly called Hijjal (Barringtonia acutangula). —लात् 5 *c. sin.*

नितम्ब *s. m.* The buttocks or posteriors in general; or as it is sometimes applied, the circumference of the hip and loins.

नित्य *adj.* Constant, continual.

निद्रा *s. f.* Sleep, slumber. निद्राम् 2 *c. sin.*

निधि *s. m.* A treasure. निधयः 1 *c. pl.*

निनाद *s. m.* Noise, sound. निनादः 1 *c. sin.*

निपतति *pres. par. of* पत 1 *cl.* Fall, *with* नि. निपातयत् *pres. p. caus. form.* निपातयन्त्यः 1 *c. pl. f.*

निपुण *adj.* Clever, skilled. निपुणाः 1 *c. pl. m.*

निभ *in comp.* Like, resembling. —भाम् 2 *c. sin. f.*

निभृत *adj.* Lonely, solitary. निभृते 8 *c. sin. f.*

निम्न *adj.* Deep.

नियत *p. p.* (*of* यम *with* नि) Fixed, settled, constant, permanent.

नियतवसतिम् *ep. of* स्कन्दम्.

नियमन *s. n.* Humiliation, coercion.

निर् *prep.* Out.

निरञ्जन *adj.* Free from passion or sorrow (*from* नि *neg. and* रञ्जन Affection, *or* निर् Without, अञ्जन Collyrium, *fig.* Darkness). निरञ्जनम् 2 *c. sin. n.*

निर्दय *adj.* Unmerciful. Close (embrace).

निर्दिशत् *pres. p. par. of* दिश 6 *cl.* Shew, point, *with* निर् Out. निर्दिशन्तः 1 *c. pl. m.*

निर्मित *p. p.* (*of* मा Measure, *with* निर्) Made, fabricated.

निर्विनोद *adj.* Void of solace, destitute of that which might divert the mind from care. निर्विनोदाम् 2 *c. sin. f.*

निर्विन्ध्या *s. f.* Name of a river issuing from the Vindhya mountain. निर्विन्ध्यायाः 6 *c. sin.*

निर्विशेः *pot. and* निर्वेक्ष्यावः 2 *fut. par. of* विश Enter, *with* निर् Arrive at, obtain, enjoy.

निवृत्त *p. p.* (*of* वृत Become, *with* नि) Returned. निवृत्तः 1 *c. sin. m.*

निशा *s. f.* Night. निशि 7 *c. sin.*

निशीथ *s. n.* Midnight. निशीथे 7 *c. sin.*

निश्शब्द *adj.* Silent. निश्शब्दः 1 *c. sin. m.*

निश्श्वास *s. m.* A sigh. निश्श्वासानाम् 6 *c. pl.*

निषण्ण *p. p.* (*of* षद Sit, *with* नि) Seated, perched, rested, reclining. निषण्णः 1 *c. sin. m.*

निष्पतन्ति *pres. par. of* पत 1 *cl.* Fall, *with* निर् Out.

निष्फल *adj.* Fruitless, useless, unprofitable.

निष्फलारम्भयत्नाः *ep. of* के.

निस्यन्दमान *pres. p. átm. of* स्यदि 1 *cl. with* नि Trickling, flowing, oozing, issuing.

निस्स्यन्द *s. m.* A dropping, a distilling.

निहित *p. p.* (*of* धा Hold, *with* नि) Laid, fixed, lodged, treasured up, deposited. निहितात्

5 *c. sin. m.* निहितम् 2 *c. sin. n.* निहितैः 3 *c. pl. n.*

निह्राद *s. m.* Sound.

निह्रादिन् *adj.* Sounding, pealing. निह्रादी 1 *c. sin. m.*

नीचैराख्यम् *ep. of* गिरिम्.

नीचैस् *ind.* Down, downward, below, underneath. Low, dwarfish.

नीड *s. m. n.* A nest.

नीत *p. p.* (*of* णी) Brought, conducted. Reduced. Passed. नीताः 1 *c. pl. m.* नीता 1 *c. sin. f.*

नीत्वा *ind. p. p.* (*of* णी) Having passed.

नीप *s. m.* The Kadamba-tree. नीपम् 2 *c. sin.* The Kadamba flower when full blown is invested with projecting antheræ like the erect bristles of a hedgehog. *In the neut.* The blossoms are denoted.

नील *adj.* Blue. नीलम् 2 *c. sin. n.*

नीलकण्ठ *s. m.* A peacock. नीलकण्ठः *nom. sin.*

नीवी *s. f.* A petticoat.

नीवीबन्धोच्छ्वसितशिथिलम् *ep. of* वासः.

नुदति *pres. par. of* णुद 6 *cl.* Send, drive, propel.

नूनम् *ind.* Assuredly, certainly. Perhaps, probably.

नृ *s. m.* A man. नृणाम् 6 *cl. pl.*

नृत्य *s. n.* Dancing, a dance. (There is a kind of dance with violent and frantic gesticulations practised by the god Śiva and his votaries. It is called Táńdava, from the inventor Tańdu, one of Śiva's doorkeepers, and an original teacher of the arts of dancing and mimicry.)

नेतृ *agt.* A leader, a guide. नेत्रा 3 *c. sin.*

नेत्र *s. n.* An eye.

नेमि *s. f.* The felly, circumference, or outer part of a wheel.

नेय *fut. p. p.* (*of* णी) To be brought. नेयम् 1 *c. sin. n.*

नेष्यन्ति 2 *fut. par. of* णी Bring, reduce.

नैदाघ *adj.* Scorching, peculiar to the hot season (May--June), called निदाघ. —म् 2 *c. sin. m.*

नैश *adj.* Nightly, nocturnal. नैशः 1 *c. sin. m.*

नौ 6 *c. du. of* अस्मद् I.

न्यस्त *p. p.* (*of* अस Throw, *with* नि) Thrown, placed, laid; leaning, resting. न्यस्तम् 1 *c. sin. n.* न्यस्ते 7 *c. sin. n.* न्यस्य *ind. p. p.* Having placed.

न्यास *s. m.* A placing, setting, laying or depositing. Impress, stamp, mark.

प

पक्व *p. p.* (*irreg. of* पच) Ripe.

पक्षिन् *s. m.* A bird. पक्षिणाम् 6 *c. pl.*

पक्ष्मन् *s. n.* An eyelash. पक्ष्मभिः 3 *c. pl.*

पङ्क *s. m. n.* Mud.

पङ्क्ति *s. f.* A line, row, series. पङ्क्तिम् 2 *c. sin.*

पञ्चबाण *s. m.* Kámadeva. पञ्चबाणः 1 *c. sin.*

पञ्जर *s. n.* A cage, an aviary.

पट *s. m. n.* Cloth. A veil or screen.

पटह *s. m.* A kettle-drum, a tabor.

पटहता *s. f.* The function, office, or noise of a drum. पटहताम् 2 *c. sin.*

पटु *adj.* Sensible, intellectual. Smart, shrill, sharp, crackling. पटुतर *compar.* Fiercer.

पटुकरणैः *ep. of* प्राणिभिः.

पण्यस्त्री *s. f.* A harlot (पण्य Vendible, स्त्री Woman.

पतन्ति *pres. par. of* पत 1 *cl.* Fall.

पति *s. m.* Lord, master.

पतित *p. p.* (*of* पत) Fallen, dropped, prostrate. पतितम् 2 *c. sin. m.* पतिताम् 2 *c. sin. f.* पतितैः 3 *c. pl. n.*

पथ *s. m.* A road. पथे 7 *c. sin.*

पथिक *s. m.* A traveller.

पथिन् *s. m.* A road, path, way. **पन्थाः** 1 *c. sin.* **पथि** 7 *c. sin.*

पद *s. n.* A foot. Step, footstep, print of a foot; a mark. A foot, or, rather, a line of a stanza. A work. Place, site. Rank, station. **पदम्** 1 *or* 2 *c. sin.* **पदैः** 3 *c. pl.*

पदवी *s. f.* A road, path, way, track. **पदवीम्** 2 *c. sin.*

पद्म *s. m. n.* A lotus. One of Kuvera's nine gems.

पद्मिनी *s. f.* A lotus.

पयस् *s. n.* Water. **पयः** 2 *c. sin.* **पयसि** 7 *c. sin.*

पयोद *s. m.* A cloud. **पयोद** 8 *c. sin.*

पयोनिधि *s. m.* The ocean. **पयोनिधिम्** 2 *c. sin.*

पर *pronom.* After, following, next, beyond. **परम्** 2 *c. sin. n.*

परम् *ind. governing the* 5*th case,* After.

पराधीन *adj.* Dependent, subject, subservient.

पराधीनवृत्तिः *ep. of* **अन्यः** *or of* **अहम्**.

परि *prep.* Round, about.

परिकीर्त्तित *p. p.* (*of* **कृत** *with* **परि**) Called.

परिगणना *s. f.* Enumeration, counting, number. **परिगणनया** 3 *c. sin.*

परिगत *p. p.* (*of* **गम** *with* **परि**) Obtained, gained. Distressed, overcome,

परिचय *s. m.* Acquaintance, intimacy. **परिचयम्** 2 *c. sin.*

परिचित *p. p.* (*of* **चि** Collect, *with* **परि**) Known, acquainted with. **परिचितः** 1 *c. sin. m.*

परिचितभ्रूलताविभ्रमाणाम् *ep. of* **कौतूहलानाम्**.

परिणत *p. p.* (*of* **णम** Bow, *with* **परि**) Bowed, bent. Stooping (as an elephant about to strike with his tusks). Ripe, mature, full grown; perfected, exalted. **परिणताम्** 2 *c. sin. f.*

परिणति *s. f.* Ripeness, maturity.

परिणमयितृ *agt.* Who or what bends down. Who causes to ripen. —**ता** 1 *c. sin. m.*

परितः *ind.* On every side, all around.

परिताप *s. m.* Heat. **परितापात्** 5 *c. sin.*

परित्राण *s. n.* Preservation.

परिदग्ध *p. p.* (*of* **दह** Burn, *with* **परि**) Burned, scorched. **परिदग्धाः** 1 *c. pl. f.*

परिभव *s. m.* Defeat, discomfiture, disgrace.

परिमल *s. m.* The fragrant scent of unguents.

परिमित *p. p.* (*of* **मा** Measure, *with* **परि**) Limited; moderate, sparing.

परिलघु *adj.* Very light.

परिसर *s. m.* Breadth, width, expansion.

परिहृत् *p. p. par.* (*of* **हृ** 1 *cl.* Take, *with* **परि**) Setting aside, taking down, humbling. **परिहरन्** 1 *c. sin. m.*

परीयाः *pot. par. of* **इ** 2 *cl.* Go, *with* **परि** Go round, circumambulate.

परुष *adj.* Harsh, grating. Violent, blustering. Rough, crisp (not softened with unguents). **परुषम्** 2 *c. sin. m. n.* **परुषैः** 3 *c. pl. n.*

पर्ण *s. n.* A leaf. **पर्णैः** 3 *c. pl.*

पर्य्यन्त *s. n.* Extremity.

पर्व्वत *s. m.* A mountain. **पर्व्वते** 7 *c. sin.*

पवन *s. m.* Air, wind, personified as a deity. **पवनः** 1 *c. sin.*

पशुपति *s. m.* A name of Śiva. **पशुपतेः** 6 *c. sin.*

पश्चात् *ind.* Afterwards. Westward.

पश्य *imp. par. of* **दृश** 1 *cl.* See, observe, behold. **पश्यत्** *pres. p.* **पश्यन्तीनाम्** 6 *c. pl. f.*

पाणि *s. m.* The hand. **पाणीन्** 2 *c. pl.* **पाणिभिः** 3 *c. pl.*

पाण्डु *adj.* Pale, straw-coloured, yellowish white. **पाण्डुः** 1 *c. sin. m.*

पाण्डुच्छाया *ep. of* **सिन्धुः**.

पाण्डुच्छायोपवनवृतयः *ep. of* **दशार्णाः**.

पाण्डुता *s. f.* Paleness. पाण्डुताम् 2 *c. sin.*

पात *s. m.* A fall, or falling. पातैः 3 *c. pl.*

पातिन् *agt.* Falling, failing. पाति 2 *c. sin. n.*

पातुम् *inf. of* पा Drink.

पात्र *s. n.* A vessel, a receptacle of any kind. पात्रीकुर्वन् 1 *c. sin. m.* Making an object.

पाथेय *s. n.* Provender, provision for a journey.

पाथेयवत् *adj.* Furnished with provisions for a journey. पाथेयवन्तः 1 *c. pl. m.*

पाद *s. m.* A foot. A ray of light. पादः 1 *c. sin.* पादे 7 *c. sin.* पादान् 2 *c. pl.*

पादचार *s. m.* A going on foot. —रेण 3 *c. sin.*

पादन्यास *s. m.* A dance, or measured step.

पादन्यासक्वणितरसनाः *ep. of* वेश्याः.

पाप *s. n.* Sin. पापम् 2 *c. sin.*

पारावत *s. m.* A dove, a pigeon.

पावक *s. m.* Fire. पावकेन 3 *c. sin.*

पार्श्व *s. m.* A side.

पाश *s. m.* A noose. *In compos. with words signifying hair,* Quantity; *as,* केशपाश Much, or flowing hair.

पास्यसि 2 *fut. par. of* पा Drink.

पिशुन *adj.* Vile, infamous. पिशुनम् 2 *c. sin. n.*

पीडयेत् *pot. par. of* पीड 10 *cl.* Pain, distress, afflict.

पीयमान *pres. p. p.* (*of* पा Drink) Being drunk or sucked in. पीयमानः 1 *c. sin. m.*

पुंस् *s. m.* The masculine gender. पुंसि 7 *c. sin.*

पुंसङ्गित *adj.* Male, masculine (*from* पुम् *s. m.* A male, *and* सङ्गित United, associated, classed). पुंसङ्गितः 1 *c. sin. m.*

पुट *s. m.* A cover, wrapper; the pod or capsule which envelopes young shoots. पुटान् 2 *c. pl.*

पुण्य *adj.* Pure, holy, sacred. Delightful. पुण्यः 1 *c. sin. m.* पुण्यम् 2 *c. sin. n.* *s. n.* A virtuous action. पुण्यैः 3 *c. pl.*

पुत्र *s. m.* A son.

पुनर् *ind.* Again.

पुमस् *s. m.* A man or male. पुंसाम् 6 *c. pl.*

पुरस् *ind.* In front, before, over against.

पुरस्तात् *ind.* Before, in presence. Eastward.

पुरा *ind.* Before, formerly.

पुरी *s. f.* A city. पुरीम् 2 *c. sin.*

पुरे *ind.* Before.

पुलकित *adj.* Bristling up with joy, enraptured, delighted. पुलकितम् 2 *c. sin. m.*

पुलिन *s. n.* An island of alluvial formation, or one from which the water has recently withdrawn, or a small island or bank left in the middle of a river.

पुलिनजघनाम् *ep.* of the Gambhírá river personified as a female.

पुष्कर *s. m.* Water. A kind of cloud. पुष्कराः 1 *c. pl.* *s. n.* The head of a drum, or place where any musical instrument is struck. पुष्करेषु 7 *c. pl.*

पुष्करावर्त्तक *s. m.* A watery cloud. पुष्करावर्त्तकानाम् 6 *c. pl.*

पुष्प *s. n.* A flower, a blossom. पुष्पैः 3 *c. pl.*

पुष्पमेघीकृतात्मा *ep. of* भवान्.

पुष्पलाव *s. m.* A flower-seller, a garland-maker. पुष्पलावी *f.*

पुष्यति *pres. par. of* पुष 4 *cl.* Nourish, maintain, keep up, retain.

पूर्णता *s. n.* Fulness.

पूर्णतागौरवाय 4 *c. s. m. ep.* Possessing the weight of abundance.

पूर्यमाण *pres. p. pass.* (*of* पृ Fill) Being filled.

पूर्व *pronom.* Before, former. पूर्वम् *n. sin. used adverbially,* Previously, already.

पूर्वार्द्धलम्बिन् *agt.* Leaning forward, having the foremost half inclined. —म्बी 1 *c. sin. m.*

पृच्छत् *pres. p. par. of* प्रच्छ 6 *cl.* Ask, inquire. पृच्छतः 6 *c. sin. m.* पृच्छन्ती 1 *c. sin. f.* पृच्छति *pres.*

पृथु *adj.* Broad, wide. पृथुम् 2 *c. sin. m.*

पृषत *s. m.* A drop of water.

पेय *fut. p. p.* (*of* पा) To be imbibed. पेयम् 2 *c. sin. m.*

पेशल *adj.* Beautiful. Smooth. पेशलैः 3 *c. pl. m.*

पौर *adj.* Belonging to a city, city, citizen.

प्याययेः *pot. par. of* प्याय Increase, swell, *caus. form,* Refresh (with cold water).

प्र *prep.* Fore, before, *pro, præ.*

प्रकल्पयेत् *pot. of* क्लृप 10 *cl.* Make, with प्र.

प्रकाम *adj.* Amorous. प्रकामाः 1 *c. pl. f.*

प्रकाश *adj.* Like, resembling. प्रकाशैः 3 *c. pl. m.*

प्रकीर्त्तित *p. p.* (*of* कृत 10 *cl.* Declare, *with* प्र) प्रकीर्त्तितम् 1 *c. sin. n.*

प्रकृति *s. f.* Nature, natural state. A requisite of regal government, of which seven are enumerated; the king, minister, ally, treasure, territory, fortresses, and army.

प्रकृतिकृपणाः *ep. of* कामार्त्ताः Feeble in their nature, (and therefore incapable of discriminating between rational and irrational beings).

प्रकृतिपुरुष *s. m.* A minister of state.

प्रकोष्ठ *s. m.* The fore-arm, or part between the elbow and the wrist. प्रकोष्ठः 1 *c. sin.*

प्रक्रमेथाः *pot. par. of* क्रम 1 *cl.* Step, *with* प्र Begin.

प्रचक्षते *pres. átm. of* चक्ष 2 *cl.* Say, call, *with* प्र.

प्रचलित *p. p.* (*of* चल Go, *with* प्र) Swinging to and fro. (The long line in page 37 is a specimen of the *Dańd́aka* metre. It contains 18 feet (2 Tribrachs and 16 Cretics), or 54 syllables; and the stanza therefore consists of 216. An error or two having crept into the printing of the text, the words are here repeated, and given separately. प्रचलित, करिन्, कृत्ति, पर्य्यन्त, चञ्चत्, नख, आघात, भिन्न, इन्दु, निस्यन्दमान, असृत, ख्योत, जीवत्, कपाल, आवली, मुक्त, चण्ड, अट्टहास, त्रसत्, भूरि, भूत, प्रवृत्त, स्तुतिः).

प्रणय *s. m.* Love, affection, affectionate regard or solicitation. Friendly acquaintance.

प्रणयिन् *adj.* Longing, anxious, affectionate, loving. प्रणयिनि 7 *c. sin. m.* प्रणयि 2 *c. sin. n.* *s. m.* A husband, or lover. A beggar, petitioner. प्रणयिनः 6 *c. sin.* प्रणयिनि 7 *c. sin.* प्रणयिभिः 3 *c. pl.* प्रणयिषु 7 *c. pl.*

प्रणिहित *p. p.* (*of* धा *with* नि *and* प्र) Outstretched.

प्रतनु *adj.* Small, minute, thin, slender, emaciated. प्रतनुम् 2 *c. sin. m.* प्रतनुषु 7 *c. pl. f.*

प्रति *prep.* Back, again, *re.*

प्रतिदिशम् *ind.* To every region.

प्रतिनव *adj.* New, young, fresh. Blown, budded.

प्रतिनवजवापुष्परक्तम् *ep. of* तेजः.

प्रतिमुख *adj.* Before, in front, in presence. प्रतिमुखगतम् *ep. of* त्वाम्.

प्रतिसार्य्यते *pres. pass. of* सृ Go, *caus. form with* प्रति Make to go back, replace.

प्रतिहत *p. p.* (*of* हन *with* प्रति) Obstructed, impeded, retarded.

प्रत्यक्ष *adj.* Evident, manifest. प्रत्यक्षम् 1 *c. s. n.*

प्रत्यग्र *adj.* New, recent, fresh. प्रत्यग्रैः 3 *c. pl. n.*

प्रत्यय *s. m.* Belief, certainty, assurance. प्रत्ययात् 5 *c. sin.*

प्रत्यादेश *s. m.* Refusal, denial, disallowance: silence. प्रत्यादेशात् 5 *c. sin.*

प्रत्यावृत्त *p. p.* (*of* वृत *with* आ *and* प्रति) Returned. प्रत्यावृत्तः 1 *c. sin. m.*

प्रत्याश्वस्त *p. p.* (*of* श्वस *with* आ *and* प्रति) Refreshed, revived, reanimated. प्रत्याश्वस्ताम् 2 *c. sin. f.*

प्रत्यासन्न *p. p.* (*of* षद Sink, *with* आ *and* प्रति) Near, nigh, contiguous, close at hand. प्रत्यासन्नः 1 *c. sin. m.* प्रत्यासन्ने 7 *c. sin. n.*

प्रत्युक्त *p. p.* (*of* वच *with* प्रति) Replied. *s. n.* A reply. प्रत्युक्तम् 1 *c. sin.*

प्रत्युद्यात *p. p.* (*of* या *with* उत् *and* प्रति) Received, met (as a guest). प्रत्युद्यातः 1 *c. sin. m.*

प्रथम *adj.* First, former, previous. Early.

प्रथयति *pres. par. of* प्रथ 10 *cl.* Reveal.

प्रथित *p. p.* (*of* प्रथ) Famous, renowned.

प्रथितविदिशालक्षणाम् *ep. of* राजधानीम्.

प्रद *agt.* Giving. प्रदाः 1 *c. pl. m.*

प्रदक्षिण *s. m. n.* Reverential salutation by circumambulating a person or object, keeping the right side towards them.

प्रदिशसि *pres. par. of* दिश 6 *cl.* Shew, *with* प्र, Give.

प्रदीप *s. m.* A lamp.

प्रधन *s. n.* War, battle.

प्रबल *adj.* Violent, strong.

प्रबलरुदितोच्छूननेत्रम् 1 *c. sin. n. ep. of* मुखम्.

प्रबुद्ध *p. p.* (*of* बुध *with* प्र) Awake.

प्रभव *s. m.* The place of receiving existence, or where an object is first perceived. प्रभवम् 2 *c. sin.*

प्रभवति *pres. par. of* भू 1 *cl.* Become, *with* प्र Come forth, appear, become visible. Be able, possess power.

प्रभा *s. f.* Radiance, lustre. प्रभाम् 2 *c. sin.*

प्रमत्त *p. p.* (*of* मद Rejoice, *with* प्र) Careless, negligent, remiss. प्रमत्तः 1 *c. sin. m.*

प्रमुख *adj.* Chief, principal, first.

प्रयाचित *p. p.* (*of* याच *with* प्र) Asked, solicited. प्रयाचितः 1 *c. sin. m.*

प्रयाण *s. n.* Going, march, journey.

प्रयाति, प्रयान्ति *pres. par. of* या 2 *cl.* Go, *with* प्र Proceed, advance.

प्ररोह *s. m.* A bud, shoot.

प्रवाह *s. m.* A stream. प्रवाहम् 2 *c. sin.*

प्रवितत *p. p.* (*of* तन Stretch, *with* वि *and* प्र) Outspread.

प्रविष्ट *p. p. of* विश Enter, *with* प्र. प्रविष्टान् 2 *c. pl. m.*

प्रवृत्त *p. p.* (*of* वृत *with* प्र) Turned, directed, proceeding, driving. Rendered by, emanating from. प्रवृत्ताः 1 *c. pl. m.*

प्रवृत्ति *s. f.* News, tidings. प्रवृत्तिम् 2 *c. sin.*

प्रवृद्ध *p. p.* (*of* वृध *with* प्र) Increased, augmented.

प्रवेश *s. m.* Entrance, admittance. प्रवेशम् 2 *c. sin.*

प्रशमन *s. n.* Alleviation, assuaging, mitigation.

प्रशमित *p. p.* (*of* शम *caus. form*) Allayed, extinguished, quenched.

प्रसन्न *p. p.* (*of* षद *with* प्र) Clear, unsullied. प्रसन्ने 7 *c. sin. n.*

प्रसर *agt.* Going forth, proceeding.

प्रसरति *pres. par. of* सृ 1 *cl.* Go, *with* प्र.

प्रसव *s. m.* A blossom, a flower.

प्रसविन् *adj.* Producing, bearing offspring. प्रसवि 2 *c. sin. n.*

प्रसारिन् *agt.* Flowing, streaming forth. —रिभिः 3 *c. pl. n.*

प्रसूत *p. p.* (*of* षू *with* प्र) Born, produced, grown. प्रसूतम् 2 *c. sin. n.*

प्रस्थ *s. m.* Table-land on the top of a mountain.

प्रस्थान *s. n.* Departure.

प्रस्थित *p. p.* (*of* ष्ठा *with* प्र) Gone, departed, set forth (on a journey, &c.). —तस्य 6 *c. sin. m.*

प्रहत *p. p.* (*of* हन *with* प्र) Struck, beat; played upon.

प्रहतमुरजाः *ep. of* **प्रासादाः**.

प्रहित *p. p.* (*of* **धा** *with* **प्र**) Sent, despatched. Discharged (as an arrow from a bow).

प्राचीमूल *s. n.* The eastern horizon.

प्राणिन् *s. m.* An animal, a sentient or living being. **प्राणिभिः** 3 *c. pl.*

प्रातर् *ind.* Early in the morning.

प्रान्त *s. m.* Edge, margin, skirt.

प्राप् *agt.* (*of* **आप** *with* **प्र**) Getting, obtaining (habitually wearing?). **प्रापि** 7 *c. sin. m.*

प्रापणीय *fut. p. p. of* **आप** Obtain, *with* **प्र**. **प्रापणीयाः** 1 *c. pl. m.*

प्राप्त *p. p.* (*of* **आप** *with* **प्र**) Obtained, gotten. Arrived. **प्राप्ते** 7 *c. sin. n.*

प्राप्तवानीरशाखम् *ep. of* **वसनम्** (Holding or detained by branches of reeds).

प्राप्ति *s. f.* Acquisition, attainment. **प्राप्तये** 4 *c. sin.*

प्राप्य *ind. p. p.* (*of* **आप** *with* **प्र**) Having obtained, received, reached, arrived at. *fut. p. p.* That may be reached, attainable.

प्रायशस्, **प्रायस्**, *or* **प्रायेण** *ind.* Usually, commonly, for the most part.

प्रार्थन *s. n.* A request. **प्रार्थनम्** 2 *c. sin.*

प्रार्थना *s. f.* Asking, begging, request, prayer.

प्रालेय *s. n.* Frost, dew.

प्रालेयाद्रि *s. m.* The Himálaya mountain. **प्रालेयाद्रेः** 6 *c. sin.*

प्रावृष् *s. f.* The rainy season. **प्रावृषा** 3 *c. sin.*

प्रासाद *s. m.* A palace.

प्रिय *adj.* Dear, beloved, favourite. **प्रियः** 1 *c. sin. m.* **प्रियम्** 2 *c. sin. n.* **प्रिया** 1 *c. sin. f.* **प्रियायाः** 6 *c. sin. f.* *s. m.* A lover, a friend. **प्रियेषु** 7 *c. pl.* *s. f.* **प्रिया** A wife.

प्रियतम *superl.* Dearest, best beloved. **प्रियतमः** 1 *c. sin. m.*

प्रीत *p. p.* (*of* **प्री** Please) Pleased, delighted, glad. **प्रीतः** 1 *c. sin. m.*

प्रीति *s. f.* Love, affection, kind regard, friendship. Joy, pleasure, delight, solace. **प्रीतिम्** 2 *c. sin.* **प्रीत्या** 3 *c. sin.*

प्रीतिप्रमुखवचनम् *ep. of* **स्वागतम्**.

प्रीतिस्निग्धैः *ep. of* **लोचनैः** (Moist with affection).

प्रेक्षण *s. n.* The eye.

प्रेक्षणीय *fut. p. p.* (*of* **ईक्ष** See, *with* **प्र**) To be seen, viewed, beheld, gazed at. Visible, apparent, looking or appearing like. **प्रेक्षणीयः** 1 *c. sin. m.* **प्रेक्षणीयम्** 2 *c. sin. m.*

प्रेक्षित *s. n.* A gaze, look, glance. **प्रेक्षिते** 7 *c. sin.* **प्रेक्षितानि** 2 *c. pl.*

प्रेक्षिष्यसे 2 *fut. átm. of* **ईक्ष** See, *with* **प्र**.

प्रेक्ष्य *ind. p. p. of* **ईक्ष** See, *with* **प्र**. *Also fut. p. p.* To be seen; visible, apparent. **प्रेक्ष्यम्** 1 *c. sin. n.*

प्रेमन् *s. m. n.* Affection, tender regard. **प्रेम्णा** 3 *c. sin.* **प्रेमराशीभवन्ति** They become a heap of affection, *i. e.* they wax more intense.

प्रेरण *s. n.* A sending or throwing.

प्रेरित *p. p.* (*of* **ईर** Send, *with* **प्र**) Instigated, excited, influenced. **प्रेरिताः** 1 *c. pl. m.*

प्रोषित *p. p.* (*of* **वस** Dwell, *with* **प्र**) Abroad, absent, away from home, sojourning in another country. **प्रोषितानाम्** 6 *c. pl. m.*

प्रौढ *p. p.* (*of* **वह** *with* **प्र**) Full grown.

प्रौढपुष्पैः *ep. of* **कदम्बैः**.

प्लुष्ट *p. p.* (*of* **प्लुष**) Burned.

फ

फल *s. n.* Fruit, product, result, consequence, reward. **फलम्** 1 *or* 2 *c. sin.* **फले** 7 *c. sin.*

फलक *s. m. n.* A slab, quadrangular pedestal.

फलति *pres. par. of* **फल** 1 *cl.* Bear fruit.

फलपरिणतिश्यामजम्बूवनान्ताः *ep. of* दशार्णाः.

फेन *s. m.* Froth, foam (compared to white teeth). फेनैः 3 *c. pl.*

ब

बद्ध *p. p.* (*of* बन्ध) Bound, tied, fixed, fastened. बद्धा 1 *c. sin. f.*

बन्ध *s. m.* A knot.

बन्धु *s. m.* A friend, kinsman, relation.

बल *s. n.* Power.

बलि *s. m.* Sacrifice, oblation, religious offering, public worship. The handle of a chowrie or fly-flapper. Name of a celebrated Daitya king. बलिम् 2 *c. sin.* बलिभिः 3 *c. pl.*

बहु *adj. n. used adverbially,* Much. बहुतर *compar.* Greater, more.

बहुशस् *ind.* Abundantly.

बाधेत *pot. átm. of* बाध 1 *cl.* Torment, ravage, devastate.

बाल *adj.* Young, tender, budding. Tall. *s. m.* A tail. Hair.

बालभार *s. m.* A weight of tail, a large bushy tail.

बाला *s. f.* A girl, or young woman. बालाम् 2 *c. sin.* बाले 8 *c. sin.*

बिभर्त्ति *pres. par. of* भृ 3 *cl.* Bear, wear, exhibit.

बुद्धि *s. f.* Thought, sentiment, feeling.

ब्रह्मावर्त्त *s. m.* Name of a country.

ब्रूयाः *pot. par. of* ब्रू 2 *cl.* Say.

भ

भक्ति *s. f.* Service, devotion, attachment. Worship, reverence. भक्त्या 3 *c. sin.*

भक्तिच्छेद *s. m.* (*from* भक्ति Devotion, *and* छेद A distinguishing mark) A coloured streak, the separating or distinguishing marks of Vaishńava devotion; certain streaks on the forehead, nose, cheeks, breast, and arms, which denote a follower of Vishńu.

भङ्ग *s. m.* Breaking, fracture. भङ्गाय 4 *c. sin.*

भङ्गी *s. f.* A bending.

भजते *pres. átm. of* भज 1 *cl.* Obtain.

भजेथाः *pot. átm. of* भज 1 *cl.* Worship, honour with a visit.

भय *s. n.* Fear, dread, alarm, fright. भयात् 5 *c. sin.*

भर *adj.* Much, excessive.

भर्तृ *s. m.* Lord, master. Mate, husband. भर्त्तुः 6 *c. sin.*

भव *s. m.* Birth.

भवानी *s. f.* The goddess Párvatí or Durgá in her pacific and amiable form. भवान्या 3 *c. sin.*

भवत् *honorif. pron.* You, your honour, worship, highness, &c. भवान् 1 *c. sin. m.* भवन्तम् 2 *c. sin. m.* भवतः 6 *c. sin. m.*

भवति, भवेत्, भव *from* भू 1 *cl.* Be, become.

भवन *s. n.* A house, dwelling. भवनम् 1 *c. sin.*

भवितृ *agt.* About to be, actually becoming or disposed to be. भविता 1 *c. sin. m.* भवित्रीम् 2 *c. sin. f.*

भानु *s. m.* The sun. भानोः 6 *c. sin.*

भाययेः *pot. par. of* भी *caus. form.* Frighten.

भार *s. m.* A burden, weight, load. भारः 1 *c. sin.* भारात् 5 *c. sin.*

भाव *s. m.* State, condition. The abstract idea conveyed by any word; दूरभाव *is therefore equivalent to* दूरता, *or* दूरत्व Distance.

भाविन् *agt.* Future, what will be, or what is about to be. भावी 1 *c. sin. m.* भावि 1 *c. sin. n.*

भास् *s. f.* Light, glare, splendour, lustre. भासम् 2 *c. sin.* भासा 3 *c. sin.*

भित्त्वा *ind. p. p. of* भिद् Break, burst.

भिन्न *p. p.* (*of* भिद्) Broken, fractured, powdered, pounded. Divided, detached, separated; deprived.

भिन्नवक्षोधरोष्ठम् 1 *c. sin. n. ep. of* मुखम्.

भीति *s. f.* Fear, dread.

भुक्त *p. p.* (*of* भुज्) Used, enjoyed.

भुज *s. m.* The arm, the hand.

भुजग *s. m.* A snake, a serpent.

भुवन *s. n.* The world.

भू *s. f.* Earth, ground, floor. भुवः 6 *c. sin.* 1 *c. pl.* भुवि 7 *c. sin.*

भूः *and* भूत् 3 *pret. par. of* भू Be, become.

भूत *p. p.* (*of* भू) Become. *s. n.* A living being, creature, spirit. *In comp.* Like, resembling.

भूति *s. f.* Ashes. Paint sometimes laid on the body of an elephant in streaks as an ornament. भूतिम् 2 *c. sin.*

भूमि *s. f.* Ground, floor. Place, spot. भूमयः 1 *c. pl.* भूमीः 2 *c. pl.*

भूयस् *ind.* Again. भूयो भूयः Again and again.

भूरि *adj.* Many, numerous.

भृगु *s. m.* Name of the Rishi Jamadagni, and father of Paraśuráma.

भृगुपति *s. m.* The hero and Avatár Paraśuráma.

भृङ्ग *s. m.* A bee.

भेद्य *fut. p. p.* (*of* भिद्) Capable of being pierced. भेद्यैः 3 *c. pl. n.*

भोग *s. m.* Enjoyment. भोगान् 2 *c. pl.*

भोग्य *fut. p. p.* (*of* भुज् Eat; also enjoy or suffer) To be endured. भोग्येन 3 *c. sin. m.*

भोजयामास 2 *pret. par. of* भुज् Enjoy, *causal form.*

भ्रंश *s. m.* A slipping, sliding, falling.

भ्रंशिन् *agt.* Falling, who or what falls. भ्रंशिभिः 3 *c. pl. n.*

भ्रमति *pres. par. of* भ्रम 1 *cl.* Whirl.

भ्रातृ *s. m.* A brother. भ्रातः 8 *c. sin.*

भ्रुकुटि *s. f.* A frown.

भ्रू *s. f.* The eyebrow.

भ्रूभङ्ग *s. m.* A contraction of the eyebrow (often compared to the bending of a bow).

भ्रूलता *s. f.* The brow compared to the gentle bends of a climbing plant.

भ्रूविकार *s. m.* Ogling (*from* भ्रू The eyebrow, *and* विकार A change).

भ्रूविकारानभिज्ञैः *ep. of* लोचनैः.

भ्रूविलास *s. m.* A waving or graceful motion of the brow.

म

मघवन् *s. m.* The god Indra. मघोनः 6 *c. sin.*

मज्जन *s. n.* Bathing, ablution. मज्जनात् 5 *c. sin.*

मणि *s. m.* A jewel, gem; crystal.

मणिबन्धन *s. n.* The wrist, or rather the forearm from the wrist to the elbow. मणिबन्धनात् 5 *c. sin.*

मणिमय *adj.* Made of precious stones.

मणिमयभुवः *ep of* प्रासादाः.

मण्डप *s. m. n.* A bower, an arbour. मण्डपात् 5 *c. sin.*

मण्डल *s. n.* An orb, a globe. मण्डलेन 3 *c. sin.*

मत् *pron. in comp.* My, mine.

मत *s. n.* Direction, command.

मत्त *p. p.* (*of* मद्) Furious, mad, ruttish (elephant). Pleased, glad, delighted. Intoxicated. मत्ताः 1 *c. pl. m.*

मत्वा *ind. p. p.* (*of* मन्) Knowing, understanding.

मत्सर *adj.* Insatiate, greedy. मत्सराः 1 *c. pl. m.*

मथित *p. p.* (*of* मथ्) Pinched, nipped. मथिताम् 2 *c. sin. f.*

मद *s. m.* The juice that flows from an elephant's temples when in rut. मदैः 3 *c. pl.*

मदकल *adj.* Indistinct, inarticulate. मदकलम् 2 *c. sin. n.*

मदिरा *s. f.* Spirituous liquor, inebriating drink. मदिराम् 2 *c. sin.*

मदीय *adj.* My. मदीयैः 3 *c. pl. n.*

मद्गोत्राङ्कम् *ep. of* गेयम् (Relating to my family).

मधु *s. n.* Honey. Any exhilarating or inebriating beverage, wine, mead. मधु 2 *c. sin.* मधुनः 6 *c. sin.*

मधुकर *s. m.* Honey-making; a bee.

मधुर *adj.* Sweet. मधुरम् *n. adv.* Sweetly.

मधुरवचनाम् *ep. of* सारिकाम्.

मध्य *s. m. n.* Middle, midst, centre, waist. मध्ये 7 *c. sin.* *adj.* Central.

मनस् *s. n.* The heart, mind, affection. मनः 1 *or* 2 *c. sin.* मनसि 7 *c. sin.*

मनोहर *adj.* Pleasing, agreeable.

मन्द *s. m.* Slow, dull, sluggish. Little. मन्दम् *n. used adverbially,* Slowly, softly.

मन्दच्छायम् *ep. of* भवनम् (Dull, dim, lustreless).

मन्दमन्दातपम् *ep. of* अहः.

मन्दायन्ते *pres. átm. nominal verb (from* मन्द*)* Relax, linger, loiter.

मन्दार *s. m.* One of the five trees of Swarga.

मन्द्र *s. m.* A bass or low tone, such as the grumbling of clouds, &c.

मन्मथ *s. m.* Kámadeva, the god of love.

मन्ये *pres. átm. of* मन 4 *cl.* Think, imagine, fancy, suspect.

मम 6 *c. sin. of* अस्मद् *pron.* I. मया 3 *c. sin.* मयि 7 *c. sin.*

मय *m.* मयी *f. an affix to form adjectives, implying,* Made up of, consisting of.

मयूर *s. m.* A peacock. मयूरम् 2 *c. sin.*

मरकत *s. m.* An emerald.

मरकतशिलाबद्धसोपानमार्गा *ep. of* वापी.

मरुत् *s. m.* Wind, air. मरुद्भिः 3 *c. pl.* मरुताम् 6 *c. pl.*

मलिन *adj.* Dirty, soiled.

मलिनवसने *ep. of* उत्सङ्गे.

महत् *adj.* Great. Excellent, illustrious. महत् 2 *c. sin. n.* महत्सु 7 *c. pl. m.*

महाकाल *s. m.* A name or rather form of Śiva in his character of the destroying deity, being then represented of a black colour, and of aspect more or less terrific. —लम् 2 *c. sin.*

महात्मन् *adj.* Magnanimous. —त्मनः 1 *c. pl. m.*

महिमन् *s. m.* Greatness. महिमा 1 *c. sin.*

महिष *s. m.* A buffalo. महिषाः 1 *c. pl.*

मही *s. f.* The earth. महीम् 2 *c. sin.*

मा *a particle of forbidding or dissuading, employed with the* 3 *pret. and usually causing the elision of the augment,* No, not.

मातङ्ग *s. m.* An elephant.

मात्र *s. n.* Measure, space. मात्रम् 2 *c. sin.* मात्र *or* मात्रेण *ind.* Only, solely, merely.

माधवी *s. f.* Name of a large creeper (Gœrtnera racemosa).

मानयिष्यत् *fut. p. par. of* मन 10 *cl.* Honour, respect, worship. मानयिष्यन् 1 *c. sin. m.* मानयिष्यन्ति 2 *fut.*

मानस *s. n.* The lake Mánasa or Mánasarovara in the Himálaya mountains. *adj.* Mental.

मानिनी *s. f.* A woman, an object of respect. मानिनीम् 2 *c. sin.*

माम् 2 *c. sin. of* अस्मद् *pron.* I.

मार्ग *s. m.* A road, way, path, passage. मार्गः 1 *c. sin.* मार्गम् 2 *c. sin.*

माल *s. m.* Name of a country. मालम् 2 *c. sin.*

मालती *s. f.* The great-flowered jasmine. मालतीनाम् 6 *c. pl.*

माला *s. f.* A garland, a wreath. मालाः 1 *c. pl.*

मास *s. m.* A month. मासान् 2 *c. pl.*

मित्र *s. n.* A friend. मित्रम् 2 *c. sin.* मित्रे 7 *c. sin.*

मिथुन *s. n.* A couple, pair, brace, male and female.

मिलित *p. p.* (*of* मिल) Met, encountered.

मीन *s. m.* A fish.

मीलयित्वा *ind. p. p.* (*of* मील *caus. form*) Close.

मुकुल *s. m.* or *n.* An opening bud. मुकुलैः 3 *c. pl.*

मुक्त *p. p.* (*of* मुच) Quitted, left, deserted, retired from. Discharged, sent forth, vented, scattered, dropped.

मुक्तध्वनिम् *ep. of* त्वाम्.

मुक्तरोधोनितम्बम् *ep. of* वसनम्.

मुक्ता *s. f.* A pearl.

मुक्ताजाल *s. n.* A string or multitude of pearls; a pearly zone.

मुक्ताजालैः *ep. of* हारैः.

मुक्तास्थूल *adj.* Big as a pearl. —लाः 1 *c. pl. m.*

मुक्ति *s. f.* Beatitude, delivery of the soul from the body, and release from further transmigrations. मुक्तिम् 3 *c. sin.*

मुख *s. n.* The face. The mouth.

मुग्ध (*p. p. of* मुह) *adj.* Lovely, beautiful.

मुच्यमान *pres. p. p.* (*of* मुच) Being left free.

मुञ्चत् *pres. p. par. of* मुच 6 *cl.* Shed. मुञ्चतः 6 *c. sin. m. ep. of* यस्य Of which (mountain).

मुनि *s. m.* A holy sage.

मुरज *s. m.* A small drum, a tabour.

मुष्टि *s. f.* A handful. मुष्टिः 1 *c. sin.*

मुहुर्मुहुः *ind.* Again and again; repeatedly.

मुहुस् *ind.* Repeatedly, again and again.

मुहूर्त्त *s. m. n.* An hour of 40 minutes. मुहूर्त्तम् 2 *c. sin.*

मूढ *p. p.* (*of* मुह) Confused, bewildered, overwhelmed. मूढानाम् 6 *c. pl. f.*

मूर्च्छना *s. f.* A musical air. —नाम् 2 *c. sin.*

मूर्त्ति *s. f.* Figure, form, shape, image. मूर्त्या 3 *c. sin.*

मूर्द्धन् *s. m.* The head. मूर्द्ध्ना 3 *c. sin.*

मूल *s. n.* Root, base. मूले 7 *c. sin.*

मृग *s. m.* A deer. मृगाणाम् 6 *c. pl.*

मृगाक्षी *s. f.* A fawn-eyed woman. मृगाक्ष्याः 6 *c. sin.*

मे 6 *c. sin. of* अस्मद् I.

मेखला *s. f.* The edge or swell of a mountain. मेखलासु 7 *c. pl.*

मेघ *s. m.* A cloud.

मेघदूताभिधम् *ep. of* काव्यम्.

मेचक *adj.* Black, dark-coloured. मेचके 7 *c. sin. n.*

मैत्री *s. f.* Friendship, association, union, contact.

मैथिली *s. f.* Maithilí, a name of Sítá, wife of Ráma (*from* मिथिला her native place).

मोक्ष *s. m.* A loosening, untying, unbinding. Escape, release. Eternal happiness.

मोघ *adj.* Fruitless, unsuccessful. मोघा 1 *c. sin. f.* मोघीकर्त्तुम् To frustrate, baffle, disappoint.

मोचयिष्यति 2 *fut. par. of* मुच *caus. form*, Cause or compel to shed.

मौलि *s. m. f.* A diadem. मौलेः 6 *c. sin.*

य

यः 1 *c. sin. m. of* यद् Who, which.

यक्ष *s. m.* A kind of demigod. यक्षः 1 *c. sin.*

यक्षेश्वर *s. m.* A Yaksha chief.

यत्न *s. m.* Effort, exertion.

यथा *ind.* As.

यद् *rel. pron.* Who, which, what.

यदपि (*more usually* यद्यपि, *but required by the metre*) What though, although.

यदि *ind.* If.

यन्त्र *s. n.* A machine, apparatus for pressing.

यन्त्रधारागृह *s. m.* A chamber containing a machine for sprinkling water; a shower-bath. यन्त्रधारागृहत्व *s. n.* The state of a यन्त्रधारागृह.

यमुना *s. f.* The Yamuná or Jumna river.

ययाचे 2 *pret. átm. of* याच Ask, request, solicit.

यव *s. m.* Barley. यवाः 1 *c. pl.*

यशस् *s. n.* Glory, fame.

यस्मिन् 7 *c. sin. m. of* यद् Which. यस्य 6 *c. sin. m.* यस्याः 6 *c. sin. f.* यस्याम् 7 *c. sin. f.*

यष्टि *s. f.* A column, pillar. यष्टिः 1 *c. sin.*

या 1 *c. sin. f. of* यद्. याः 2 *c. pl. f.*

याचित *p. p. of* याच Ask, solicit.

याञ्चा *s. f.* A request, petition.

यापयत् *pres. p. par. of* या *caus. form,* Cause to pass, spend. यापयन्तीम् 2 *c. sin. f.*

याम् 2 *c. sin. f. of* यद् Who, which.

याम *s. m.* The eighth of a day, three hours.

यायाः *pot. par. of* या 2 *cl.* Go.

यावत् *ind.* As soon as, as long as. Until.

यास्यति 2 *fut. par. of* या Go.

यियासु *agt.* Desirous of going. यियासोः 6 *c. sin.*

युक्त *p. p.* (*of* युज) Possessed, endued. युक्तम् 2 *c. sin. n.*

युवति *s. f.* A young woman.

यूथ *s. n.* A swarm. यूथैः 3 *c. pl.*

यूथिका *s. f.* The great flowered jasmine.

ये 1 *c. pl. m. of* यद् Who, which. येन 3 *c. sin. n.*

योषित् *s. f.* A woman. योषिताम् 6 *c. pl.*

यौवन *s. n.* A youthful prank, juvenile act.

र

रक्त *adj.* Red, crimson, orange-scarlet. रक्तम् 2 *c. sin. n.* *s. n.* Saffron.

रक्षा *s. f.* Preservation, protection, deliverance.

रघु *s. m.* Name of a sovereign of Ayodhyá, and great-grandfather of Rámachandra.

रचना *s. f.* Formation. रचनाम् 2 *c. sin.*

रचित *p. p.* (*of* रच) Arranged, made, composed. Decorated, strung. रचितानि 2 *c. pl. n.*

रचितशिखरः 1 *c. sin. m. ep. of* शैलः.

रजस् *s. n.* Dust. The dust or pollen of a flower. रजसा 3 *c. sin.*

रण *s. m. n.* Battle, war. रणे 7 *c. sin.*

रत *s. n.* Pleasure, enjoyment. रतैः 3 *c. pl.*

रति *s. f.* Pleasure, enjoyment.

रतिरसम् *ep. of* मधु (Producing pleasurable emotions).

रत्न *s. m. n.* A gem, a jewel.

रत्नच्छायाखचितवलिभिः *ep. of* चामरैः.

रन्तिदेव *s. m.* Name of a king.

रन्ध्र *s. n.* A hole, fissure, cavity, chasm.

रभस *s. m.* Joy, delight, eagerness.

रमण *s. m.* A husband. A lover, gallant.

रमयत् *pres. p. par. of* रम *caus. form,* Enjoy. रमयन् 1 *c. sin. m.*

रमसे *pres. átm. of* रम 1 *cl.* Sport, play.

रम्य *adj.* Pleasing, charming, delightful, agreeable.

रम्यसानौ *ep. of* शैले.

रय *s. m.* The stream or current of a river.

रवि *s. m.* The sun. रवेः 6 *c. sin.*

रस *s. m.* Water. Taste, flavour. Feeling.

रसना *s. f.* A woman's girdle, a sort of chain worn round the loins.

राग *s. m.* Colour, tint, dye.

राजधानी *s. f.* A royal city, metropolis.

राजन् *s. m.* A king. A Yaksha.

राजन्य *s. m.* A man of the military tribe.

राजराज *s. m.* Kuvera, king of the Yakshas.

राजहंस *s. m.* A white goose with red legs and bill, or more properly, perhaps, the flamingo.

राज्य *s. n.* Dominion, regal authority.

रात्रि *s. f.* Night. रात्रौ 7 *c. sin.*

राम *s. m.* Ráma, son of Daśaratha.

राशि *s. m.* A heap, pile, immense quantity. राशीभूत Heaped, piled, like an enormous pile.

रिक्त *p. p.* (*of* रिच्) Empty, void, bared.

रुच् *s. f.* Light, lustre. Beauty, loveliness. रुचा 3 *c. sin.*

रुचि *s. f.* Lustre, brilliancy, glitter.

रुजा *s. f.* or 3 *c. sin. of* रुज् *s. f.* Sickness, toil, weariness, plague, trouble.

रुणद्धि *pres. par. of* रुध 7 *cl.* Close, shut.

रुदत् *pres. p. par. of* रुद 2 *cl.* Weep, cry. रुदित *p.p.* Wept, crying, weeping. *s. n.* Weeping.

रुद्ध *p. p. of* रुध Shut, obstruct, bar, block, prevent.

रुद्धापाङ्गप्रसरम् *ep. of* नयनम्.

रुद्धालोके *ep. of* नरपतिपथे.

रुह *agt.* Growing; who or what grows.

रूढ *p. p.* (*of* रुह) Grown. रूढैः 3 *c. pl. m. n.*

रूपिन् *adj.* Shaped. रूपिणः 1 *c. pl. m.*

रेवती *s. f.* Revatí, wife of Balaráma.

रेवतीलोचनाङ्काम् *ep. of* हालाम् (Reflecting the eyes of Revatí).

रेवा *s. f.* Name of a river. रेवाम् 2 *c. sin.*

रोधस् *s. n.* A bank, a shore.

ल

लक्षण *s. n.* A name, appellation. An indication, predicate, any thing by which an object is designated or distinguished. लक्षणैः 3 *c. pl.*

लक्षयेथाः *pot. par. of* लक्ष 10 *cl.* See, perceive, know.

लक्ष्य *fut. p. p.* (*of* लक्ष) To be seen, visible. लक्ष्यम् 1 *c. sin. n.* *s. n.* A mark for archers. लक्ष्येषु 7 *c. pl.*

लग्न *p. p.* (*of* लग) Attached, adhering, sticking, clinging, in contact. लग्ना 1 *c. sin. f.*

लघु *adj.* Light. Swift, quick. Mean, insignificant, weak, feeble. लघुः 1 *c. sin. m.*

लघुगतिः *ep. of* त्वम् *understood.*

लङ्घयिष्यन्ति 2 *fut. par. of* लघि 10 *cl.* Pass over, or attempt to surmount.

लता *s. f.* A creeper, a creeping or winding plant.

लप्स्यते, लप्स्यसे 2 *fut. átm. of* लभ Gain.

लब्ध *p. p. of* लभ Get, acquire, obtain, find. लब्धस्य 6 *c. sin. m.* लब्धे 7 *c. sin. m.* लब्धायाः 6 *c. sin. f.*

लब्धकामा *ep. of* याच्ञा.

लब्धनिद्रासुखा *ep. of* सा.

लब्धा 1 *fut. átm. of* लभ Gain, *agreeing with* भवान् *understood.*

लम्ब *agt.* Hanging, pendulous, pendent. लम्बम् 2 *c. sin. m. n.*

लम्बमान *pres. p. átm. of* लबि 1 *cl.* Hanging down, superincumbent. लम्बमानस्य 6 *c. sin. m.*

ललित *adj.* Beautiful, lovely, graceful. Gay, cheerful, careless, sprightly, wanton.

ललितवनिताः *ep. of* प्रासादाः; *one of the five particulars, wherein the palaces of Alaká are said to vie with the cloud.*

ललितवनितापादरागाङ्कितेषु *ep. of* हर्म्येषु.

लव *s. m.* A drop. लवमय *adj.* Made of drops.

लाङ्गल *s. n.* A plough.

लाङ्गलिन् Balaráma (as armed with a plough).

लाव *agt.* Cutting, gathering.

लिखत् *pres. p. par. of* लिख 6 *cl.* Draw, sketch, paint. लिखन्ती 1 *c. sin. f.* लिखित *p. p.*

लिखितवपुषौ *ep. of* पक्षौ.

लीला *s. f.* Play, sport, pastime, wantonness. Grace.

लेखा *s. f.* A row, a line.

लेश *s. m.* A drop. लेशाः 1 *c. pl.*

लोचन *s. n.* An eye. लोचने 2 *c. du.* लोचनाभ्याम् 3 *c. du.* लोचनैः 3 *c. pl.*

लोध्र *s. m.* A tree, the bark whereof is used in dyeing (Symplocos racemosa).

लोभ *s. m.* An earnest desire, coveting, lust. लोभेन 3 *c. sin.* लोभात् 5 *c. sin.*

लोल *adj.* Rolling, tremulous: fickle, unsteady. Desirous, wishing. लोलः 1 *c. sin. m.*

लोलापाङ्गैः *ep. of* लोचनैः (Arch, leering).

व

वंश *s. m.* A bambu, or its shoot. Race, line, lineage. वंशे 7 *c. sin.*

वः 6 *c. pl. of* युष्मद् *pron.* Thou.

वक्तुम् *inf. of* वच 2 *cl.* Speak, address.

वक्र *adj.* Crooked, indirect, circuitous. Austere, cruel. वक्रः 1 *c. sin. m.*

वक्ष्यति, वक्ष्यसि 2 *fut. par. of* वह Bear, support, sustain; wear.

वचन *s. n.* Language, speech, word, accent.

वचस् *s. n.* A word. वचोभिः 3 *c. pl.*

वञ्चित *p. p. of* वञ्च Cheat, trick, defraud.

वडभि *s. f.* A temporary building or awning on the top of a palace, or a room or turret so situated. वडभौ 7 *c. sin.*

वत्सा *s. f.* A child, *a term of endearment.* वत्से 8 *c. sin.*

वदन *s. n.* The face. The mouth.

वधू *s. f.* A woman, a young woman, one recently married. वधूनाम् 6 *c. pl.*

वन *s. n.* A wood, forest, thicket.

वनगज *s. m.* The wild elephant.

वनचर *s. m.* A forester.

वनचरवधूभुक्तकुञ्जे *ep. of* तस्मिन्.

वनद्विप *s. m.* The wild elephant.

वनान्त *s. m.* The skirt of a forest. A grove.

वनिता *s. f.* A woman. A wife.

वन्द्य *fut. p. p. of* वदि Praise, eulogize. वन्द्यैः 3 *c. pl. n.*

वपु *s. m.* Body, form, figure. वपुः 1 *c. sin.*

वपुष् *s. n.* Body, form, figure. वपुः 1 *c. sin.* वपुषि 7 *c. sin.*

वप्र *s. m. n.* A rampart, a mud wall; earth taken from the ditch of a town, and raised as a wall or buttress.

वप्रक्रीडापरिणतगजप्रेक्षणीयम् *ep. of* मेघम्.

वयम् 1 *c. pl. of* अस्मद् I.

वरम् *ind.* Rather, better, preferable.

वराह *s. m.* A boar. वराहाः 1 *c. pl.*

वर्ग *s. m.* A class, tribe. वर्गम् 2 *c. sin.*

वर्ण *s. m.* Colour, hue.

वर्त्तिन् *agt.* Abiding, being. वर्त्ती 1 *c. sin. m.*

वर्त्मन् *s. n.* A road, path. वर्त्म 2 *c. sin.*

वर्द्धित *p. p.* (*of* वृध *caus. form*) Made to grow, reared, brought up. वर्द्धितः 1 *c. sin. m.*

वर्ष *s. m.* A year. Rain.

वर्षभोग्येन *ep. of* शापेन.

वर्ह *s. n.* The tail of a peacock. वर्हम् 2 *c. sin.* वर्हेण 3 *c. sin.*

वर्हभार *s. m.* A peacock's train.

वर्हिन् *s. m.* A peacock. वर्हिणः 1 *c. pl.*

वलय *s. m. n.* A bracelet, an armlet. A boundary, circle. वलयम् 1 or 2 *c. sin.*

वलयकुलिशोद्घट्टनोद्गीर्णतोयम् *ep. of* त्वाम्.

वलाका *s. f.* A small kind of crane. वलाकाः 1 or 2 *c. pl.*

वलाहक *s. m.* A cloud. वलाहकाः 1 *c. pl.*

वल्मीक *s. m.* A hillock, especially the large accumulation of soil sometimes made by the white ant.

वश *s. m.* Subjection, thraldom. वशात् *abl. sin.*

वशिष्ठ *s. m.* Vaśishṭha, a certain divine sage.

वसत् *pres. p. par. of* वस 1 *cl.* Dwell.

वसति *s. f.* Abode, residence. वसतिम् 2 *c. sin.*

वसन *s. n.* A garment, vesture, clothes, raiment.

वसुधा *s. f.* Earth, ground.

वस्तु *s. n.* A thing, token. वस्तुनि 7 *c. sin.*

वहति, वहसि *pres. par. of* वह 1 *cl.* Carry, bear, wear.

वा *ind.* Or, either, whether. Like.

वाचाल *adj.* Talkative, chattering, boastful.

वात *s. m.* Wind, breeze.

वातायन *s. n.* A window. वातायनस्थः 1 *c. sin. m.* Standing or being at the window.

वानीर *s. m.* A sort of cane or rattan.

वान्त *p. p.* (*of* वम) Vomited, ejected.

वान्तवृष्टिः *ep. of* त्वम् *understood.*

वापी *s. f.* A large oblong pond. वापी 1 *c. sin.*

वाम *adj.* Left. Beautiful, pleasing. वामगाः 1 *c. pl. m.* Going to the left.

वायु *s. m.* Wind. वायुः 1 *c. sin.* वायौ 7 *c. sin.*

वारि *s. n.* Water, fluid. वारिभिः 3 *c. pl.*

वार्त्ता *s. f.* News, tidings, intelligence. वार्त्ताम् 2 *c. sin.*

वाष्प *s. m.* A tear. Vapour, hot mist, steam (such as rises from the ground on the falling of the first rain). वाष्पम् 2 *c. sin.*

वि *prep.* Apart, away, without, *dis, di.*

विकच *adj.* Blown, open, expanded, spread (as a flower).

विकार *s. m.* A change.

विक्लव *adj.* Bewildered, perplexed, confounded. विक्लवाः 2 *c. pl. f.*

विक्षिपत् *pres. p. par. of* क्षिप 6 *cl. with* वि Throw aside. विक्षिपन्तीम् 2 *c. sin. f.*

विगणय *imp. par. of* गण 10 *cl. with* वि Reckon, calculate; reflect, consider, deliberate, ponder. विगणयन् 1 *c. sin. m. pres. p.*

विगम *s. m.* Separation, departure. विगमात् 5 *c. sin.* विगमे 7 *c. sin.*

विगलित *p. p.* (*of* गल *with* वि) Removed, gone, dissipated, dispersed.

विगलितशुचा *ep. of* मया.

विगलितशुचौ *ep. of* दम्पती.

विचर *imp. par. of* चर 1 *cl.* Go, *with* वि Roam, wander.

विजय *s. m.* Victory, conquest.

विटप *s. m. n.* The branch of a tree with its new sprouts or shoots.

वितत्य *ind. p. p.* (*of* तन Stretch, *with* वि) Stretching into, extending far.

विदधति *pres. par. of* धा 3 *cl.* Hold, *with* वि Cause, create.

विदित *p. p. of* विद् Know. विदिते 7 *c. sin. m.* विदित्वा *ind. p. p.*

विदिशा *s. f.* Vidiśá, the capital of the district of Daśárńa.

विदुर *adj.* Agitated, distressed. Separated, absent. विदुरः 1 *c. sin. m.*

विद्ध *p. p.* (*of* विध Pierce, *or* व्यध Beat) Thrown, sent, directed, wafted. विद्धः 1 *c. sin. m.*

विद्धि *imp. par. of* विद् 2 *cl.* Know.

विद्युत् *s. f.* Lightning. विद्युता 3 *c. sin.*

विद्युत्वत् *adj.* Having, or containing lightning (as a cloud, &c.). विद्युत्वन्तम् 2 *c. sin. m.*

विद्युद्दामन् *s. n.* The lightning's flash, a streak of zig-zag lightning.

विद्युद्दामस्फुरणचकितैः *ep. of* लोचनैः.

विधि *s. m.* Fate, luck, destiny. Mode, manner, method, way. विधिना 3 *c. sin.*

विधुर *adj.* Distressed, disquieted, filled with anxiety. विधुराम् 2 *c. sin. f.*

विनयन *s. n.* A removing, a taking away. विनयने 7 *c. sin.*

विनिष्क्रिय *adj.* Abstaining from ceremonial rites.

विनोद *s. m.* Amusement, diversion, pastime. विनोदाः 1 *c. pl.*

विन्दु *s. m.* A drop. विन्दून् 2 *c. pl.*

विन्ध्य *s. m.* The Vindhya range of mountains.

विन्यस्यत् *pres. p. par.* (*of* अस् 4 *cl.* Throw, *with* नि *and* वि Adjust, ascertain, determine, settle. विन्यस्यन्ती 1 *c. sin. f.*

विप्रबुद्ध *p. p.* (*of* बुध *with* प्र *and* वि) Wakened, awake. विप्रबुद्धा 1 *c. sin. f.*

विप्रयुक्त *p. p.* (*of* युज Join, *with* प्र *and* वि) Separated, disjoined, sundered, severed. विप्रयुक्तः 1 *c. sin. m.*

विप्रयोग *s. m.* Absence, separation, disjunction. विप्रयोगः 1 *c. sin.* विप्रयोगे 7 *c. sin.*

विफल *adj.* Fruitless, useless.

विफलप्रेरणा *ep. of* चूर्णमुष्टिः (Flung in vain).

विभ्रंशिन् *agt.* Dropping, fallen, dropt. विभ्रंशिभिः *c. pl. n.*

विभ्रम *s. m.* Agitation, perturbation, flurry. Blandishment, grace, elegance. विभ्रमः 1 *c. sin.* विभ्रमैः 3 *c. pl.* विभ्रमाणाम् 6 *c. pl.*

विमल *adj.* Clean, pure, white. Beautiful.

विमलोत्पलप्रभाः *ep. of* देशाः.

विमान *s. n.* A palace. विमानैः 3 *c. pl.*

विमुख *adj.* Turning away, having the face averted, averse, disinclined; desisting, forbearing, withholding, restraining. विमुखः 1 *c. sin. m.*

विम्ब *s. m. n.* A reflected image, a disk (of the sun or moon). *s. n.* A curcurbitaceous plant with red fruit.

वियुक्त *p. p.* (*of* युज *with* वि) Severed, separated.

वियोग *s. m.* Absence, separation. वियोगः 1 *c. sin.* वियोगेन 3 *c. sin.*

विरचित *p. p.* (*of* रच *with* वि) Made, contrived, constructed, arranged, composed, written. Worn, used. विरचिताम् 2 *c. sin. f.* विरचितम् 1 or 2 *c. sin. n.*

विरचितपदम् *ep. of* गेयम्.

विरचितवपुः *ep. of* त्वम्.

विरह *s. m.* Separation, parting, absence, especially the separation of lovers. विरहात् 5 *c. sin.* विरहे 7 *c. sin.*

विरहज *adj.* Arising from, produced by absence.

विरहव्यापदः *ep. of* स्नेहान् (Impaired by absence).

विलसत् *pres. p. par. of* लस 1 *cl. with* वि Sport.

विलसत्कृष्णसारप्रभाणाम् *ep. of* कौतूहलानाम्.

विलसन *s. n.* Sport, play. विलसनात् 5 *c. sin.*

विलसित *s. n.* Sporting.

विल्व *s. m.* A fruit-tree, commonly called Bél.

विवर्ण *adj.* Colourless. विवर्णमणीकृतम् 1 *c. sin. n.* Having the gems sullied or tarnished.

विशति *pres. par. of* विश 6 *cl.* Enter, become joined or united to.

विशद *adj.* White, bright, clear, pellucid.

विशाल *adj.* Great, eminent. विशाला *s. f.* The city of Oujein. विशालाम् 2 *c. sin.*

विशीर्ण *p. p.* (*of* शॄ *with* वि) Withered, wasted, shrunk, slender. Parted into many streamlets. *Comment. in loc.* विशीर्णाम् 2 *c. sin. f.*

विशेष *s. m.* A particular, a property or quality. A particular spot, any distinguished place. विशेषान् 2 *c. pl.* विशेषैः 3 *c. pl.*

विश्रान्त *p. p.* (*of* श्रम *with* वि) Rested, reposed. विश्रान्तः 1 *c. sin. m.*

विश्राम *s. m.* Rest, repose.

विश्लेषित *p. p.* (*of* श्लिष Embrace, *with* वि) Severed, separated. विश्लेषितस्य 6 *c. sin. m.*

विषम *adj.* Uneven, rough, rugged.

विषय *s. m.* Sphere, department, order, range, reach. विषयम् 2 *c. sin.* विषये 7 *c. sin.*

विष्णु *s. m.* Vishńu. **विष्णोः** 6 *c. sin.*

विस *s. n.* The fibre of the stalk of the water-lily.

विस्तार *s. m.* A spreading, extension, largeness, swell, breadth, amplitude.

विस्मरत् *pres. p. par. of* **स्मृ** 1 *cl.* Remember, *with* **वि** Forget. **विस्मरन्ती** 1 *c. sin. f.* **विस्मृत** *p. p.* Forgotten; forgetful.

विस्मृतभ्रूविलासम् *ep. of* **नयनम्**.

विहग *s. m.* A bird. Waterfowl.

विहरेत् *pot. par. of* **हृ** 1 *cl.* Take, *with* **वि** Saunter, stroll for pleasure or amusement.

विहस्य *ind. p. p. of* **हस** Laugh, *with* **वि** Having smiled; laughing at, contemning.

विहातुम् *inf. of* **हा** Quit, leave, *with* **वि**.

वीक्षमाण *pres. p. átm. of* **ईक्ष** 1 *cl.* See, *with* **वि**. **वीक्ष्य** *ind. p. p.* **वीक्ष्यमाण** *pres. p. pass.* Being beheld.

वीचि *s. f.* A wave, a small ripple. **वीचिषु** 7 *c. pl.*

वीचिक्षोभस्तनितविहगश्रेणिकाञ्चीगुणायाः *ep. of* **निर्विन्ध्यायाः** (Whose girdle of a line of water-fowl tinkles with the dashing of the waves).

वीणा *s. f.* A lute.

वीणिन् *s. m.* A player on the lute, a lutanist.

वृक्ष *s. m.* A tree. **वृक्षात्** 5 *c. sin.*

वृति *s. f.* A fence. **वृतेः** 6 *c. sin.* **वृतयः** 1 *c. pl.*

वृत्ति *s. f.* Being, existence, position in life, character, style, state, condition.

वृद्ध *p. p.* (*of* **वृध**) Grown: great, illustrious.

वृद्धि *s. f.* Augmentation, increase.

वृन्द *s. n.* A heap, a multitude.

वृष *s. m.* A bull.

वृष्टि *s. f.* Rain, a shower.

वृहत् *adj.* Great, large. **वृहतः** 1 *c. pl.*

वेग *s. m.* Velocity, rapidity, impetuosity, violence, vehemence. **वेगेन** 3 *c. sin.*

वेणि *or* **वेणी** *s. f.* Unornamented and braided hair; the hair as worn especially by widows and women whose husbands are absent, when it is simply collected from the forehead and temples as well as the back of the head, and twisted together into a single braid, which is then suffered to fall like a tail down the back, no sort of ornament being worn on the head. The term is also applied generally to any braid of hair, or to a braid of the long hair, of which many are made; and the whole are then twisted together, and worn as a sort of rose or flower at the back of the head. **वेणीम्** 2 *c. sin.*

वेणीभूतप्रतनुसलिला *ep. of* **सिन्धुः**.

वेत्रवती *s. f.* Name of a river. **वेत्रवत्याः** 6 *c. sin.*

वेदि *s. f.* An altar. **वेदिम्** 2 *c. sin.*

वेश्मन् *s. n.* A house. **वेश्मभिः** 3 *c. pl.*

वेश्या *s. f.* A courtezan. **वेश्याः** 1 *c. pl.*

वेष *s. m.* Dress, guise, garb.

वेष्टन *s. n.* A fence, inclosure.

वै *ind.* Indeed. *An expletive.*

वैदूर्य्य *s. n.* Lapis lazuli.

वैरिन् *adj.* Hostile, inimical. **वैरिणा** 3 *c. sin. m.*

व्यक्त *p. p.* (*of* **अञ्ज** Make clear, *with* **वि**) Distinct, plain, evident. **व्यक्तम्** 2 *c. sin. m.*

व्यक्ति *s. f.* Appearance, manifestation, display.

व्यञ्जयत् *pres. p. par. of* **अञ्ज** 10 *cl. with* **वि** Make visible, manifest, shew plainly. **व्यञ्जयन्ती** 1 *c. sin. f.*

व्यतिकर *s. m.* Contact, union, a blending or intermingling. **व्यतिकरः** 1 *c. sin.*

व्यथा *s. f.* Pain, distress. **व्यथाभिः** 3 *c. pl.*

व्यपगत *p. p.* (*of* **गम** *with* **अप** *and* **वि**) Gone off.

व्यपगतशुचः *ep. of* **हंसाः**.

व्यवसित *p. p.* (*of* षो Destroy, *with* अव *and* वि) Resolved, determined, undertaken. व्यवसिता: 1 *cl. pl. m.* व्यवसितम् 1 *c. sin. n.*

व्यवस्येत् *pot. par. of* षो 4 *cl.* Destroy, *with* अव *and* वि Try, endeavour, essay.

व्यस्त *p. p.* (*of* अस *with* वि) Driven away, dispelled.

व्याकुल *adj.* Confounded, bewildered, perplexed, flurried, excited. व्याकुलेन 3 *c. sin. m.* व्याकुला 1 *c. sin. f.*

व्याजहार 2 *pret. par. of* हृ Take, *with* आ *and* वि Utter, speak, address.

व्यापद् *s. f.* Calamity, death, decease.

व्यापार *s. m.* Occupation, employment.

व्यालम्बेथा: *pot. átm. of* लबि 1 *cl. with* आ *and* वि Hang down. Move slowly, delay.

व्यालुम्पन्ति *pres. par. of* लुप 6 *cl. with* आ *and* वि Remove, take away.

व्योमन् *s. n.* Sky.

व्रज *imp. par.* व्रजेयु: *pot. par.* व्रजते *pres. átm. of* व्रज 1 *cl.* Go.

श

शक्ष्यति 2 *fut. par. of* शक्ल Be able.

शङ्का *s. f.* Fear, terror, apprehension.

शङ्के *pres. átm. of* शकि 1 *cl.* Fear, dread. Think likely, suspect.

शङ्ख *s. m.* The conch-shell. One of Kuvera's treasures.

शत *s. n.* A hundred. शतै: 3 *c. pl.*

शब्द *s. m.* Sound. A word. शब्दाख्येय To be spoken aloud, to be communicated orally.

शब्दायन्ते *pres. átm. a nominal verb, from* शब्द Sound.

शब्दित *p. p.* (*of* शब्द) Called.

शनकैस् *ind.* Softly, gently.

शमयितुम् *inf.* शमये: *pot. par. of* शम *caus. form,* Extinguish, allay.

शम्भु *s. m.* Śiva. शम्भुना 3 *c. sin.*

शयन *s. n.* A bed. शयनात् 5 *c. sin.* शयने 7 *c. sin.*

शय्या *s. f.* A bed, a couch.

शर *s. m.* A sort of reed or grass. An arrow.

शरण *s. n.* Refuge, succour, aid. शरणम् 1 *c. sin. n.*

शरद् *s. f.* The season of autumn; the two months succeeding the rains.

शरभ *s. m.* A fabulous animal, supposed to have eight legs, and to inhabit particularly the snowy mountains.

शरवनभवम् *ep. of* देवम्.

शशिन् *s. m.* The moon. शशिनि 7 *c. sin.*

शश्वत् *ind.* Perpetually.

शष्प *s. n.* Young grass.

शस्त्रपाणि *ep.* Having a weapon in the hand. शस्त्रपाणय: 1 *c. pl.*

शाखा *s. f.* A branch.

शान्त *p. p.* (*of* शम) Allayed, alleviated, pacified, calm.

शान्ति *s. f.* Alleviation, assuagement, cessation, rest. शान्तिम् 2 *c. sin.*

शान्तोद्वेगस्तिमितनयनम् *n. sin. used adverbially,* (Her) eye moist, (her) disquietude allayed.

शाप *s. m.* A curse, malediction. शापेन 3 *c. sin.* शापस्य 6 *c. sin.*

शारङ्ग *s. m.* The chátaka. शारङ्गा: 1 *c. pl.*

शार्ङ्ग *adj.* Made of horn, horny. *s. n.* A bow in general. The bow of Vishńu.

शार्ङ्गपाणि *s. m.* Vishńu. शार्ङ्गपाणौ 7 *c. sin.*

शार्ङ्गिन् *s. m.* A bowman. Vishńu. शार्ङ्गिण: 6 *c. sin.*

शाल्मलि *s. m. f.* The silk-cotton or *seemul*-tree.

शिखर s. m. n. The peak or summit of a mountain. A piece of ruby or gem described as of the colour of the ripe pomegranate-seed.

शिखरिन् s. m. A mountain. शिखरिषु 7 c. pl.

शिखा s. f. A lock of hair on the crown of the head.

शिखिकुलकलकेका: 1 c. pl. m. ep. Vocal with the soft and shrill cries of flocks of peafowl.

शिखिन् s. m. A peacock. शिखिन: 1 c. pl.

शिञ्जत् pres. p. par. of शिजि 2 cl. Tinkle.

शित p. p. (of शो) Pointed, whetted.

शिथिल adj. Loose, drooping. —लम् 2 c. sin. n.

शिरस् s. n. The head. शिरसा 3 c. sin.

शिरीष s. m. A kind of tree. *In the neuter gender*, its blossom.

शिला s. f. A flat stone, a slab. A rock.

शिलावेश्मन् s. n. A rocky recess. शिलावेश्मभ्य: 5 c. pl.

शिशिर s. m. n. The cold season, comprising two months from the middle of January to that of March. adj. Cool. शिशिरान् 2 c. pl. m.

शीत p. p. (of श्यै) Cold, cool.

शीतल adj. Cold, cool.

शीर्ण p. p. (of शॄ) Withered, sere.

शुक्ल adj. White.

शुक्लापाङ्ग s. m. A peacock.

शुच् s. f. Sorrow, grief, regret.

शुद्ध p. p. (of शुध) Purified, pure, clean.

शुभ्र adj. White.

शुभ्रत्रिनयनवृषोत्खातपङ्कोपमेयाम् ep. of शोभाम्.

शुष्क adj. Dry.

शून्य adj. Destitute. शून्यम् 1 c. sin. n.

शूलिन् s. m. The trident-bearer, *i. e.* Śiva.

शृङ्ग s. n. A horn. The peak of a mountain. शृङ्गम् 2 c. sin. शृङ्गे 7 c. sin.

शृणु imp. par. of श्रु 1 cl. irreg. Hear.

शेष s. m. Remainder, leavings, rest, whatever remains or is left. शेषम् 2 c. sin. शेषै: 3 c. pl. adj. Left, remaining.

शेषविस्तारपाण्डु: ep. of स्तन:.

शैल s. m. A mountain, a mount.

शैलराज s. m. Himálaya, king of mountains.

शोभा s. f. Splendour, lustre, beauty, comeliness. शोभाम् 2 c. sin.

शोभिन् adj. Beautiful, graceful. शोभी 1 c. sin. m.

श्च्योत s. m. Aspersion, sprinkling.

श्याम adj. Black or dark blue, sable.

श्यामा s. f. A woman described as one who has not borne children; also as of slender make; or one from eight to sixteen; or one who resembles in darkness of complexion the blossom of the Priyangu or its stalk in shape. Name of a plant commonly called *Priyangu*. श्यामासु 7 c. pl.

श्रद्दधान pres. p. átm. (of धा 3 cl. Hold, *with* श्रत् *a particle implying*, Faith) Faithful, believing. श्रद्दधाना: 1 c. pl. m.

श्रम s. m. Weariness, fatigue.

श्रवण s. n. The ear.

श्राम्यत् pres. p. par. of श्रम 4 cl. Lag, rest, repose. श्राम्यताम् 6 c. pl. m.

श्रित p. p. (of श्रि) Covered, overspread. श्रिता: 1 c. pl. m.

श्री s. f. Beauty. Lustre, brightness, splendour. Prosperity, wealth. Fame, glory. श्री: 1 c. sin.

श्रुत्वा ind. p. p. (of श्रु) Having heard.

श्रेणि s. f. A line, a row. श्रेणीभूत Ranged in a line, forming a row. श्रेणीभूता: 2 c. pl. f.

श्रोणी s. f. The hip, the haunch.

श्रोतस् s. n. The ear. An organ of sense.

श्रोत्र s. n. The ear. श्रोत्रपेयम् ep. of सन्देशम्.

श्रोष्यति, श्रोष्यसि 2 *fut. par. of* श्रु Hear, listen.

श्लाघनीय *fut. p. p.* (*of* श्लाघ) To be praised, deserving of commendation, praiseworthy. श्लाघनीयाम् 2 *c. sin. f.* श्लाघमान *pres. p. átm.* Praising, flattering, or congratulating one's self, rejoicing. श्लाघमानः 1 *c. sin. m.*

ष

षट्पद *s. m.* A bee (six-foot).

षट्पदज्य *adj.* Strung with bees (Cupid's bow).

स

स *contraction of* सह With, having.

संयोग *s. m.* Intimate union, close contact.

संयोज्य *ind. p. p.* (*of* युज *caus. form, with* सम्) Having united.

संवाहन *s. n.* A rubbing of the persons, a kneeding of the limbs (shampooing?). संवाहनानाम् 6 *c. pl.*

संविधाय *ind. p. p.* (*of* धा Hold, *with* वि *and* सम्) Having made.

संरक्त *p. p.* (*of* रञ्ज *with* सम्) Empassioned. संरक्ताभिः 3 *c. pl. f.*

संरोध *s. m.* Obstacle, impediment.

संशुष्क *adj.* Withered, dry, sere.

संश्रय *s. m.* Protection, refuge, succour. संश्रयाय 4 *c. sin.*

संसक्त *p. p.* (*of* षञ्ज *with* सम्) Adhering, sticking close to.

संसर्पत् *pres. p. par. of* सृप 1 *cl.* Go, *with* सम् Glide, flow. संसर्पन्त्याः 6 *c. sin. f.*

संस्कार *s. m.* Decoration, adorning, dressing.

संस्थ *agt.* Staying, sojourning; a sojourner.

संस्थित *p. p.* (*of* स्था Stand, *with* सम्) Standing, stationary, fixed, residing.

संहार *s. m.* A collection, assemblage.

सः 1 *c. sin. m. of* तद् He, she, it, that. *For the elision of* : *see Grammar.*

सख *s. m. in comp. for* सखि A friend. सखम् 2 *c. sin.*

सखि *s. m.* A friend. सखे 8 *c.* सखीनाम् 6 *c. pl.*

सखी *s. f.* A female friend. सखीम् 2 *c. sin.* सख्याः 6 *c. sin.* सखीनाम् 6 *c. pl.*

सगर *s. m.* Name of a king, sovereign of Ayodhyá (Oude).

सगरतनयस्वर्गसोपानपङ्क्तिम् *ep. of* कन्याम्.

सगर्व *adj.* Joyful, glad, exulting.

सङ्कल्प *s. m.* The working of the mind, thought, imagination, fancy. सङ्कल्पैः 3 *c. pl.*

सङ्क्षिप्येत *pot. pass. of* क्षिप Throw, *with* सम् Shorten, contract.

सङ्गम *s. m.* Meeting, union, interview; confluence of rivers.

सङ्गीत *s. n.* Song, singing and dancing.

सङ्घट्ट *s. m.* Friction, a chafing or rubbing together.

सचित्र *adj.* Having pictures. Variegated, painted of divers colours. सचित्राः *ep. of* प्रासादाः.

सजल *adj.* Watery, having water.

सजलकणिकाः *ep. of* जलमुचः.

सजलनयनैः *ep. of* शुक्लापाङ्गैः.

सजलपृषतैः *ep. of* वातैः.

सत् *pres. p. par.* (*of* अस 2 *cl.* Be) Being. Good, virtuous. सन् 1 *c. sin. m.* सताम् 6 *c. pl. m.* सति 7 *c. sin. n.*

सतत *adj.* Eternal, perpetual, constant.

सततगति *s. m.* Wind. सततगतिना 3 *c. sin.*

सत्वरम् *ind.* Quickly, speedily, suddenly.

सदयहृदय *adj.* Tender-hearted. सदयहृदयः 1 *c. sin. m.*

सदृश *adj.* Like, resembling. सदृशम् 2 *c. sin. n.*

सद्भाव *s. m.* Kind feeling, good nature.

सद्यःकृत्तद्विरददशनच्छेदगौरस्य *ep. of* अद्रेः.

सद्यःपातिन् *adj.* Quickly falling, drooping, frail. सद्यःपाति 2 *c. sin. n.*

सद्यस् *s. n.* Instantly, suddenly, immediately, forthwith, straightway.

सद्यस्सीरोत्कषणसुरभिक्षेत्रम् *ep. of* मालम्.

सनाथ *adj.* Having, possessing: possessed of, occupied by. सनाथे 7 *c. sin. m.*

सन्तप्त *p. p.* (*of* तप *with* सम्) Inflamed, scorched; afflicted, tortured, distressed, wretched. सन्तप्तानाम् 6 *c. pl. m.*

सन्दर्शन *s. n.* A vision. सन्दर्शनेषु 7 *c. pl.*

सन्देश *s. m.* News, tidings, information; a message; direction.

सन्धि *s. m.* Compactness, closeness. सन्धेः 6 *c.*

सन्ध्या *s. f.* Twilight, morning or evening.

सन्न *p. p.* (*of* षद Go) Near, adjacent, neighbouring, close by, *usually with* आ.

सन्नद्ध *p. p.* (*of* णह *with* सम्) Near, at hand. सन्नद्धे 7 *c. sin. m.*

सन्निकीर्ण *p. p.* (*of* कॄ Scatter, *with* नि *and* सम्) Flung, thrown; lying, laid.

सन्निकीर्णैकपाश्वाम् *ep. of* साध्वीम्.

सन्निकृष्ट *p. p.* (*of* कृष Draw, *with* नि *and* सम्) Near, neighbouring, adjacent. सन्निकृष्टम् 2 *c. sin. n.*

सन्निपत्य *ind. p. p. of* पत Fall, *with* नि *and* सम् Alight, descend.

सन्निपात *s. m.* Collection, assemblage, aggregate.

सन्निवृत्त *p. p.* (*of* वृत Be, *with* नि *and* सम्) Returned, turned back, shrinking, withdrawing. सन्निवृत्तम् 2 *c. sin. n.*

सन्न्यस्त *p. p.* (*of* अस Throw, *with* नि *and* सम्) Laid aside, relinquished, discarded.

सन्न्यस्ताभरणम् *ep. of* गात्रम्.

सपदि *ind.* Instantly, in a moment, at the moment.

सफर *s. m.* Name of a small glittering fish.

सभ्रूभङ्गयूथैः *ep. of* वारिभिः.

सभ्रूभङ्ग *adj.* With a frown, frowning. सभ्रूभङ्गम् 2 *c. sin. n.*

सभ्रूभङ्गप्रहितनयनैः *ep. of* विभ्रमैः (Having glances shot from the arched brow).

सम् *prep.* Together, with, *con*, *col*, &c.

समग्र *adj.* All, whole, entire. समग्रः 1 *c. sin. m.*

समधिकतर *compar.* (*of* अधिक *adj.* Much, *with* सम्) Exceeding, excessive.

समन्तात् *ind.* On every side, all around. Altogether, wholly.

समम् *ind.* With, along with, together with.

समय *s. m.* Time. समये 7 *c. sin.*

समर *s. m. n.* War, strife.

समर्थ *adj.* Able. समर्थः 1 *c. sin. m.*

समीपम् *adj. n. used adverbially*, Near.

समुचित *adj.* Worthy, becoming; fit, suitable, proper. —तः 1 *c. sin. m.* —तम् 1 *c. sin. n.*

सम्पत्स्यन्ते 2 *fut. átm. of* पद Go, *with* सम् Be, become.

सम्पद् *s. f.* Wealth, riches. Success. सम्पदः 1 *c. pl.*

सम्पर्क *s. m.* Contact, mixture, mingling, union. सम्पर्कात् 5 *c. sin.*

सम्पूर्ण *p. p.* (*of* पॄ *with* सम्) Completed, finished.

सम्भाष्य *ind. p. p. of* भाष Speak, *with* सम् Accost, address.

सम्भृत *p. p.* (*of* भृ Bear, *with* सम्) Nourished, cherished, maintained. Filled, full. Collected. Cast. सम्भृतम् 1 *c. sin. n.*

सम्भृतश्रीः 1 *c. sin. m.* Richly stored. Beautiful.

सम्भृतस्नेहम् *ep. of* मनः.

सम्भोग *s. m.* Enjoyment.

सम्भ्रम *s. m.* Flurry, hurry, haste.

सम्मिश्र *adj.* Mingled. सम्मिश्रम् 2 *c. sin. n.*

सरत् *pres. p. par. of* सृ 1 *cl.* Go, move, stir: blow (as the wind). सरति 7 *c. sin. m.*

सरल *s. m.* A sort of pine.

सरलस्कन्धसङ्घट्टजन्मा *ep. of* दवाग्निः (Originating in the friction of the trunks of pines).

सरस *adj.* Fresh, moist.

सरसनिचुलात् *ep. of* स्थानात्.

सरित् *s. f.* A river. सरितः 6 *c. sin.*

सर्पिस् *s. n.* Clarified butter. सर्पिः 1 *c. sin.*

सर्व्व *pronom.* All, every. सर्व्वम् 2 *c. sin. m.*

सर्व्वग *agt.* Going everywhere, omnipresent. सर्व्वगम् 2 *c. sin. n.*

सर्व्वगत *adj.* All-pervading. सर्व्वगतः 1 *c. sin. m.*

सर्व्वतस् *ind.* On all sides.

सर्व्वत्र *ind.* Everywhere.

सर्व्वविद् *agt.* All-knowing. सर्व्ववित् 1 *c. sin.*

सलिल *s. n.* Water. -लम् 2 *c. sin.* -लैः 3 *c. pl.*

सलिलोद्गारम् *ep. of* अभ्रवृन्दम्.

सवर्ण *adj.* Like, resembling. सवर्णे 7 *c. sin. m.*

सवितृ *s. m.* The sun. सवितुः 6 *c. sin.*

सव्यापार *adj.* Employed, occupied, busily engaged. सव्यापाराम् 2 *c. sin. f.*

सह *ind.* With.

सहचर *s. m.* सहचरी *s. f.* A companion, partner, mate.

सहते *pres.* सहेथाः *pot. átm. of* षह 1 *cl.* Endure, suffer, allow, permit, wait, forbear, have patience.

सहभार्य्य *adj.* With a wife. सहभार्य्याः 1 *c. pl. m.*

सहस्र *s. n.* A thousand. सहस्रैः 3 *c. pl.*

सहाय *s. m.* A companion, follower, adherent. सहायाः 1 *c. pl.*

सा 1 *c. sin. f. of* तद् He, she, it, that.

साक्षात् *ind.* Visibly, openly, in presence.

साक्षिन् *s. m.* A witness. साक्षी 1 *c. sin.* साक्षिणम् 2 *c. sin.*

सादरम् *ind.* Respectfully, affectionately.

सादृश्य *s. n.* Likeness, resemblance, parallel. सादृश्यम् 1 or 2 *c. sin.*

साधु *adj.* Clever, intelligent. साधौ 8 *c. sin.* *n. used adverbially,* Worthily, fitly, properly.

साध्वी *s. f.* A virtuous wife. साध्वीम् 2 *c. sin.*

सानु *s. m. n.* Table-land, level ground on the top or edge of a mountain. The summit of a mountain. सानुम् 2 *c. sin.* सानौ 7 *c. sin.*

सानुमत् *s. m.* A mountain. सानुमान् 1 *c. sin.*

सान्तर्हासम् *ind.* Smilingly, with an inward laugh.

सान्ध्य *adj.* Produced at, relating to, the evening, vespertine. सान्ध्यम् 2 *c. sin. n.*

साभ्र *adj.* With clouds, cloudy. साभ्रे 7 *c. sin. n.*

सामान्य *adj.* Common, general, universal.

सार *s. n.* Water. Substance, essence.

सारयत् *pres. p. par. of* सृ Go, *caus. form,* Remove, replace. सारयन्तीम् 2 *c. sin. f.* सारयित्वा *ind. p. p.* Having caused to move or vibrate; touching, playing upon.

सारस *s. m.* The Indian crane. —सानाम् 6 *c. pl.*

सारस्वत *adj.* Belonging to the river Saraswatí. सारस्वतीनाम् 6 *c. pl. f.*

सारिका *s. f.* A sort of bird. सारिकाम् 2 *c. sin.*

सार्द्धम् *ind.* With, along with, *govern. 3d case.*

सास्र *adj.* Tearful. सास्रेण 3 *c. sin. n.*

सिक्त *p. p.* (*of* षिच) Sprinkled, wetted.

सिञ्चत् *pres. p. par. of* षिच 6 *cl.* Sprinkle, wet. सिञ्चन् 1 *c. sin. m.*

सित *adj.* White.

सितमणि *s. m.* A white precious stone, as crystal, &c. सितमणिमय *adj.* Made of crystal.

सिद्ध *p. p.* (*of* षिध) Accomplished, realised, effected, achieved. Perfected. सिद्धः 1 *c. sin. m.* *s. m.* A sort of demigod inhabiting the region between the earth and the sun. सिद्धाः 1 *c. pl.*

सिद्धार्थक *s. n.* White mustard.

सिन्दूर *s. n.* Red lead, minium.

सिन्धु *s. f.* A river. Name of a river. सिन्धुः 1 *c. sin.* सिन्धोः 6 *c. sin.*

सिप्रा *s. f.* The Siprá (a river at Ougein).

सिषेवे 2 *pret. átm. of* षेव Serve, resort to.

सीमन्त *s. m.* A separation of the hair on each side, so as to leave a distinct line on the top of the head. सीमन्ते 7 *c. sin.*

सीमन्तिनी *s. f.* A woman. सीमन्तिनीनाम् 6 *c. pl.*

सीर *s. m.* A plough.

सु *prep.* Very, good, well.

सुकृत *s. n.* A good deed, a kindness.

सुख *s. n.* Happiness, pleasure, ease, comfort. सुखम् 1 or 2 *c. sin. n.* *adj.* Comfortable, grateful, soothing. सुखान् 2 *c. pl. m.*

सुखयितुम् *inf. of* सुख 10 *cl.* Render happy, cheer.

सुखस्पर्श *adj.* Agreeable to the touch or feelings. सुखस्पर्शम् 2 *c. sin. n.*

सुखिन् *adj.* Happy. सुखिनम् 2 *c. sin. m.* सुखिनः 6 *c. sin. m.*

सुचरित *s. n.* Good or virtuous course of life.

सुतनु *adj.* Very thin, emaciated. सुतनु 2 *c. sin. n.*

सुतराम् *ind.* Exceedingly.

सुप्त *p. p.* (*of* ष्वप) Sleeping, asleep.

सुप्तपारावतायाम् *ep. of* वडभौ.

सुभग *adj.* Agreeable, pleasing, grateful (to the eye or ear). Beloved, liked. सुभगः 1 *c. sin. m.* सुभगम् 2 *c. sin. m. n.* सुभग 8 *c. sin. m.* सुभगैः 3 *c. pl. m.* सुभगम् *n. used adverbially*, Gratefully, delightfully.

सुभगम्मन्य *s. m.* One who fancies himself beloved.

सुभगम्मन्यभाव *s. m.* The state of supposing one's self beloved; vanity, self-conceit.

सुर *s. m.* A god, a deity.

सुरत *s. n.* Pleasure. Sexual intercourse.

सुरपति *s. m.* Indra, chief of the gods.

सुरपतिधनुश्चारुणा *ep. of* तोरणेन (Beautiful as the rainbow).

सुरभि *adj.* Fragrant, sweet-smelling. सुरभिम् 2 *c. sin. m.* सुरभिणः 6 *c. sin.* सुरभौ 7 *c. sin. m.* सुरभयः 1 *c. pl. m.* सुरभिषु 7 *c. pl. n.* *s. f.* A fabulous cow, the cow of plenty, granting every wish.

सुरभित *adj.* Perfumed, scented.

सुरभितशिलम् *ep. of* अचलम्.

सुरयुवति *s. f.* A youthful goddess. —तयः 1 *c. pl.*

सुलभ *adj.* Easy of access. सुलभा 1 *c. sin. f.*

सुहृद् *s. m.* A friend. सुहृदाम् 6 *c. pl.*

सूचयिष्यन्ति 2 *fut. par. of* सूच 10 *cl.* Make known, report, give information, tell, discover, reveal, disclose. सूच्यते *pres. pass.*

सूचि *s. f.* A needle. सूचिभिन्नैः 3 *c. pl. m.* Aculeated, prickly.

सूत्र *s. n.* A thread.

सूर्य *s. m.* The sun. सूर्ये 7 *c. sin.*

सृष्टि *s. f.* Creation. सृष्टिः 1 *c. sin.*

सेन्द्रचापम् *ep. of* त्वाम्.

सेविष्यन्ते 2 *fut. átm. of* षेव Serve, wait upon, honour, pay homage.

सैन्य *s. n.* An army.

सोत्कम्प *adj.* Tremulous, trembling. सोत्कम्पानि 2 *c. pl. n.*

सोपान *s. n.* Stairs, steps, a staircase.

सोपानत्व *s. n.* The state, condition, or uses of a staircase. सोपानत्वम् 2 *c. sin.*

सौदामिनी *s. f.* Lightning. सौदामिन्या 3 *c. sin.*

सौध *s. n.* A mansion, palace. The side or angle (of a house).

सौभाग्य *s. n.* Affection, favour. —ग्यम् 2 *c. sin.*

सौम्य *adj.* Handsome, pleasing, mild, gentle, amiable, *generally in the vocative case.*

सौहार्द *s. n.* Friendship. सौहार्दात् 5 *c. sin.*

स्कन्द *s. m.* Skanda or Kártikeya, son of Śiva, and military deity of the Hindus. स्कन्दम् 2 *c.*

स्कन्ध *s. m.* The trunk of a tree.

स्खलित *p. p.* (*of* स्खल्) Stumbling, tripping, dashing. स्खलितसुभगम् *n. sin. used adverbially*, Tripping beautifully.

स्तन *s. m.* The female breast or bosom. स्तनः 1 *c. sin.* स्तनाभ्याम् 3 *c. du.*

स्तनपरिसरच्छिन्नसूत्रैः *ep. of* हारैः.

स्तनित *p. p.* (*of* स्तन्) Sounding loud, noisy. *s. n.* The rattling of thunder, the grumbling of thunder-clouds. Thunder. The purling or murmuring of a rippling stream.

स्तम्भ *s. m.* The stem of a tree.

स्तम्भित *p. p.* (*of* ष्टभि) Stopped (as a hemorrhage), suppressed.

स्तम्भितान्तर्जलौघः *ep. of* त्वम् *understood.*

स्तबक *s. m.* A cluster of blossoms.

स्तिमित *p. p.* (*of* ष्टिम Steam) Moist. Steady, pleased, gratified (eye).

स्तिमितनयनाम् *ep. of* ताम्.

स्तुति *s. f.* Praise. स्तुतिः 1 *c. sin.*

स्तोक *adv.* A little, slightly. स्तोकनम्रा 1 *c. sin. f.* Slightly bending (forwards).

स्त्री *s. f.* A woman, or female. स्त्रियः 1 *c. pl.* स्त्रीणाम् 6 *c. pl.*

स्थल *s. m.* A place, site, or spot. A chamber. स्थलानि 2 *c. pl.*

स्थलकमलिनी *s. f.* Name of a shrub (Hibiscus mutabilis). स्थलकमलिनीम् 2 *c. sin.*

स्थली *s. f.* Dry or firm ground. स्थलीषु 7 *c. pl.*

स्थलीदेवता *s. f.* A deity of the soil, a faun, a dryad.

स्थातव्य *fut. p. p. of* ष्ठा Stand, stop, stay. स्थातव्यं ते Thou must halt.

स्थान *s. n.* A place. स्थानात् 5 *c. sin.* स्थाने 7 *c. sin.* स्थानेषु 7 *c. pl.*

स्थापित *p. p.* (*of* ष्ठा *caus. form*) Fixed, appointed. स्थापितस्य 6 *c. sin. m.*

स्थायिन् *agt.* Staying, tarrying, waiting.

स्थित *p. p. of* ष्ठा Standing, stationed, steady. Obedient. स्थितः 1 *c. sin.* स्थिताः 1 *c. pl. m.*

स्थित्वा *ind. p. p.* (*of* ष्ठा) Having stood, stayed, or halted.

स्थिर *adj.* Permanent, durable.

स्थूल *adj.* Great, big, large, huge, bulky.

स्थूलमध्येन्द्रनीलम् *ep. of* मुक्तागुणम्.

स्नपयतु *imp. par. of* ष्णा Bathe, *caus. form.*

स्नान *s. n.* Bathing, washing, ablution.

स्निग्ध *p. p.* (*of* ष्णिह Be smooth) Smooth, glossy; oily, moist. Cool. Thick, dense. Pleasing, agreeable. Sweet, harmonious. स्निग्धैः 3 *c. pl. m. n.*

स्निग्धगम्भीरघोषम् *ep. of* त्वाम्.

स्निग्धच्छायातरुषु *ep. of* आश्रमेषु. च्छ *for* छ *is allowed by grammar, and required by the metre.* (स्निग्ध, छाया, तरुषु).

स्निग्धभिन्नाञ्जनाभे *ep. of* त्वयि.

स्निग्धवेणीसवर्णे *ep. of* त्वयि.

स्नेह *s. m.* Affection. Oiliness. स्नेहान् 2 *c. pl.*

स्पन्दिन् *agt.* Beating, throbbing, tremulous. स्पन्दि 1 *c. sin. n.*

स्पर्श *s. m.* Touch, contact.

स्पृष्ट *p. p.* (*of* स्पृश्) Touched, moved, filled. स्पृष्टाः 1 *c. pl. m.* स्पृष्टम् 1 *c. sin. n.*

स्फटिक *s. m.* Crystal.

स्फटिकफलका *ep. of* यष्टिः.

स्फुट *adj.* Bursting.

स्फुटित *p. p.* (*of* स्फुट) Opened, expanded.

स्फुटितकमलामोदमैत्रीकषायः *ep. of* वातः.

स्फुरण *s. m.* A throbbing, quivering, darting.

स्फुरति *pres. par. of* स्फुर् 6 *cl.* Quiver, crackle.

स्फुरित *p. p.* (*of* स्फुर्) Quivering, trembling, shaking, flashing, glittering, gleaming, playing, unsteady.

स्फुरितरुचिना *ep. of* चर्हेण.

स्मरसि, स्मरामि *pres. par. of* स्मृ 1 *cl.* Remember, call to mind, think of.

स्यन्दिन् *agt.* Dropping, distilling, shedding. स्यन्दिनः 1 *c. pl. m.*

स्याः, स्यात्, स्युः *pot. par. of* अस् 2 *cl.* Be.

स्रस्त *p. p.* (*of* स्रंस्) Fallen, slipped. स्रस्तम् 1 *c. sin. n.*

स्रस्तगङ्गादुकूलाम् *ep. of* सलकाम् (Let fall her Gangetic silken garment).

स्रुति *s. f.* Exudation, oozing.

स्रोतस् *s. n.* A current, a stream. A river. स्रोतसि 7 *c. sin.* स्रोतसाम् 6 *c. pl.*

स्व *pronom.* (My, thy, his, her, our, your, their) Own. स्वम् 2 *c. sin. m.* स्वाम् 2 *c. sin. f.*

स्वच्छ *adj.* Pure, transparent. (सु *and* अच्छ).

स्वन *s. m.* Sound. स्वनैः 3 *c. pl.*

स्वनत् *pres. p. par. of* स्वन् 1 *cl.* Sound, roar. स्वनताम् 6 *c. pl. m.*

स्वप्न *s. m.* Sleep, a dream. स्वप्ने 7 *c. sin.* स्वप्नजः 1 *c. sin. m.* Produced in sleep.

स्वयम् *ind.* Of one's own self. स्वयङ्कृत Made by self, self-made.

स्वर्ग *s. m.* Paradise, Indra's heaven.

स्वर्गिन् *s. m.* An inhabitant of Indra's heaven. स्वर्गिणाम् 6 *c. pl.*

स्वल्प *adj.* (सु *and* अल्प Little) Very little, too small. स्वल्पीभूते 7 *c. sin. n.* Being too small.

स्वागत *s. n.* Welcome (सु Well, आगत Come). स्वागतीकृत्य Having made into welcome, giving (to a cry) the sound *swágata*, welcome.

स्वादु *s. m.* A sweet taste or flavour, sweetness.

स्वाधिकारप्रमत्तः *ep. of* यक्षः. (स्व, अधिकार, प्रमत्तः).

स्वेद *s. m.* Sweat, perspiration.

ह

हंस *s. m.* A goose. हंसाः 1 *c. pl.*

हति *s. f.* A blow.

हन्त *ind.* Ah! oh!

हन्तुम् *inf. of* हन् 2 *cl.* Kill, slay. हन्युः *pot. par.*

हर *s. m.* Śiva. *imp. par.*, हरति *pres. of* हृ 1 *cl.* Take, convey, take away, remove.

हरि *s. m.* Vishńu. हरे 8 *c. sin.*

हरिचन्दन *s. m. n.* One of the trees of paradise.

हरिणी *s. f.* A female deer, a roe.

हरित *adj.* Green.

हर्तुम् *inf. of* हृ Take, remove.

हर्म्य *s. n.* A palace, mansion. हर्म्येषु 7 *c. pl.*

हल *s. n.* A plough.

हलधर *or* हलभृत् *s. m.* A name of Balaráma, elder brother of Krishńa. हलभृतः 6 *c. sin.*

हस्त *s. m.* The hand. The trunk of an elephant.

हार *s. m.* A string or garland (of pearls, &c.), a necklace. हारैः 3 *c. pl.*

हारयिष्यत् *part.* 2 *fut. par. of* हृ Take, *caus. form*, About to transmit. —ष्यन् 1 *c. sin. m.*

हाला *s. f.* Wine, any intoxicating draught. हालाम् 2 *c. sin.*

हास *s. m.* A laugh, a smile.

हि *ind.* For, since, because.

हित्वा *ind. p. p. of* हा Leave, quit, desert, discard.

हिमांशु *s. m.* The moon (cold-ray). हिमांशोः 6 *c. sin.*

हुत *s. n.* An oblation.

हुतवह *s. m.* Agni, or fire.

हुताग्नि *s. m.* Sacrificial fire. हुताग्नीन् 2 *c. pl.*

हृत् *agt. in comp.* Taking away, removing, who or what makes riddance. हृत् 2 *c. sin. n.*

हृत *p. p.* (*of* हृ) Taken, brought. हृतम् 2 *c. sin. m.*

हृत्वा *ind. p. p. of* हृ Having taken, laying hold.

हृदय *s. n.* Heart, mind. हृदयम् 2 *c. sin. m.*

हृदयनिहितारम्भम् *ep. of* संयोगम्.

हृष्ट *p. p.* (*of* हृष) Pleased. हृष्टाः 1 *c. pl. m.*

हृष्टचित्त *adj.* Rejoiced at heart. हृष्टचित्तौ 2 *c. du.*

हेतु *s. m.* Cause, reason, motive, sake; means, origin. हेतोः 6 *c. sin.* For the sake, on account of.

हेमन् *s. n.* Gold.

हैम *adj.* Golden. हैमैः 3 *c. pl. m. n.*

ह्री *s. f.* Shame.

The metre in which the Megha Dúta is written is called Mandákrántá; referring probably to the slow and stately movement of the measure. It is a variety of the order termed Atyashtí; which, as a class, denotes a stanza of four equal lines, each containing seventeen syllables, variously divided and disposed. In the Mandákrántá species, each line consists of a Molossus, a Dactyl, a Tribrach, two Antibacchics, and two long syllables, or a spondee; as,

– – –| – ◡◡|◡◡◡|– – ◡| – –◡| – –

कश्चित् कान्ताविरहगुरुणा स्वाधिकारप्रमत्तः

Kaśchit kántá-viraha-guruńá swádhikára-pramattah,

and a cæsura or pause occurs after the fourth, tenth, and seventeenth syllables—

शापेनास्तं | गमितमहिमा | वर्षभोग्येन भर्त्तुः

Śápenástang gamita-mahimá varsha-bhogyena bharttuh.

The following verse from the Śruta bodha defines and exemplifies the Mandákrántá stanza:—

मन्दाक्रान्ता तदनु नियतं वश्यतामेति बाला

Mandákrántá, tad anu niyatam, vaśyatám eti bálá.

ADDITIONS.

प्रत्यूष *s. m.* Morning. प्रत्यूषेषु 7 *c. pl.*
मुखर *adj.* Noisy. मुखरः 1 *c. sin. m.*
यत्र *ind.* Where.
वास *s. m.* A dwelling. A roosting-place.
वासर *s. n.* A day. वासराणि 1 *c. pl.*
वासव *adj.* Belonging to, commanded by वासव Vásava or Indra. वासवीनाम् 6 *c. pl. f.*
वासस् *s. n.* Clothes, raiment. वासः 2 *c. sin.* वाससि 7 *c. sin.*
वासित *p. p.* (*of* वास) Perfumed, scented. वासितम् 2 *c. sin. n.*
वास्यति 2 *fut. par. of* वा 2 *cl.* Blow.
वाहयेत् *pot. par. of* वह Carry, *caus. form*, Continue, prosecute.
वाह्य *adj.* Outer.
वाह्योद्यानस्थितहरशिरश्चन्द्रिकाधौतहर्म्या *ep. of* अलका.

CORRECTIONS.

Page 89, *for* كهقي *read* كهتي.
... 112, .. उल्लिङ्घिताध्वा ... उल्लङ्घिताध्वा.
... 113, .. करोनि ... करोति.
... 126, .. पञ्च ... पञ्जर.